VALIANT

#1

FRED VAN LENTE / CLAYTON HENRY / BRIAN REBER

Ivar, Timewalker

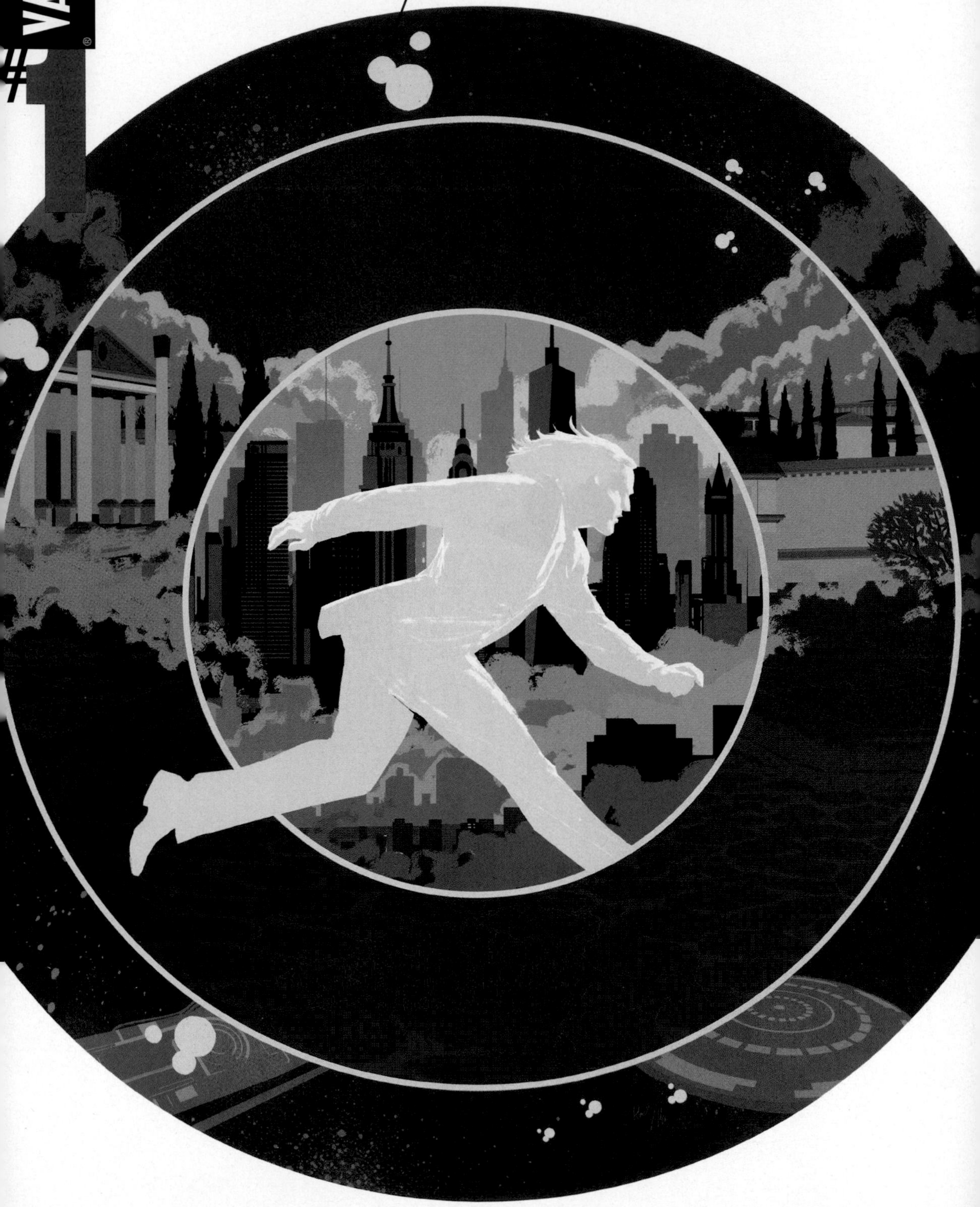

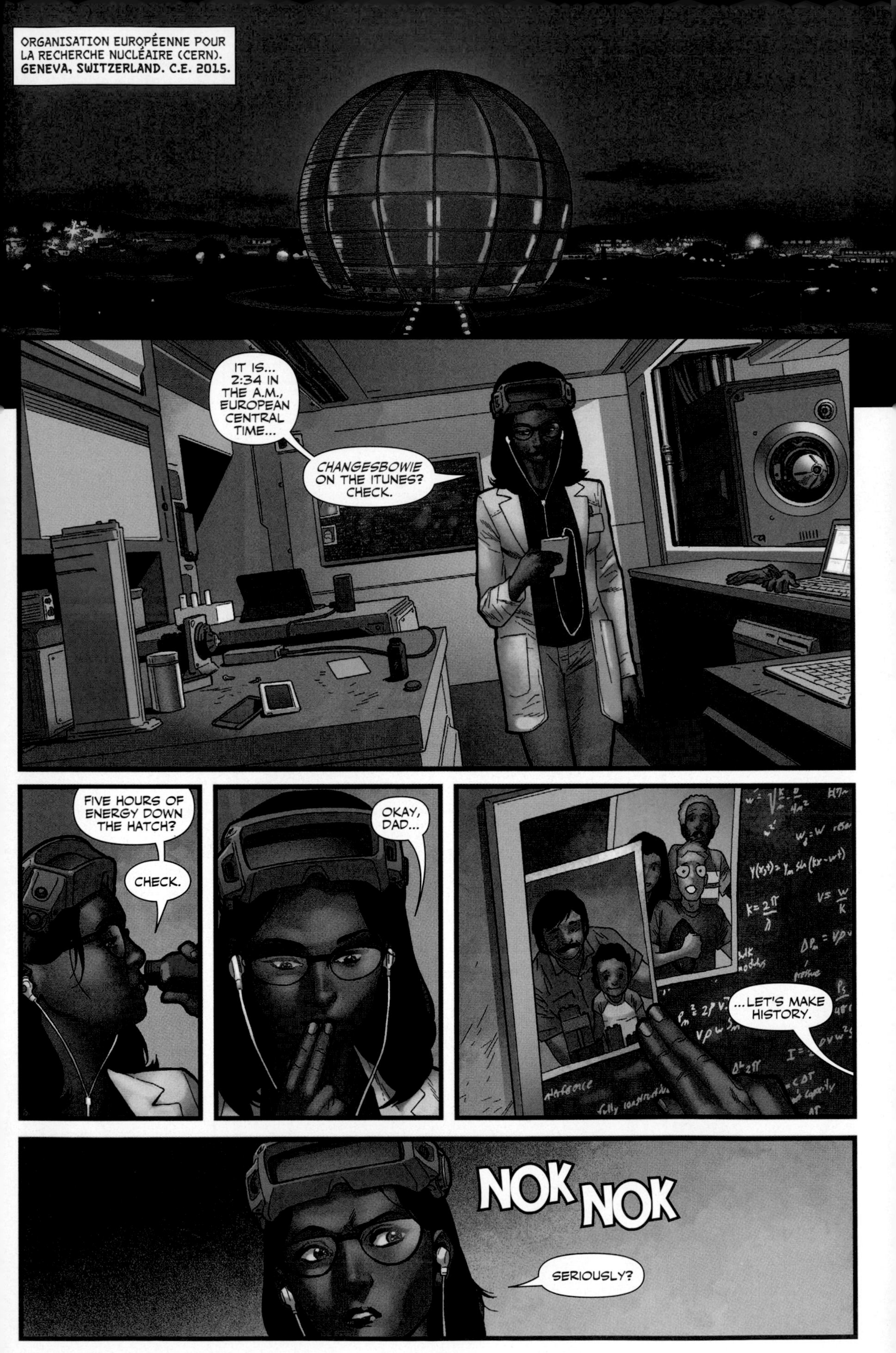
ORGANISATION EUROPÉENNE POUR LA RECHERCHE NUCLÉAIRE (CERN). GENEVA, SWITZERLAND. C.E. 2015.
IT IS... 2:34 IN THE A.M., EUROPEAN CENTRAL TIME...
CHANGESBOWIE ON THE ITUNES? CHECK.
FIVE HOURS OF ENERGY DOWN THE HATCH?
CHECK.
OKAY, DAD...
...LET'S MAKE HISTORY.
NOK NOK
SERIOUSLY?

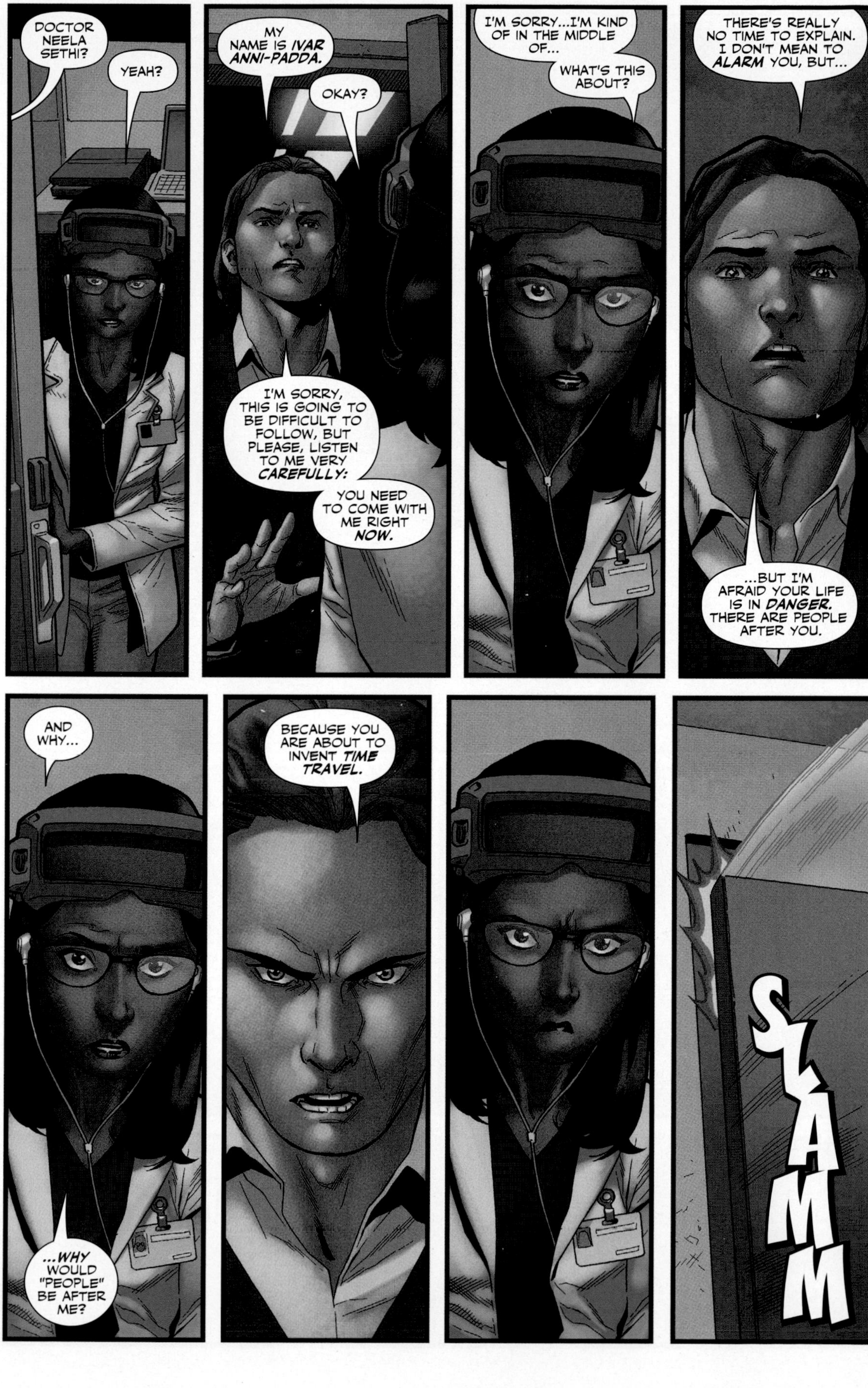
DOCTOR NEELA SETHI?
YEAH?
MY NAME IS IVAR ANNI-PADDA.
OKAY?
I'M SORRY, THIS IS GOING TO BE DIFFICULT TO FOLLOW, BUT PLEASE, LISTEN TO ME VERY CAREFULLY:
YOU NEED TO COME WITH ME RIGHT NOW.
I'M SORRY...I'M KIND OF IN THE MIDDLE OF...
WHAT'S THIS ABOUT?
THERE'S REALLY NO TIME TO EXPLAIN. I DON'T MEAN TO ALARM YOU, BUT...
...BUT I'M AFRAID YOUR LIFE IS IN DANGER. THERE ARE PEOPLE AFTER YOU.
AND WHY...
...WHY WOULD "PEOPLE" BE AFTER ME?
BECAUSE YOU ARE ABOUT TO INVENT TIME TRAVEL.
SLAMM

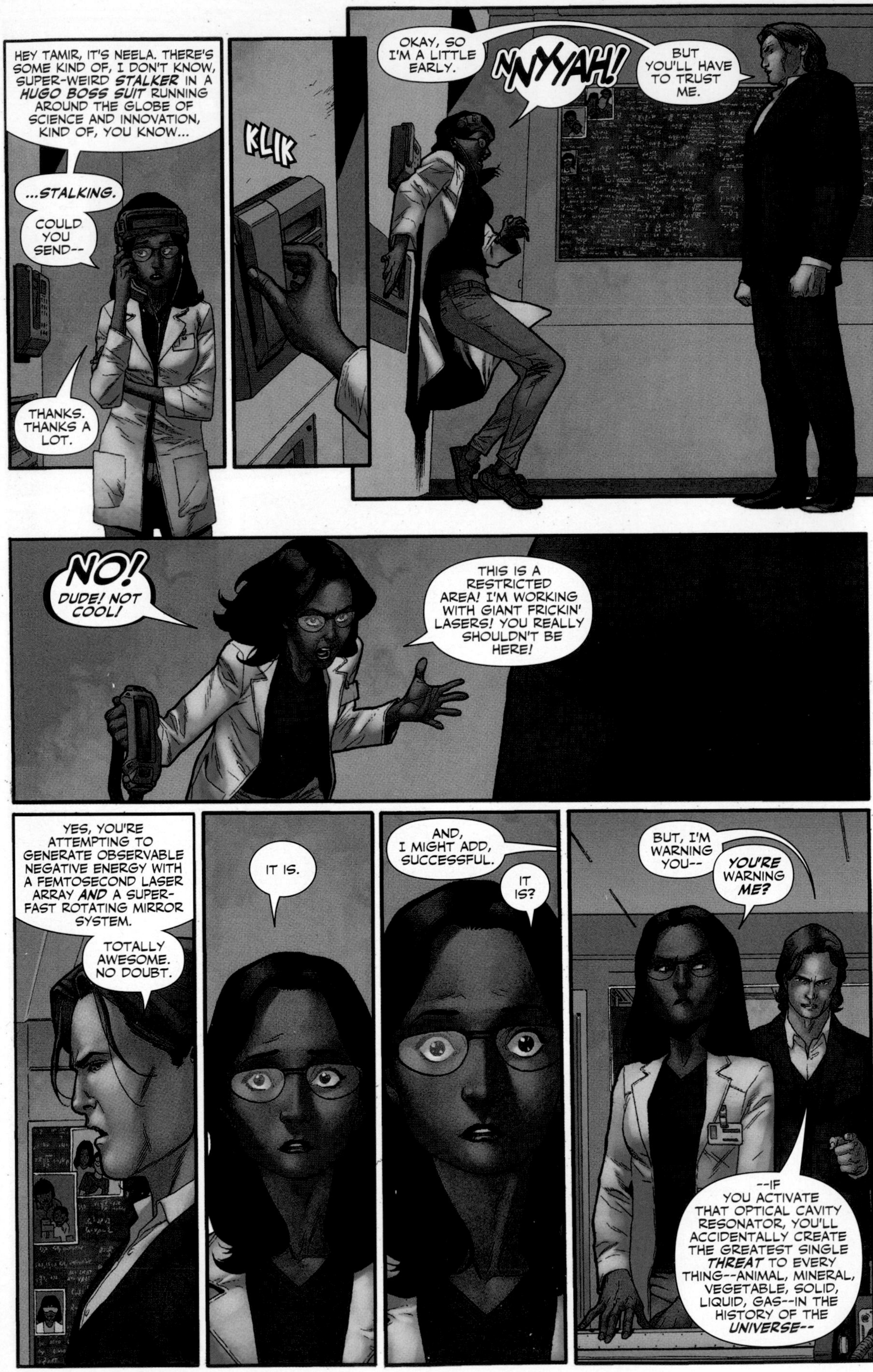
HEY TAMIR, IT'S NEELA. THERE'S SOME KIND OF, I DON'T KNOW, SUPER-WEIRD STALKER IN A HUGO BOSS SUIT RUNNING AROUND THE GLOBE OF SCIENCE AND INNOVATION, KIND OF, YOU KNOW...
...STALKING.
COULD YOU SEND--
THANKS. THANKS A LOT.
KLIK
OKAY, SO I'M A LITTLE EARLY.
NNYYAH!
BUT YOU'LL HAVE TO TRUST ME.
NO! DUDE! NOT COOL!
THIS IS A RESTRICTED AREA! I'M WORKING WITH GIANT FRICKIN' LASERS! YOU REALLY SHOULDN'T BE HERE!
YES, YOU'RE ATTEMPTING TO GENERATE OBSERVABLE NEGATIVE ENERGY WITH A FEMTOSECOND LASER ARRAY AND A SUPER-FAST ROTATING MIRROR SYSTEM.
TOTALLY AWESOME. NO DOUBT.
IT IS.
AND, I MIGHT ADD, SUCCESSFUL.
IT IS?
BUT, I'M WARNING YOU--
YOU'RE WARNING ME?
--IF YOU ACTIVATE THAT OPTICAL CAVITY RESONATOR, YOU'LL ACCIDENTALLY CREATE THE GREATEST SINGLE THREAT TO EVERY THING--ANIMAL, MINERAL, VEGETABLE, SOLID, LIQUID, GAS--IN THE HISTORY OF THE UNIVERSE--

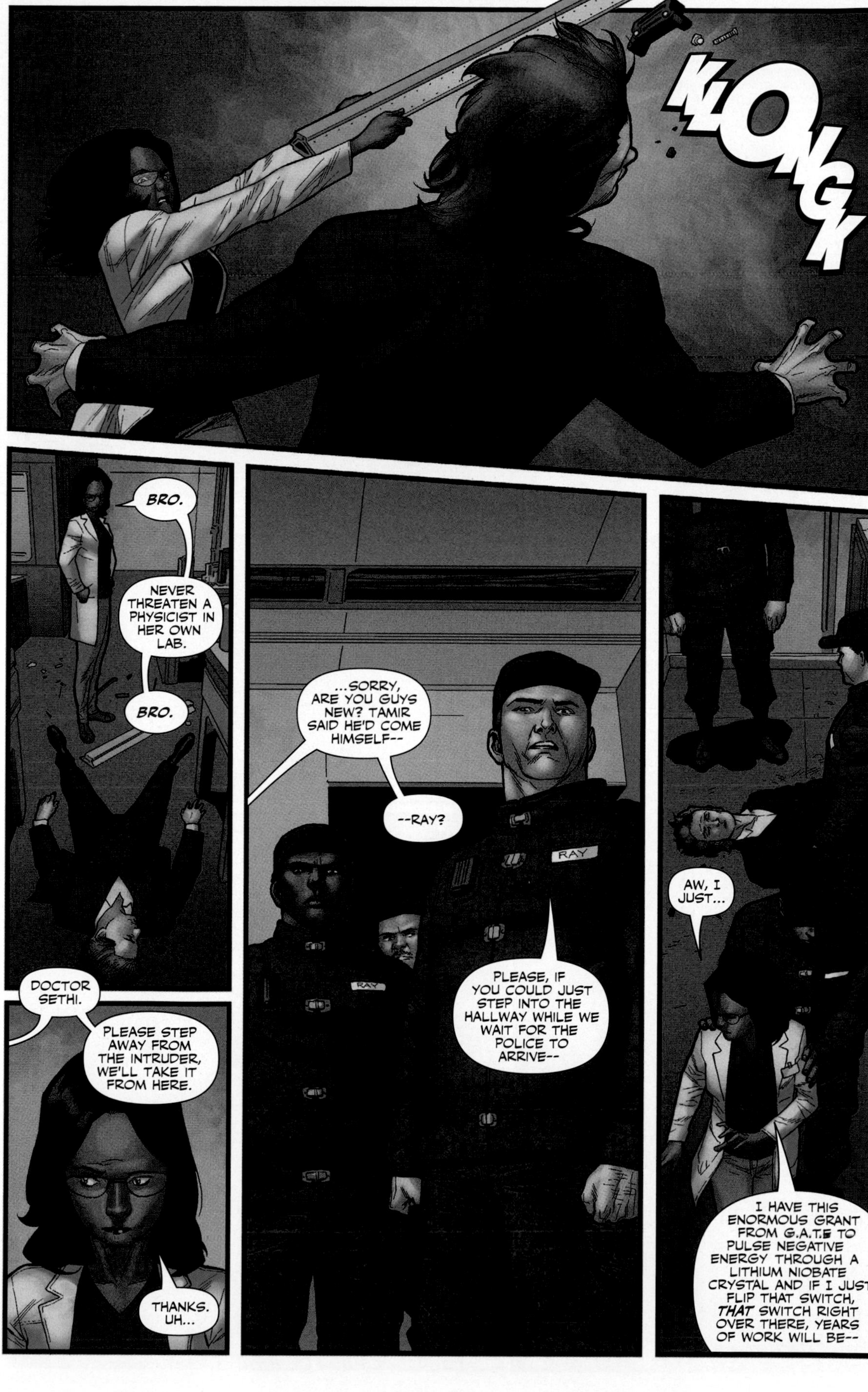
KLONGK
BRO.
NEVER THREATEN A PHYSICIST IN HER OWN LAB.
BRO.
DOCTOR SETHI.
PLEASE STEP AWAY FROM THE INTRUDER, WE'LL TAKE IT FROM HERE.
THANKS. UH...
...SORRY, ARE YOU GUYS NEW? TAMIR SAID HE'D COME HIMSELF--
--RAY?
RAY
RAY
PLEASE, IF YOU COULD JUST STEP INTO THE HALLWAY WHILE WE WAIT FOR THE POLICE TO ARRIVE--
AW, I JUST...
I HAVE THIS ENORMOUS GRANT FROM G.A.T.E TO PULSE NEGATIVE ENERGY THROUGH A LITHIUM NIOBATE CRYSTAL AND IF I JUST FLIP THAT SWITCH, *THAT* SWITCH RIGHT OVER THERE, YEARS OF WORK WILL BE--

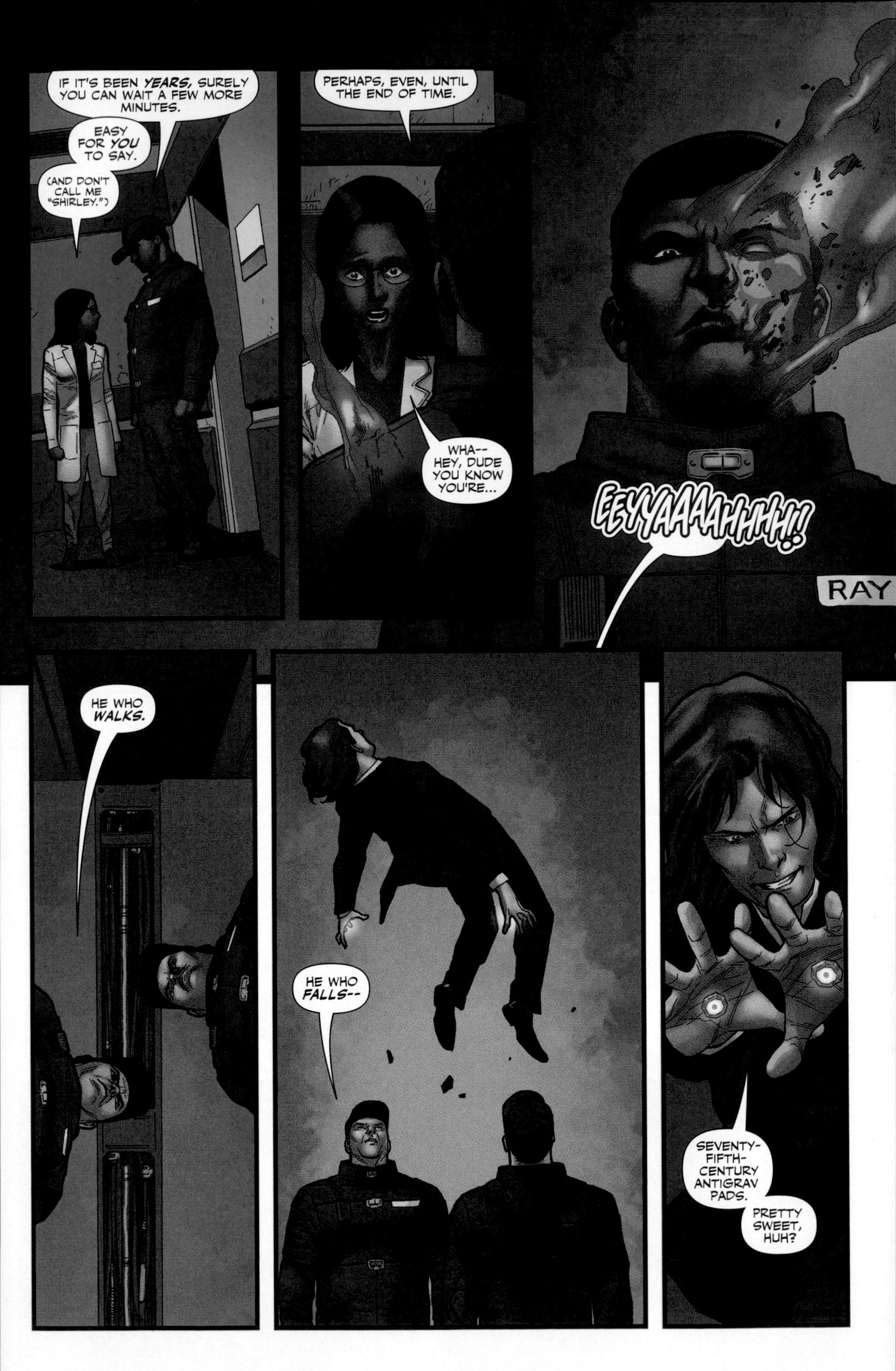
IF IT'S BEEN YEARS, SURELY YOU CAN WAIT A FEW MORE MINUTES.
EASY FOR YOU TO SAY.
(AND DON'T CALL ME "SHIRLEY.")
PERHAPS, EVEN, UNTIL THE END OF TIME.
WHA-- HEY, DUDE YOU KNOW YOU'RE...
EEYYAAAAHHHH!!
RAY
HE WHO WALKS.
HE WHO FALLS--
SEVENTY-FIFTH-CENTURY ANTIGRAV PADS.
PRETTY SWEET, HUH?

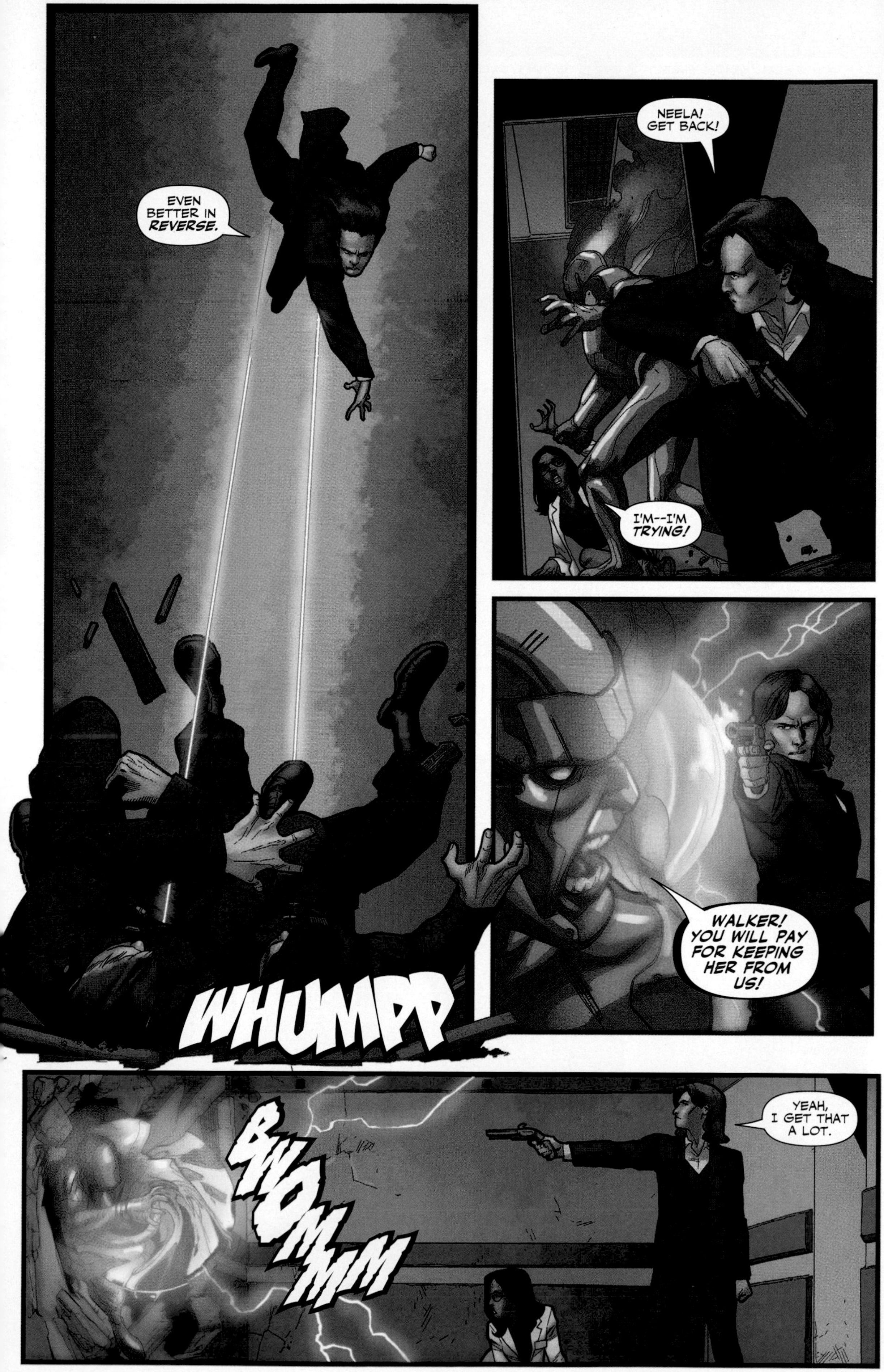
EVEN BETTER IN REVERSE.
WHUMPP
NEELA! GET BACK!
I'M--I'M TRYING!
WALKER! YOU WILL PAY FOR KEEPING HER FROM US!
BWOMMM
YEAH, I GET THAT A LOT.

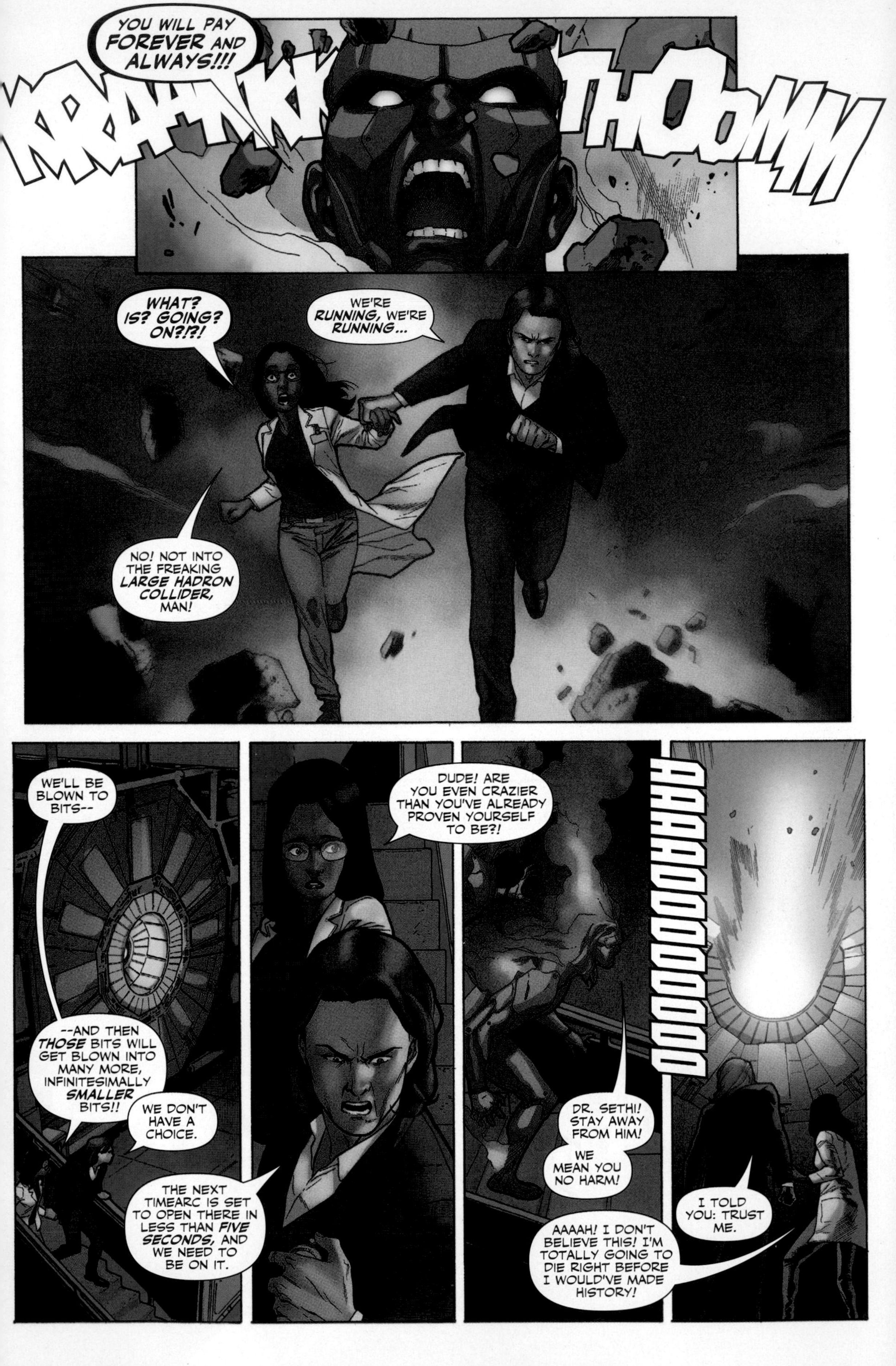
YOU WILL PAY FOREVER AND ALWAYS!!!
KRAAKKK THOOMM
WHAT? IS? GOING? ON?!?!
WE'RE RUNNING, WE'RE RUNNING...
NO! NOT INTO THE FREAKING LARGE HADRON COLLIDER, MAN!
WE'LL BE BLOWN TO BITS--
--AND THEN THOSE BITS WILL GET BLOWN INTO MANY MORE, INFINITESIMALLY SMALLER BITS!!
WE DON'T HAVE A CHOICE.
DUDE! ARE YOU EVEN CRAZIER THAN YOU'VE ALREADY PROVEN YOURSELF TO BE?!
THE NEXT TIMEARC IS SET TO OPEN THERE IN LESS THAN FIVE SECONDS, AND WE NEED TO BE ON IT.
AAAAAOOOOOOOOOO
DR. SETHI! STAY AWAY FROM HIM!
WE MEAN YOU NO HARM!
I TOLD YOU: TRUST ME.
AAAAH! I DON'T BELIEVE THIS! I'M TOTALLY GOING TO DIE RIGHT BEFORE I WOULD'VE MADE HISTORY!

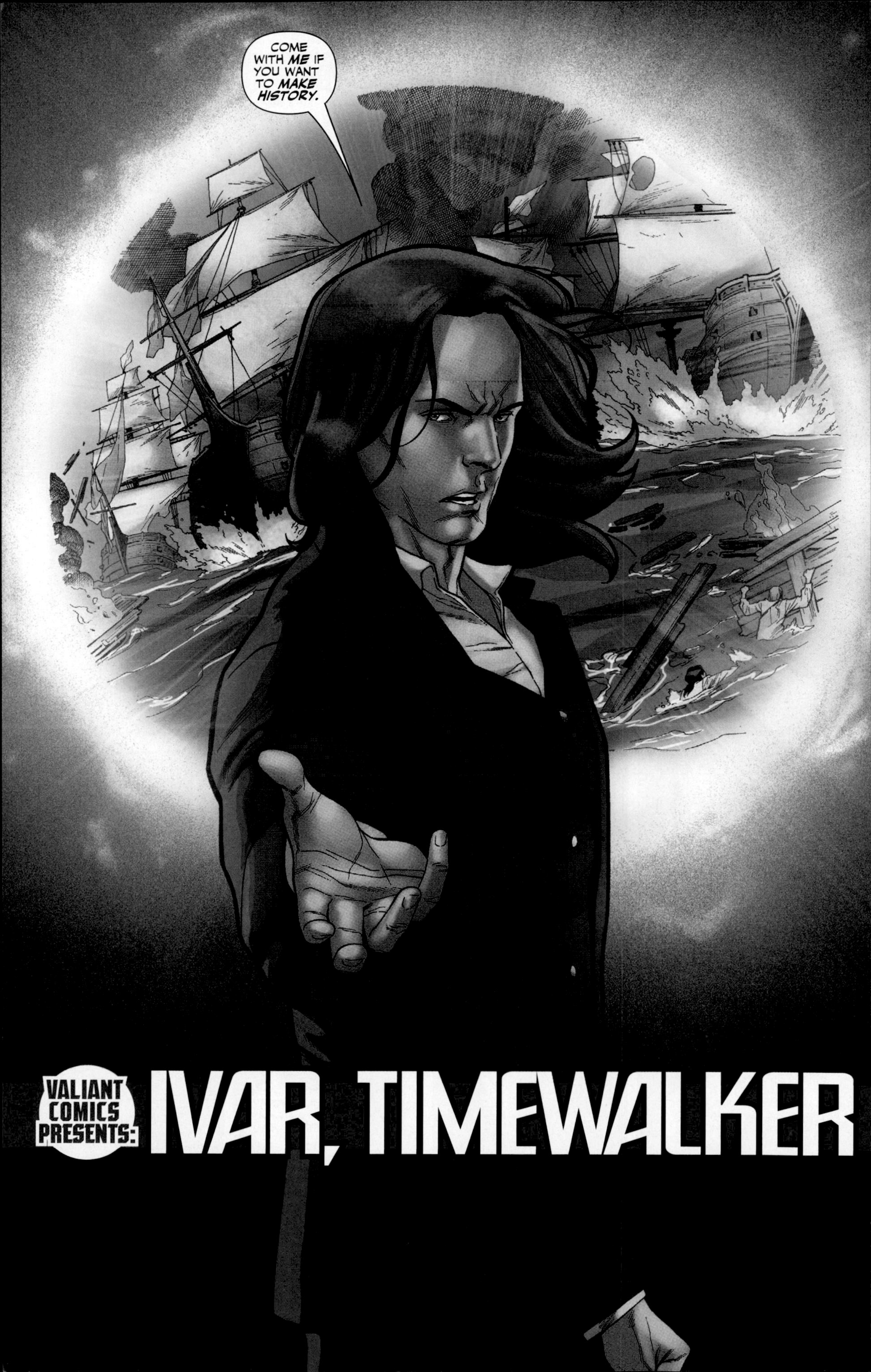
COME WITH ME IF YOU WANT TO MAKE HISTORY.
VALIANT COMICS PRESENTS: IVAR, TIMEWALKER

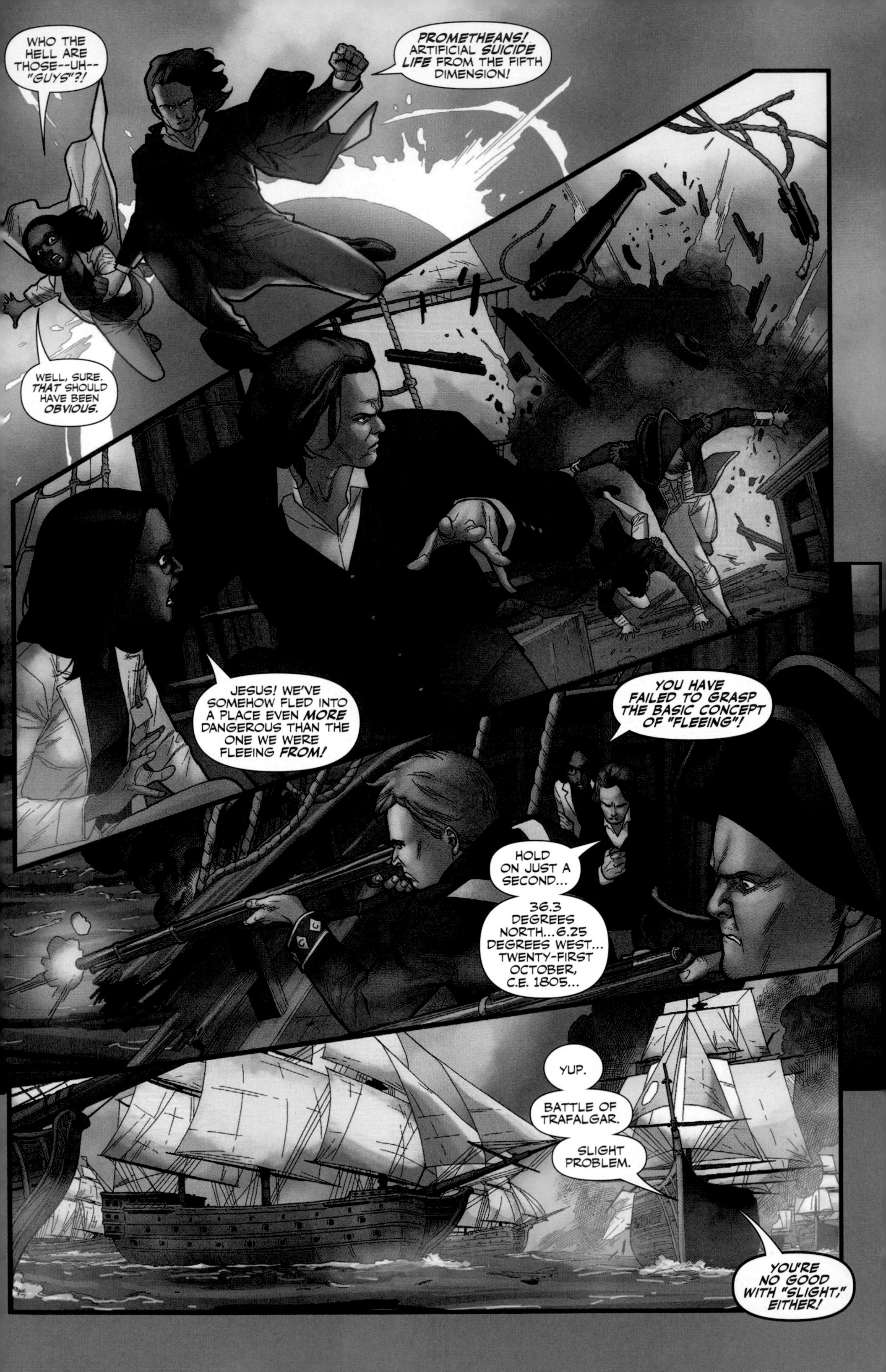
WHO THE HELL ARE THOSE--UH--"GUYS"?!
PROMETHEANS! ARTIFICIAL SUICIDE LIFE FROM THE FIFTH DIMENSION!
WELL, SURE. THAT SHOULD HAVE BEEN OBVIOUS.
JESUS! WE'VE SOMEHOW FLED INTO A PLACE EVEN MORE DANGEROUS THAN THE ONE WE WERE FLEEING FROM!
YOU HAVE FAILED TO GRASP THE BASIC CONCEPT OF "FLEEING"!
HOLD ON JUST A SECOND...
36.3 DEGREES NORTH...6.25 DEGREES WEST... TWENTY-FIRST OCTOBER, C.E. 1805...
YUP.
BATTLE OF TRAFALGAR.
SLIGHT PROBLEM.
YOU'RE NO GOOD WITH "SLIGHT," EITHER!

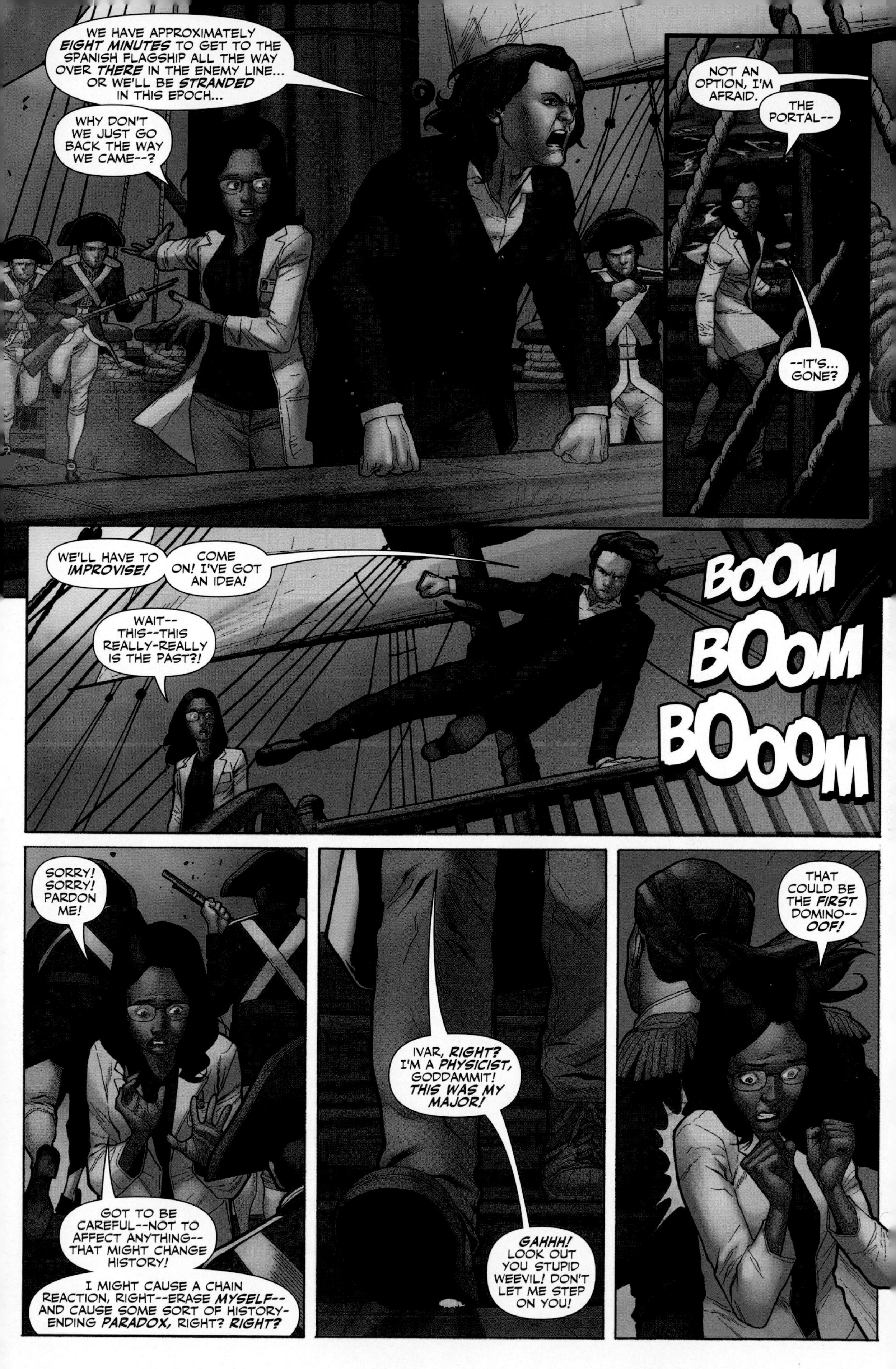
WE HAVE APPROXIMATELY EIGHT MINUTES TO GET TO THE SPANISH FLAGSHIP ALL THE WAY OVER THERE IN THE ENEMY LINE... OR WE'LL BE STRANDED IN THIS EPOCH...
WHY DON'T WE JUST GO BACK THE WAY WE CAME--?
NOT AN OPTION, I'M AFRAID.
THE PORTAL--
--IT'S... GONE?
WE'LL HAVE TO IMPROVISE!
COME ON! I'VE GOT AN IDEA!
WAIT-- THIS--THIS REALLY-REALLY IS THE PAST?!
BOOM
BOOM
BOOOM
SORRY! SORRY! PARDON ME!
GOT TO BE CAREFUL--NOT TO AFFECT ANYTHING-- THAT MIGHT CHANGE HISTORY!
I MIGHT CAUSE A CHAIN REACTION, RIGHT--ERASE MYSELF-- AND CAUSE SOME SORT OF HISTORY-ENDING PARADOX, RIGHT? RIGHT?
IVAR, RIGHT? I'M A PHYSICIST, GODDAMMIT! THIS WAS MY MAJOR!
GAHHH! LOOK OUT YOU STUPID WEEVIL! DON'T LET ME STEP ON YOU!
THAT COULD BE THE FIRST DOMINO-- OOF!

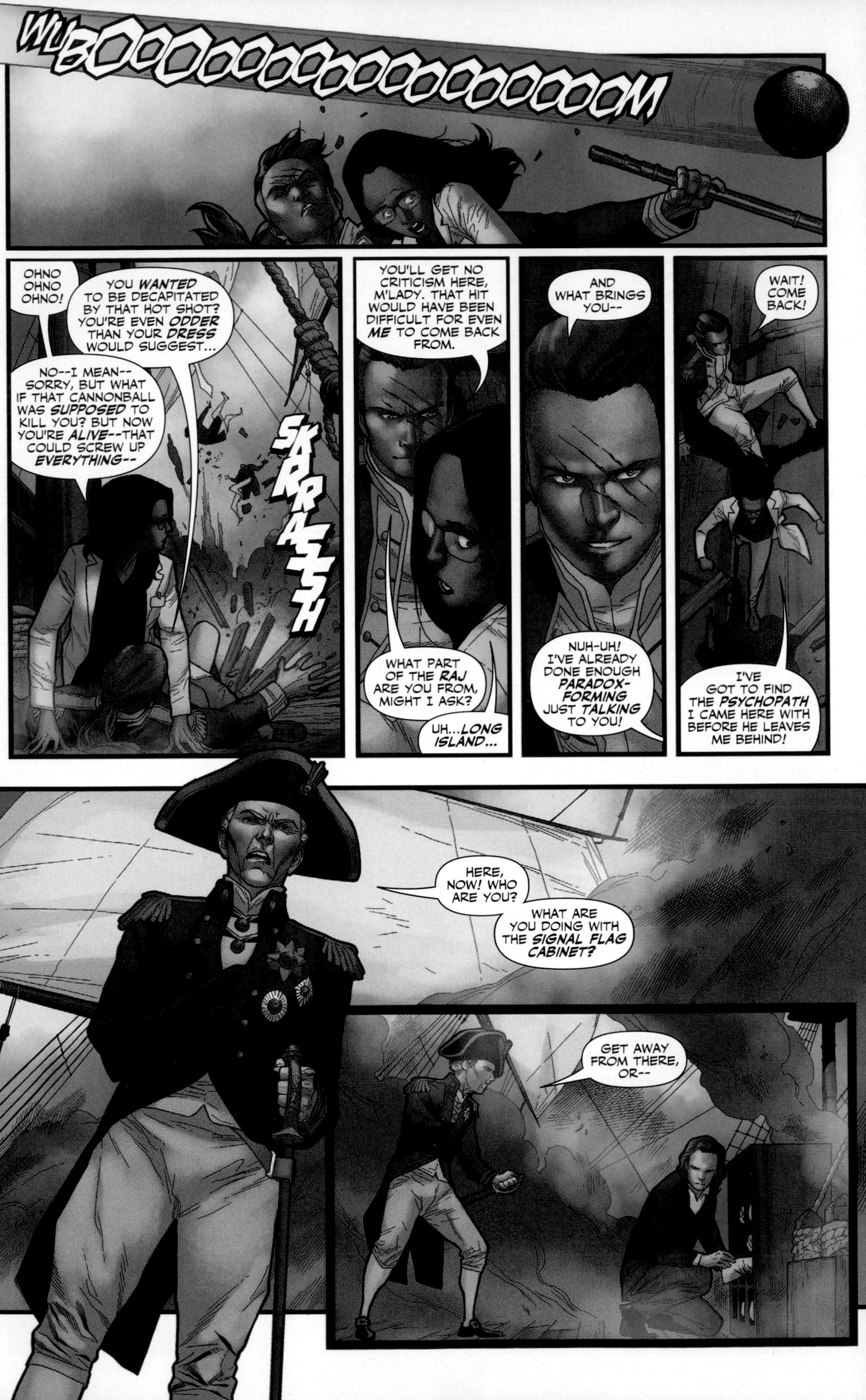
WUBOOOOOOOOOOOOOOOOOOM
OHNO OHNO OHNO!
YOU WANTED TO BE DECAPITATED BY THAT HOT SHOT? YOU'RE EVEN ODDER THAN YOUR DRESS WOULD SUGGEST...
NO--I MEAN--SORRY, BUT WHAT IF THAT CANNONBALL WAS SUPPOSED TO KILL YOU? BUT NOW YOU'RE ALIVE--THAT COULD SCREW UP EVERYTHING--
SKRASSSH
YOU'LL GET NO CRITICISM HERE, M'LADY. THAT HIT WOULD HAVE BEEN DIFFICULT FOR EVEN ME TO COME BACK FROM.
WHAT PART OF THE RAJ ARE YOU FROM, MIGHT I ASK?
UH...LONG ISLAND...
AND WHAT BRINGS YOU--
NUH-UH! I'VE ALREADY DONE ENOUGH PARADOX-FORMING JUST TALKING TO YOU!
WAIT! COME BACK!
I'VE GOT TO FIND THE PSYCHOPATH I CAME HERE WITH BEFORE HE LEAVES ME BEHIND!
HERE, NOW! WHO ARE YOU?
WHAT ARE YOU DOING WITH THE SIGNAL FLAG CABINET?
GET AWAY FROM THERE, OR--

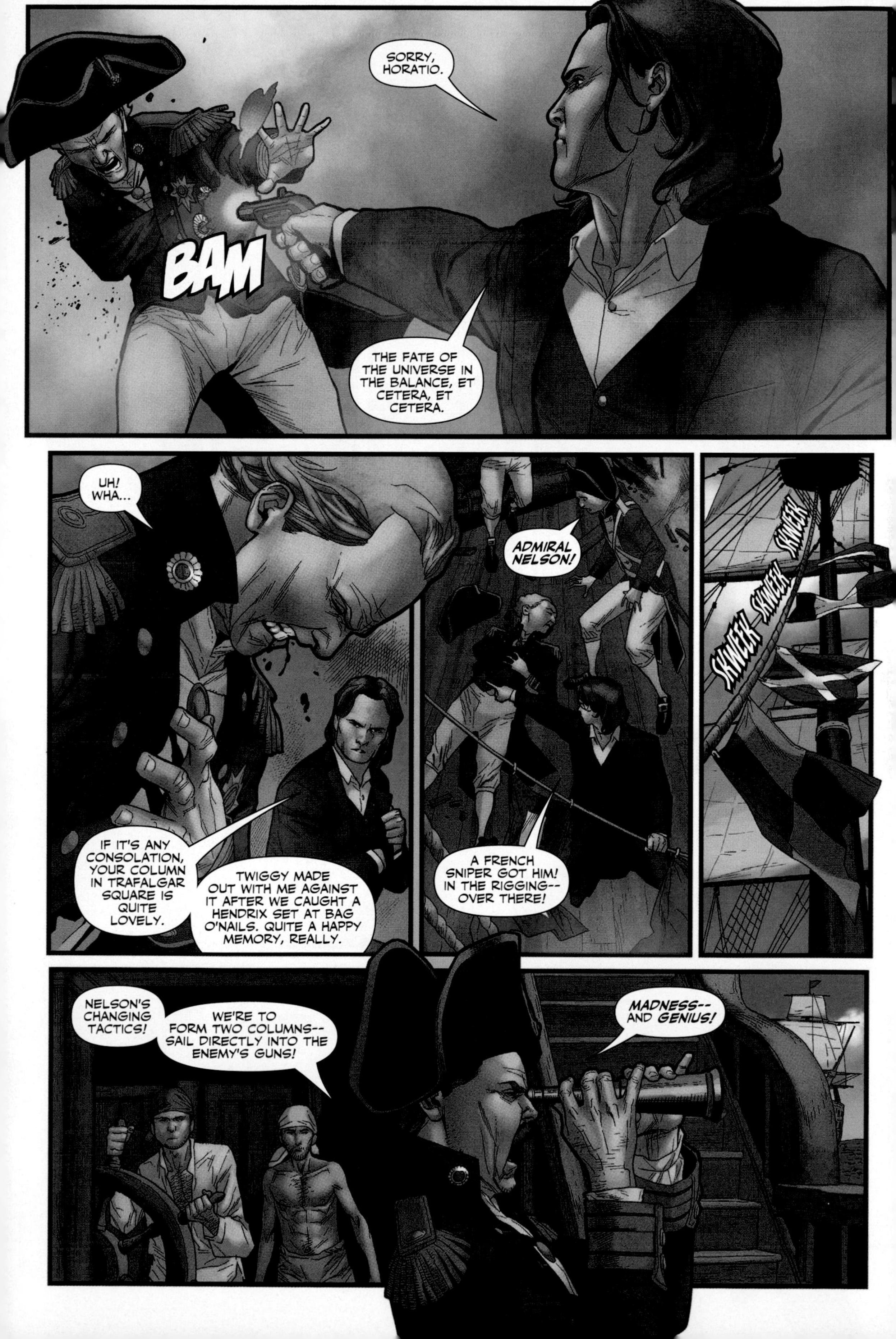
SORRY, HORATIO.
BAM
THE FATE OF THE UNIVERSE IN THE BALANCE, ET CETERA, ET CETERA.
UH! WHA...
IF IT'S ANY CONSOLATION, YOUR COLUMN IN TRAFALGAR SQUARE IS QUITE LOVELY.
TWIGGY MADE OUT WITH ME AGAINST IT AFTER WE CAUGHT A HENDRIX SET AT BAG O'NAILS. QUITE A HAPPY MEMORY, REALLY.
ADMIRAL NELSON!
A FRENCH SNIPER GOT HIM! IN THE RIGGING-- OVER THERE!
SKWEEK SKWEEK SKWEEK
NELSON'S CHANGING TACTICS!
WE'RE TO FORM TWO COLUMNS-- SAIL DIRECTLY INTO THE ENEMY'S GUNS!
MADNESS-- AND GENIUS!

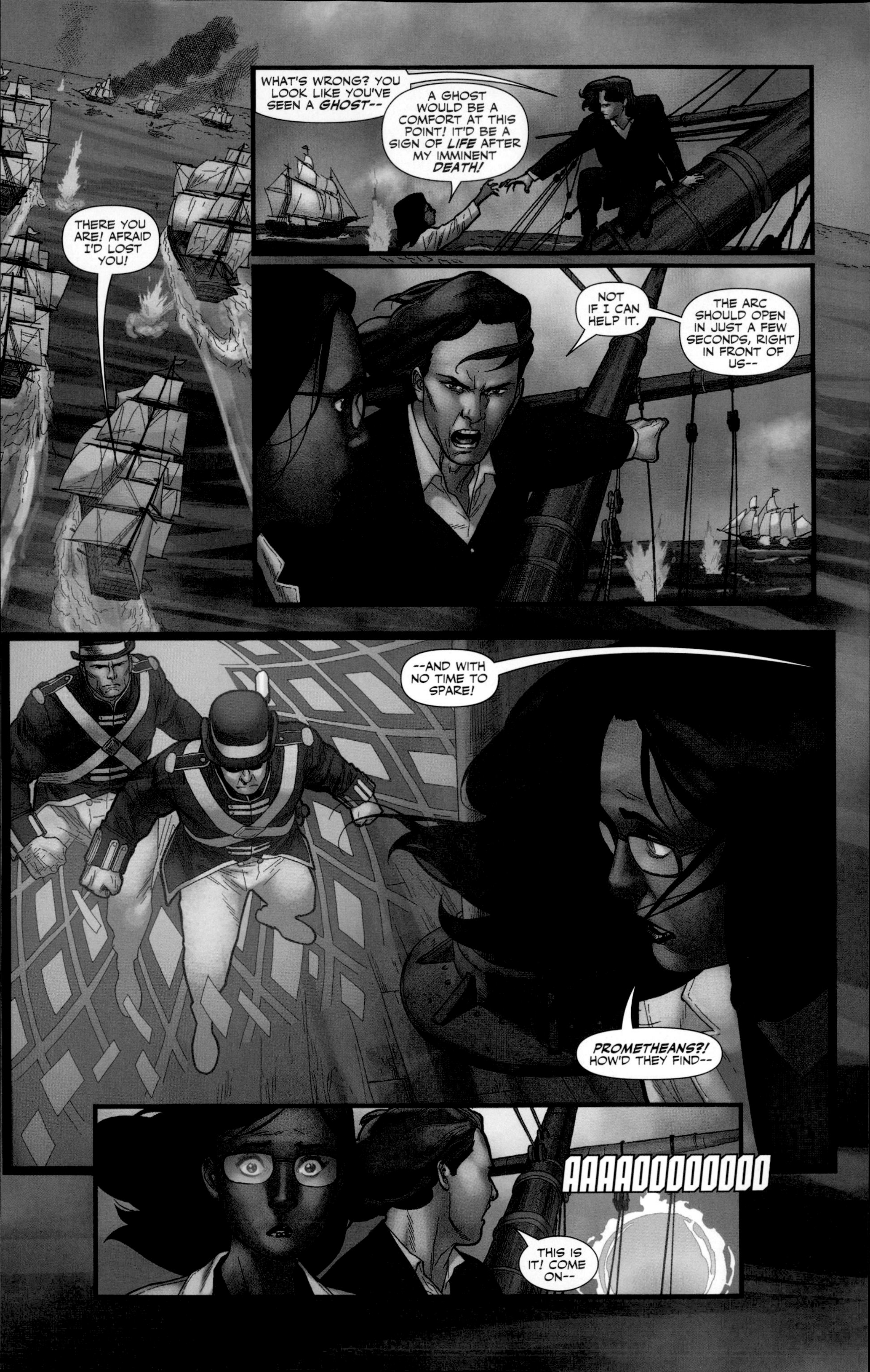

THERE YOU ARE! AFRAID I'D LOST YOU!
WHAT'S WRONG? YOU LOOK LIKE YOU'VE SEEN A GHOST--
A GHOST WOULD BE A COMFORT AT THIS POINT! IT'D BE A SIGN OF LIFE AFTER MY IMMINENT DEATH!
NOT IF I CAN HELP IT.
THE ARC SHOULD OPEN IN JUST A FEW SECONDS, RIGHT IN FRONT OF US--
--AND WITH NO TIME TO SPARE!
PROMETHEANS?! HOW'D THEY FIND--
AAAADDDDDDDD
THIS IS IT! COME ON--

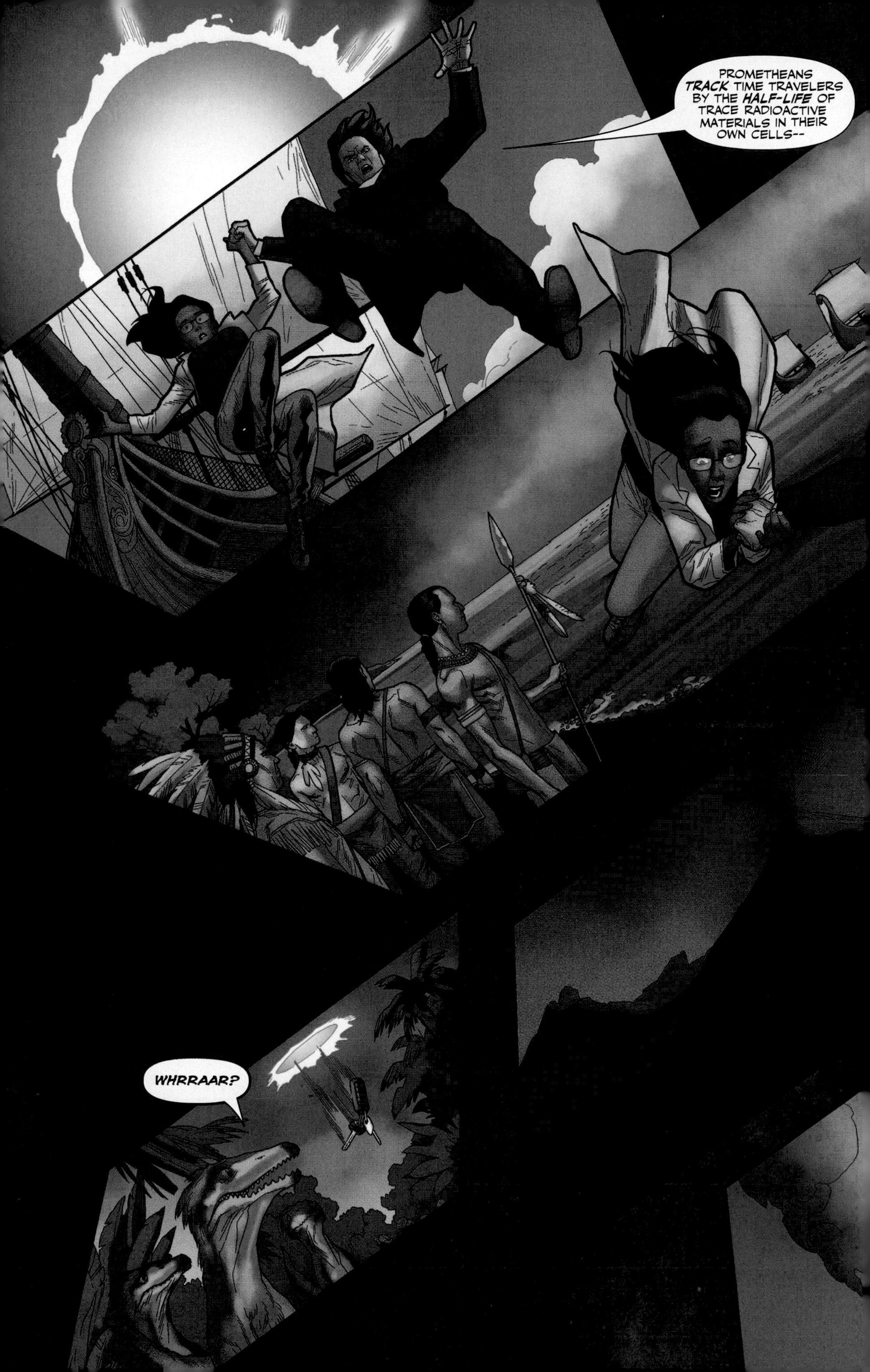
PROMETHEANS TRACK TIME TRAVELERS BY THE HALF-LIFE OF TRACE RADIOACTIVE MATERIALS IN THEIR OWN CELLS--
WHRRAAR?

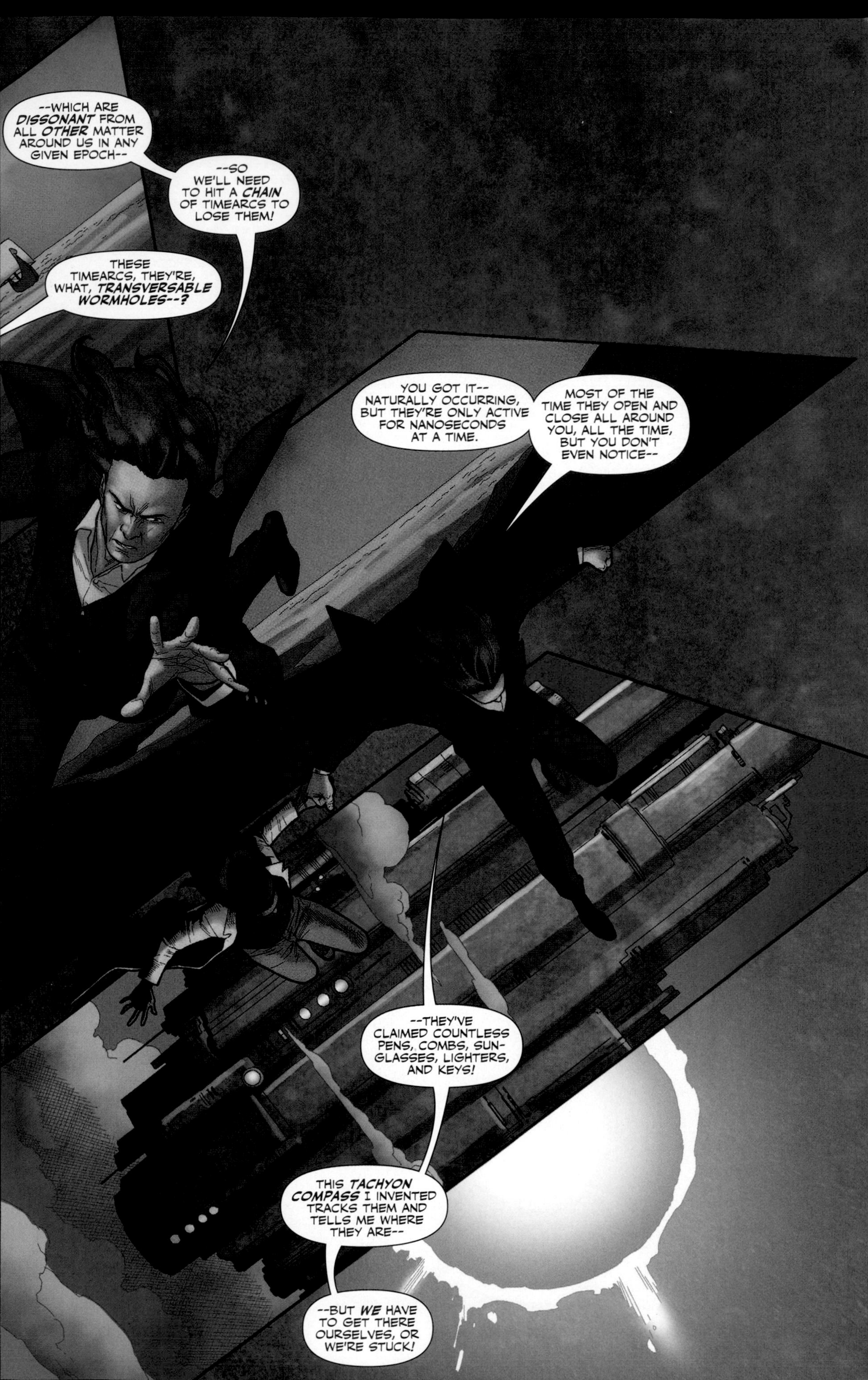
--WHICH ARE DISSONANT FROM ALL OTHER MATTER AROUND US IN ANY GIVEN EPOCH--
--SO WE'LL NEED TO HIT A CHAIN OF TIMEARCS TO LOSE THEM!
THESE TIMEARCS, THEY'RE, WHAT, TRANSVERSABLE WORMHOLES--?
YOU GOT IT-- NATURALLY OCCURRING, BUT THEY'RE ONLY ACTIVE FOR NANOSECONDS AT A TIME.
MOST OF THE TIME THEY OPEN AND CLOSE ALL AROUND YOU, ALL THE TIME, BUT YOU DON'T EVEN NOTICE--
--THEY'VE CLAIMED COUNTLESS PENS, COMBS, SUN-GLASSES, LIGHTERS, AND KEYS!
THIS TACHYON COMPASS I INVENTED TRACKS THEM AND TELLS ME WHERE THEY ARE--
--BUT WE HAVE TO GET THERE OURSELVES, OR WE'RE STUCK!

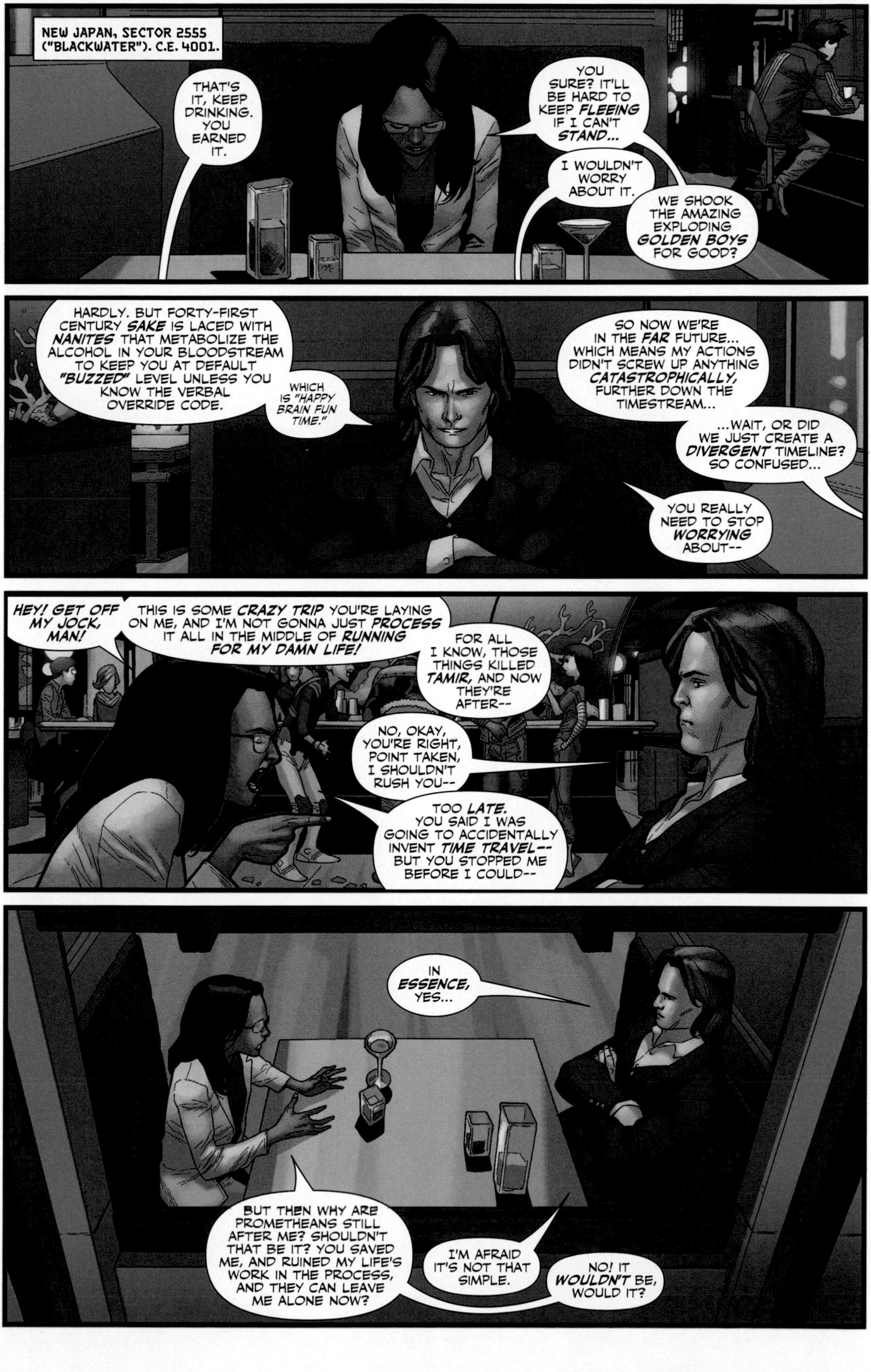
NEW JAPAN, SECTOR 2555 ("BLACKWATER"). C.E. 4001.
THAT'S IT, KEEP DRINKING. YOU EARNED IT.
YOU SURE? IT'LL BE HARD TO KEEP FLEEING IF I CAN'T STAND...
I WOULDN'T WORRY ABOUT IT.
WE SHOOK THE AMAZING EXPLODING GOLDEN BOYS FOR GOOD?
HARDLY. BUT FORTY-FIRST CENTURY SAKE IS LACED WITH NANITES THAT METABOLIZE THE ALCOHOL IN YOUR BLOODSTREAM TO KEEP YOU AT DEFAULT "BUZZED" LEVEL UNLESS YOU KNOW THE VERBAL OVERRIDE CODE.
WHICH IS "HAPPY BRAIN FUN TIME."
SO NOW WE'RE IN THE FAR FUTURE... WHICH MEANS MY ACTIONS DIDN'T SCREW UP ANYTHING CATASTROPHICALLY, FURTHER DOWN THE TIMESTREAM...
...WAIT, OR DID WE JUST CREATE A DIVERGENT TIMELINE? SO CONFUSED...
YOU REALLY NEED TO STOP WORRYING ABOUT--
HEY! GET OFF MY JOCK, MAN!
THIS IS SOME CRAZY TRIP YOU'RE LAYING ON ME, AND I'M NOT GONNA JUST PROCESS IT ALL IN THE MIDDLE OF RUNNING FOR MY DAMN LIFE!
FOR ALL I KNOW, THOSE THINGS KILLED TAMIR, AND NOW THEY'RE AFTER--
NO, OKAY, YOU'RE RIGHT, POINT TAKEN, I SHOULDN'T RUSH YOU--
TOO LATE. YOU SAID I WAS GOING TO ACCIDENTALLY INVENT TIME TRAVEL-- BUT YOU STOPPED ME BEFORE I COULD--
IN ESSENCE, YES...
BUT THEN WHY ARE PROMETHEANS STILL AFTER ME? SHOULDN'T THAT BE IT? YOU SAVED ME, AND RUINED MY LIFE'S WORK IN THE PROCESS, AND THEY CAN LEAVE ME ALONE NOW?
I'M AFRAID IT'S NOT THAT SIMPLE.
NO! IT WOULDN'T BE, WOULD IT?

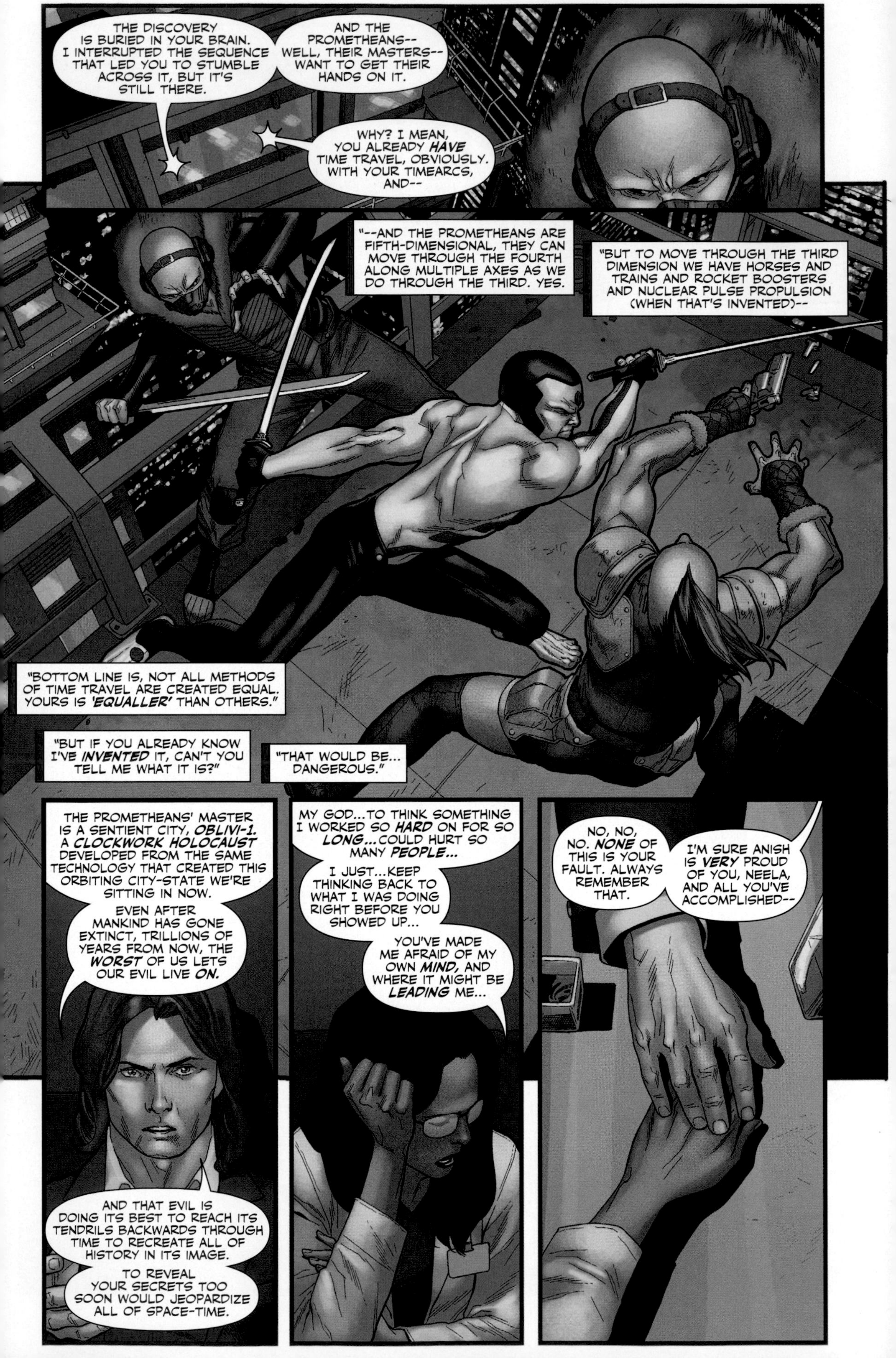
THE DISCOVERY IS BURIED IN YOUR BRAIN. I INTERRUPTED THE SEQUENCE THAT LED YOU TO STUMBLE ACROSS IT, BUT IT'S STILL THERE.
AND THE PROMETHEANS--WELL, THEIR MASTERS--WANT TO GET THEIR HANDS ON IT.
WHY? I MEAN, YOU ALREADY HAVE TIME TRAVEL, OBVIOUSLY. WITH YOUR TIMEARCS, AND--
"--AND THE PROMETHEANS ARE FIFTH-DIMENSIONAL, THEY CAN MOVE THROUGH THE FOURTH ALONG MULTIPLE AXES AS WE DO THROUGH THE THIRD. YES.
"BUT TO MOVE THROUGH THE THIRD DIMENSION WE HAVE HORSES AND TRAINS AND ROCKET BOOSTERS AND NUCLEAR PULSE PROPULSION (WHEN THAT'S INVENTED)--
"BOTTOM LINE IS, NOT ALL METHODS OF TIME TRAVEL ARE CREATED EQUAL. YOURS IS 'EQUALLER' THAN OTHERS."
"BUT IF YOU ALREADY KNOW I'VE INVENTED IT, CAN'T YOU TELL ME WHAT IT IS?"
"THAT WOULD BE... DANGEROUS."
THE PROMETHEANS' MASTER IS A SENTIENT CITY, OBLIVI-1. A CLOCKWORK HOLOCAUST DEVELOPED FROM THE SAME TECHNOLOGY THAT CREATED THIS ORBITING CITY-STATE WE'RE SITTING IN NOW.
EVEN AFTER MANKIND HAS GONE EXTINCT, TRILLIONS OF YEARS FROM NOW, THE WORST OF US LETS OUR EVIL LIVE ON.
AND THAT EVIL IS DOING ITS BEST TO REACH ITS TENDRILS BACKWARDS THROUGH TIME TO RECREATE ALL OF HISTORY IN ITS IMAGE.
TO REVEAL YOUR SECRETS TOO SOON WOULD JEOPARDIZE ALL OF SPACE-TIME.
MY GOD...TO THINK SOMETHING I WORKED SO HARD ON FOR SO LONG...COULD HURT SO MANY PEOPLE...
I JUST...KEEP THINKING BACK TO WHAT I WAS DOING RIGHT BEFORE YOU SHOWED UP...
YOU'VE MADE ME AFRAID OF MY OWN MIND, AND WHERE IT MIGHT BE LEADING ME...
NO, NO, NO. NONE OF THIS IS YOUR FAULT. ALWAYS REMEMBER THAT.
I'M SURE ANISH IS VERY PROUD OF YOU, NEELA, AND ALL YOU'VE ACCOMPLISHED--

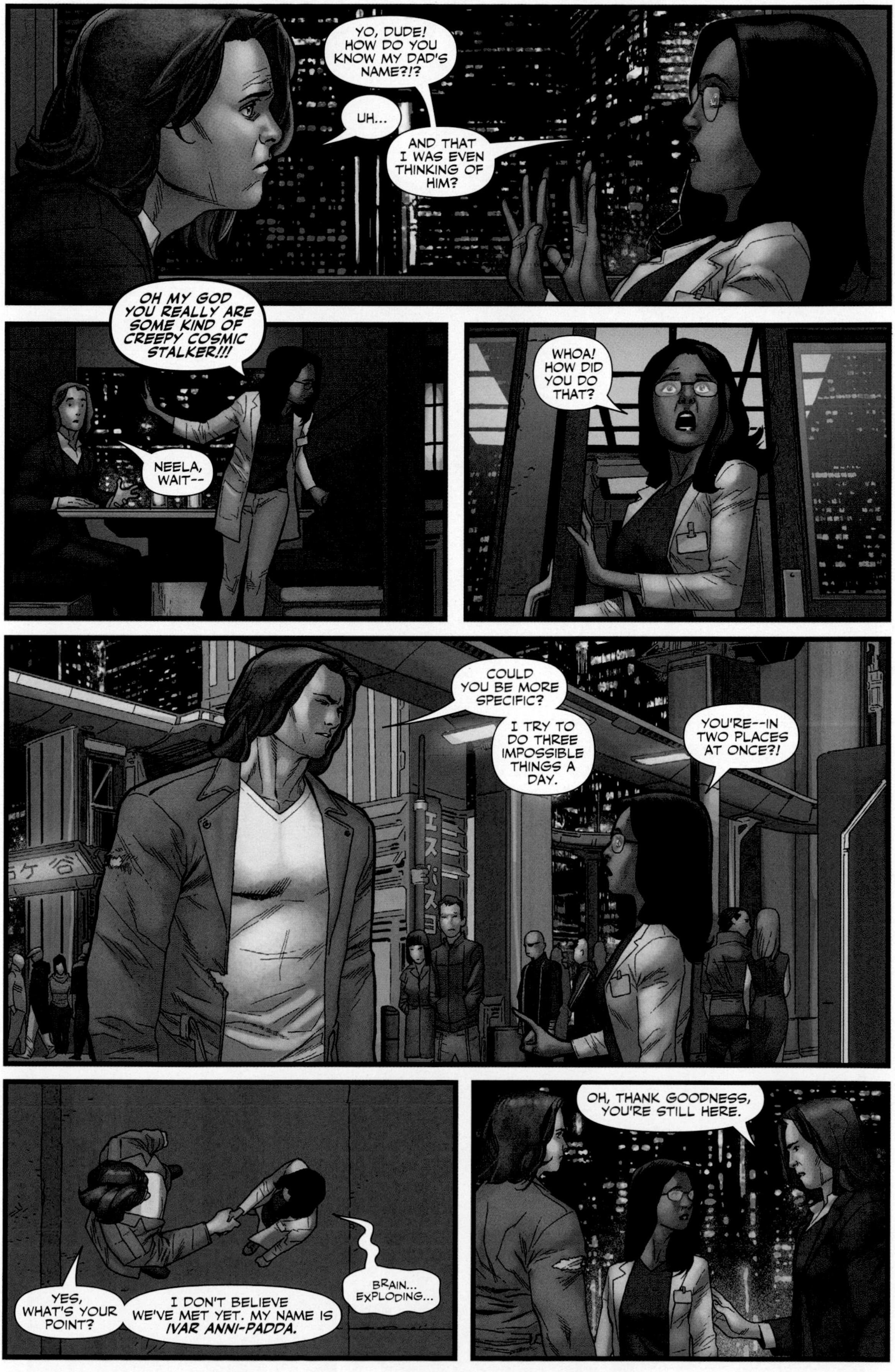
YO, DUDE! HOW DO YOU KNOW MY DAD'S NAME?!?
UH...
AND THAT I WAS EVEN THINKING OF HIM?
OH MY GOD YOU REALLY ARE SOME KIND OF CREEPY COSMIC STALKER!!!
NEELA, WAIT--
WHOA! HOW DID YOU DO THAT?
COULD YOU BE MORE SPECIFIC?
I TRY TO DO THREE IMPOSSIBLE THINGS A DAY.
YOU'RE--IN TWO PLACES AT ONCE?!
BRAIN... EXPLODING...
YES, WHAT'S YOUR POINT?
I DON'T BELIEVE WE'VE MET YET. MY NAME IS *IVAR ANNI-PADDA.*
OH, THANK GOODNESS, YOU'RE STILL HERE.

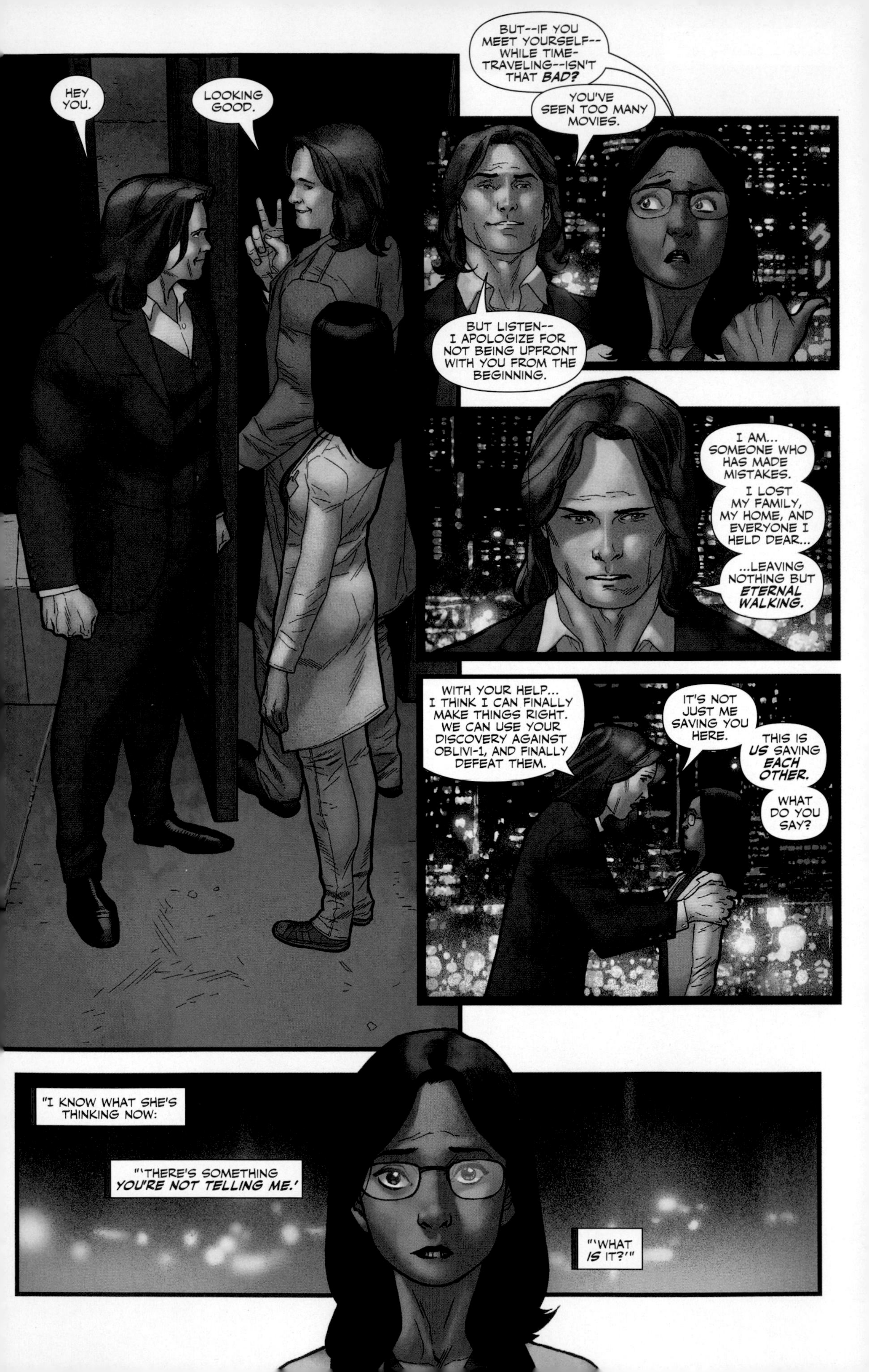
HEY YOU.
LOOKING GOOD.
BUT--IF YOU MEET YOURSELF--WHILE TIME-TRAVELING--ISN'T THAT *BAD?*
YOU'VE SEEN TOO MANY MOVIES.
BUT LISTEN--I APOLOGIZE FOR NOT BEING UPFRONT WITH YOU FROM THE BEGINNING.
I AM... SOMEONE WHO HAS MADE MISTAKES.
I LOST MY FAMILY, MY HOME, AND EVERYONE I HELD DEAR...
...LEAVING NOTHING BUT ***ETERNAL WALKING.***
WITH YOUR HELP... I THINK I CAN FINALLY MAKE THINGS RIGHT. WE CAN USE YOUR DISCOVERY AGAINST OBLIVI-1, AND FINALLY DEFEAT THEM.
IT'S NOT JUST ME SAVING YOU HERE.
THIS IS ***US*** SAVING ***EACH OTHER.***
WHAT DO YOU SAY?
"I KNOW WHAT SHE'S THINKING NOW:
"'THERE'S SOMETHING *YOU'RE NOT TELLING ME.'*
"'WHAT *IS* IT?'"

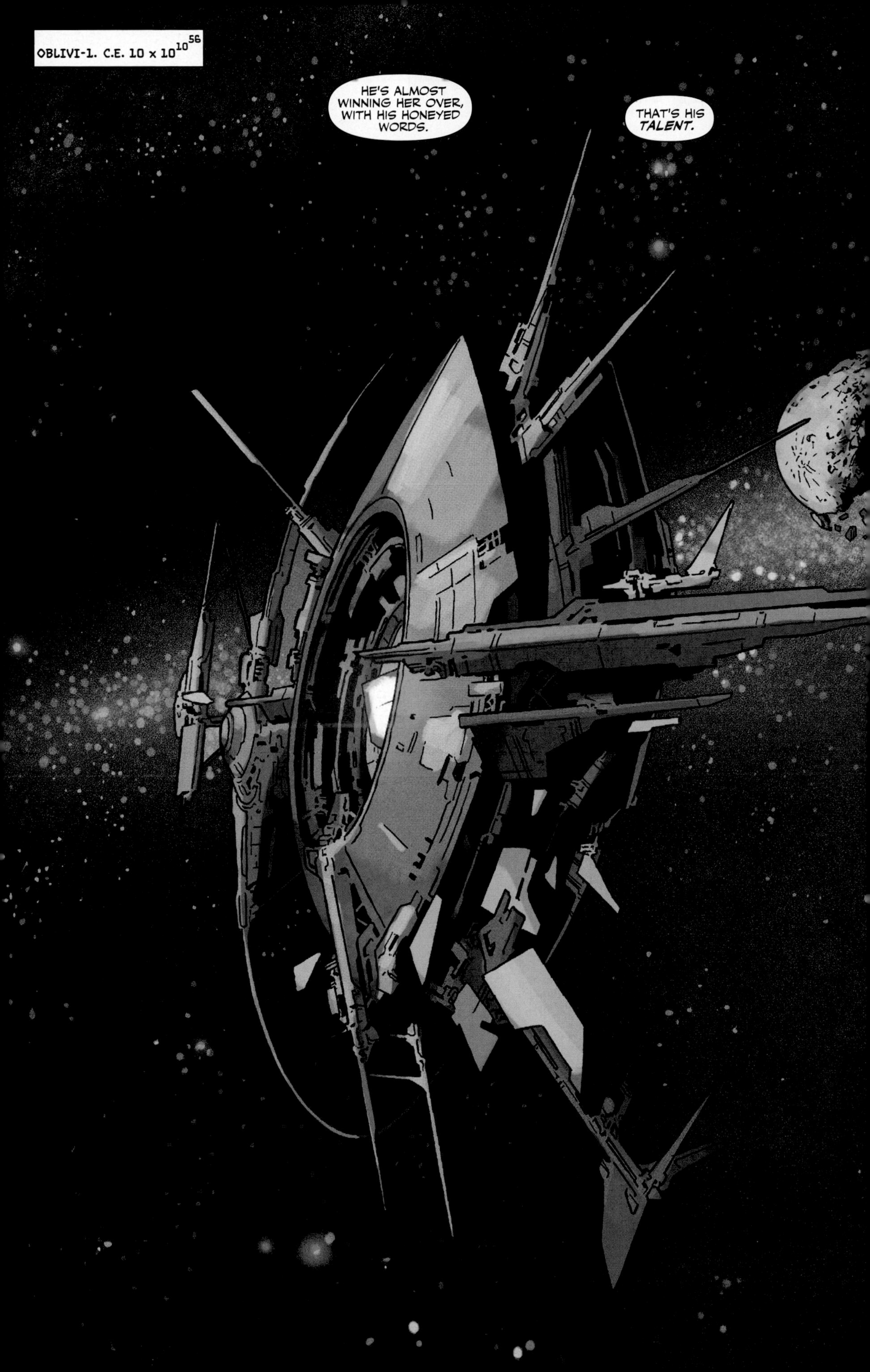
OBLIVI-1. C.E. $10 \times 10^{10^{56}}$
HE'S ALMOST WINNING HER OVER, WITH HIS HONEYED WORDS.
THAT'S HIS *TALENT.*

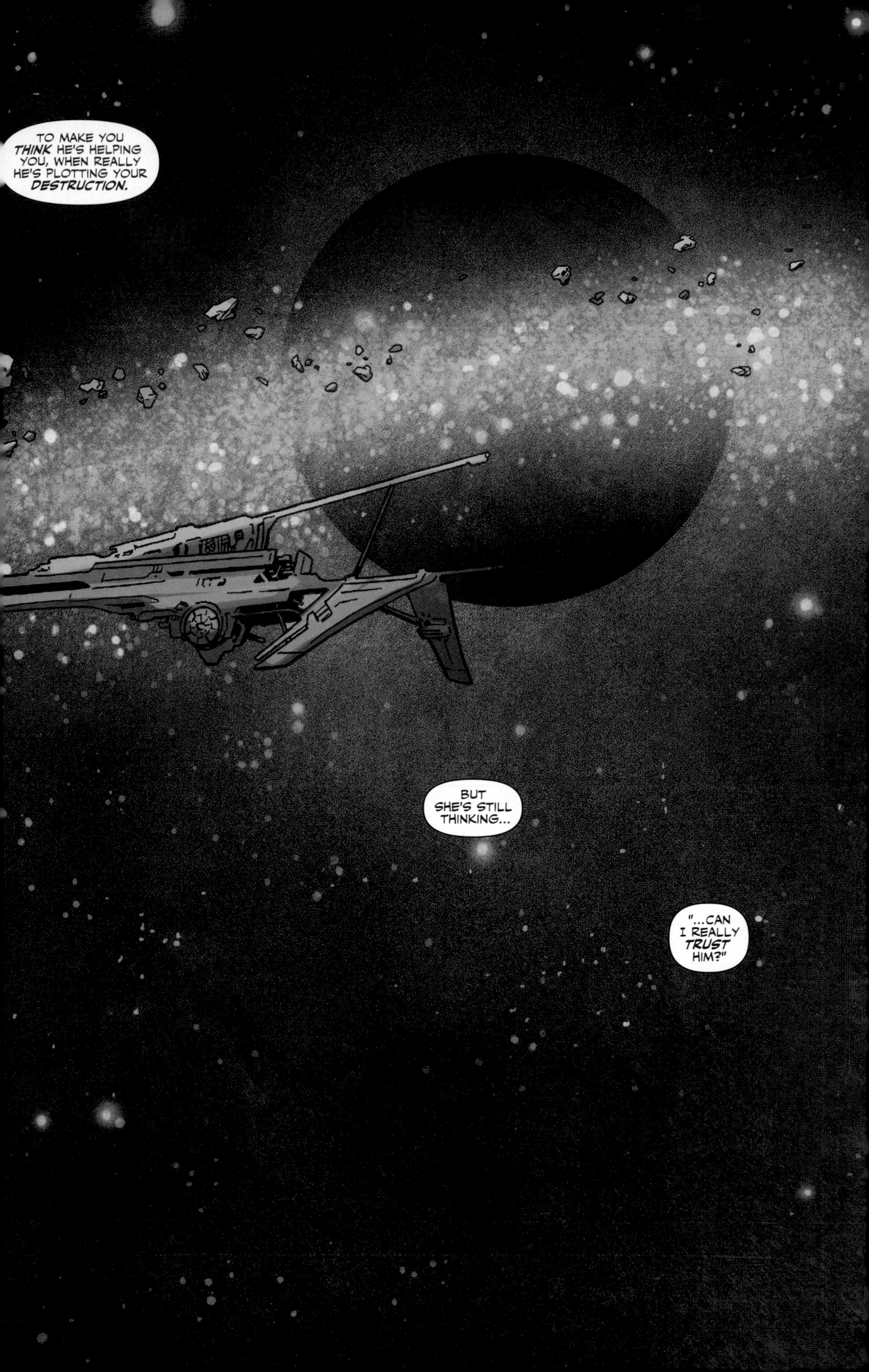
TO MAKE YOU *THINK* HE'S HELPING YOU, WHEN REALLY HE'S PLOTTING YOUR *DESTRUCTION.*
BUT SHE'S STILL THINKING...
"...CAN I REALLY *TRUST* HIM?"

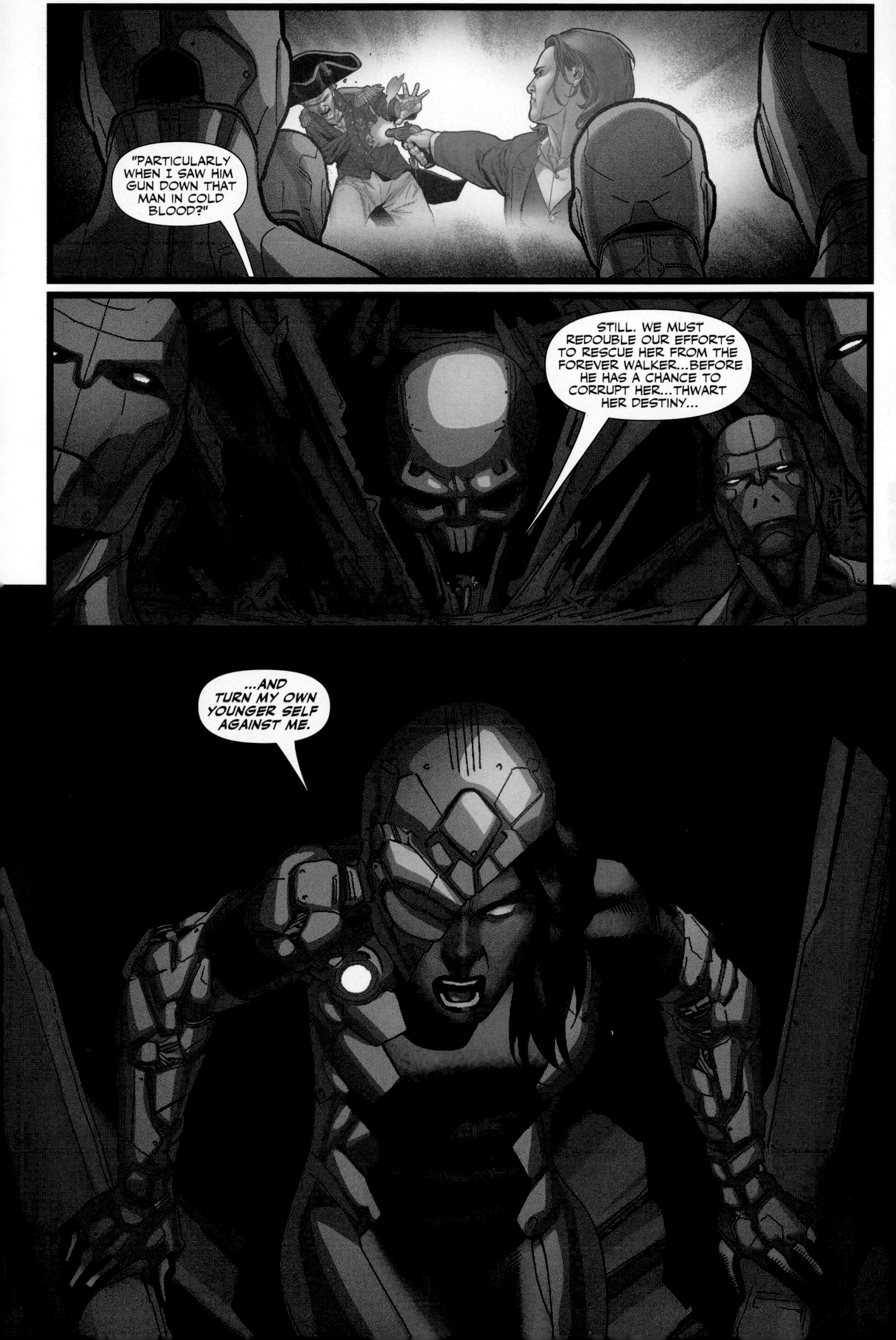
"PARTICULARLY WHEN I SAW HIM GUN DOWN THAT MAN IN COLD BLOOD?"
STILL. WE MUST REDOUBLE OUR EFFORTS TO RESCUE HER FROM THE FOREVER WALKER...BEFORE HE HAS A CHANCE TO CORRUPT HER...THWART HER DESTINY...
...AND TURN MY OWN YOUNGER SELF AGAINST ME.

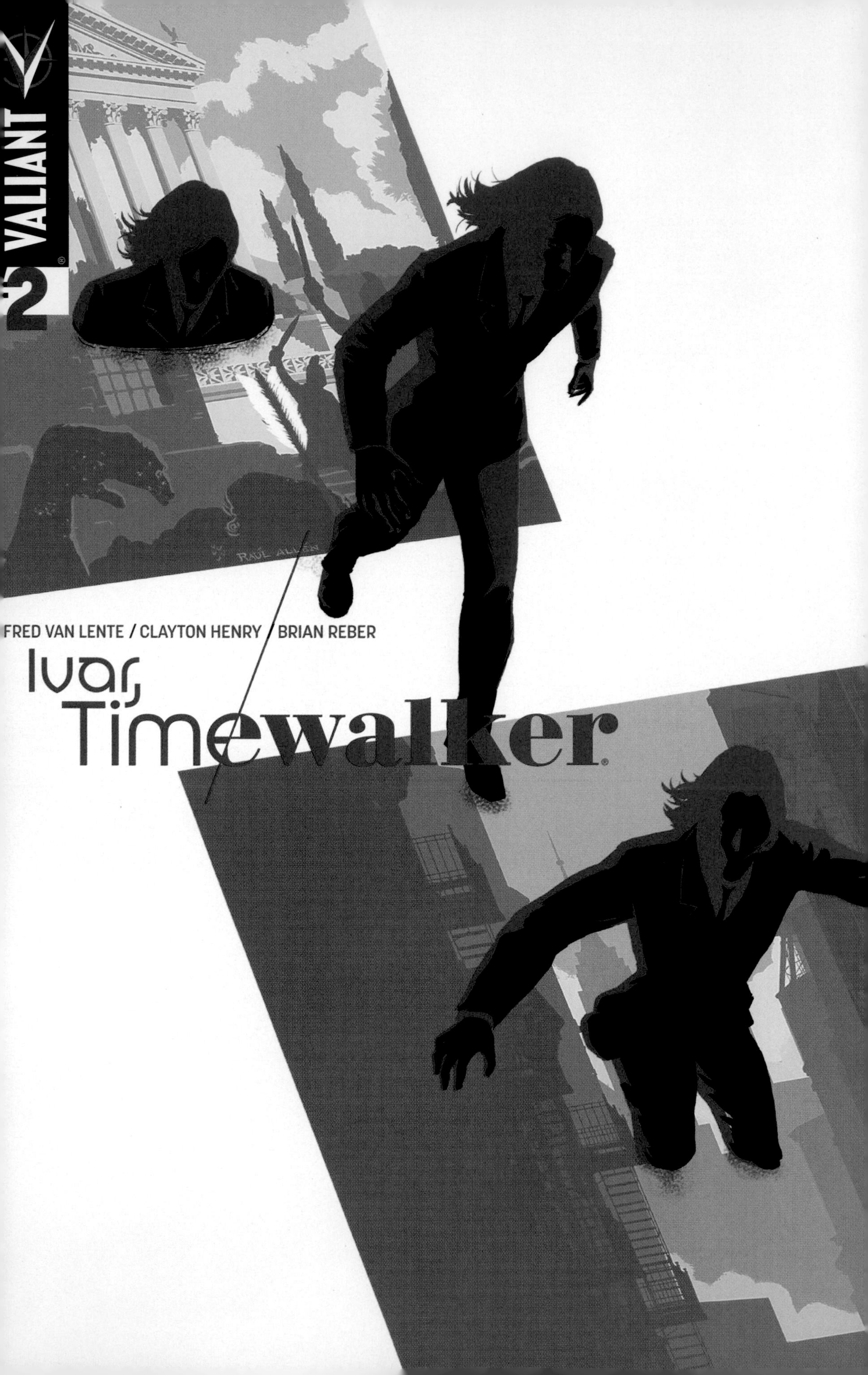
VALIANT
2
RAÚL ALLEN
FRED VAN LENTE / CLAYTON HENRY / BRIAN REBER
Ivar, Timewalker

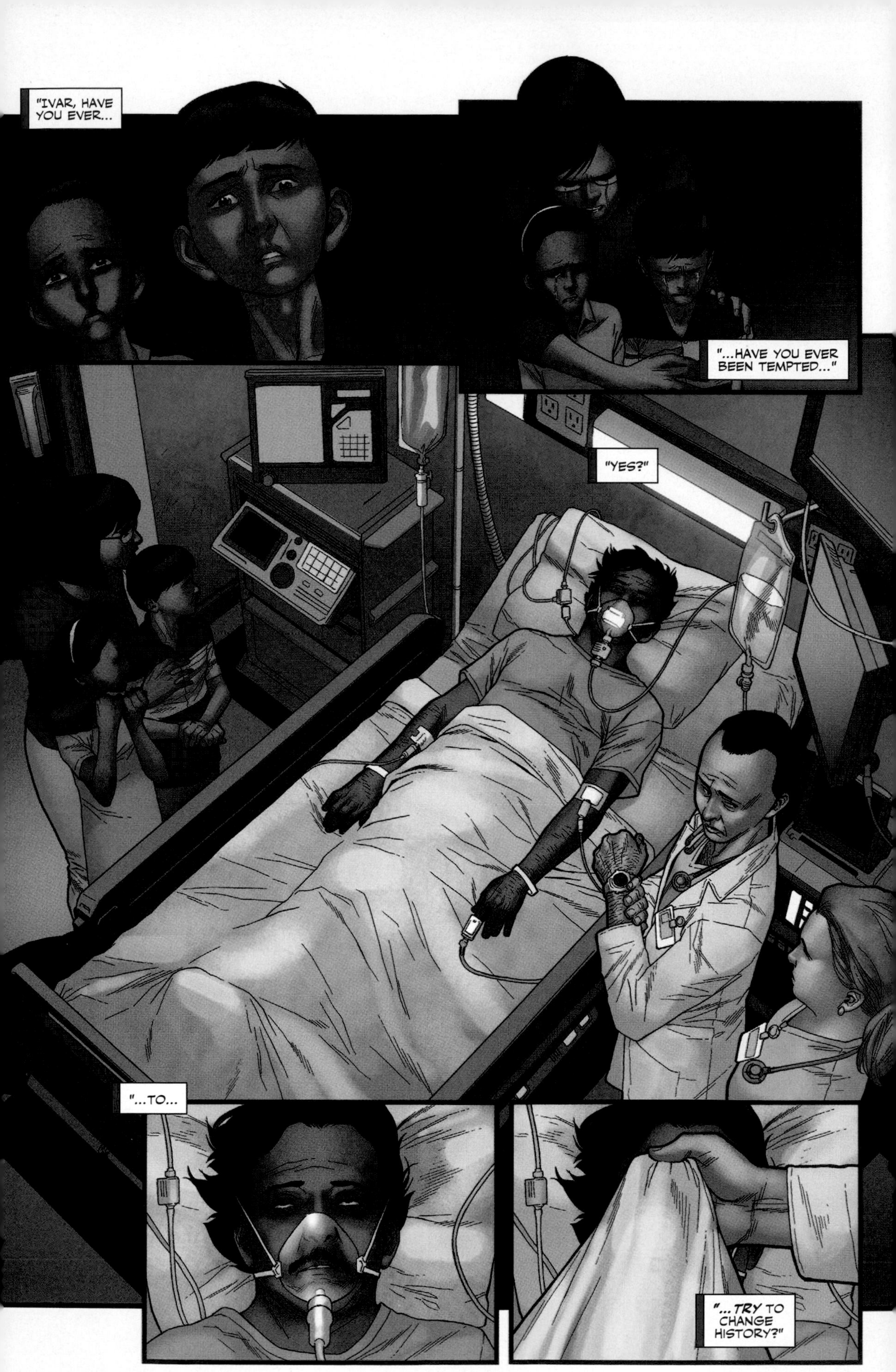
"IVAR, HAVE YOU EVER...
"...HAVE YOU EVER BEEN TEMPTED..."
"YES?"
"...TO...
"...TRY TO CHANGE HISTORY?"

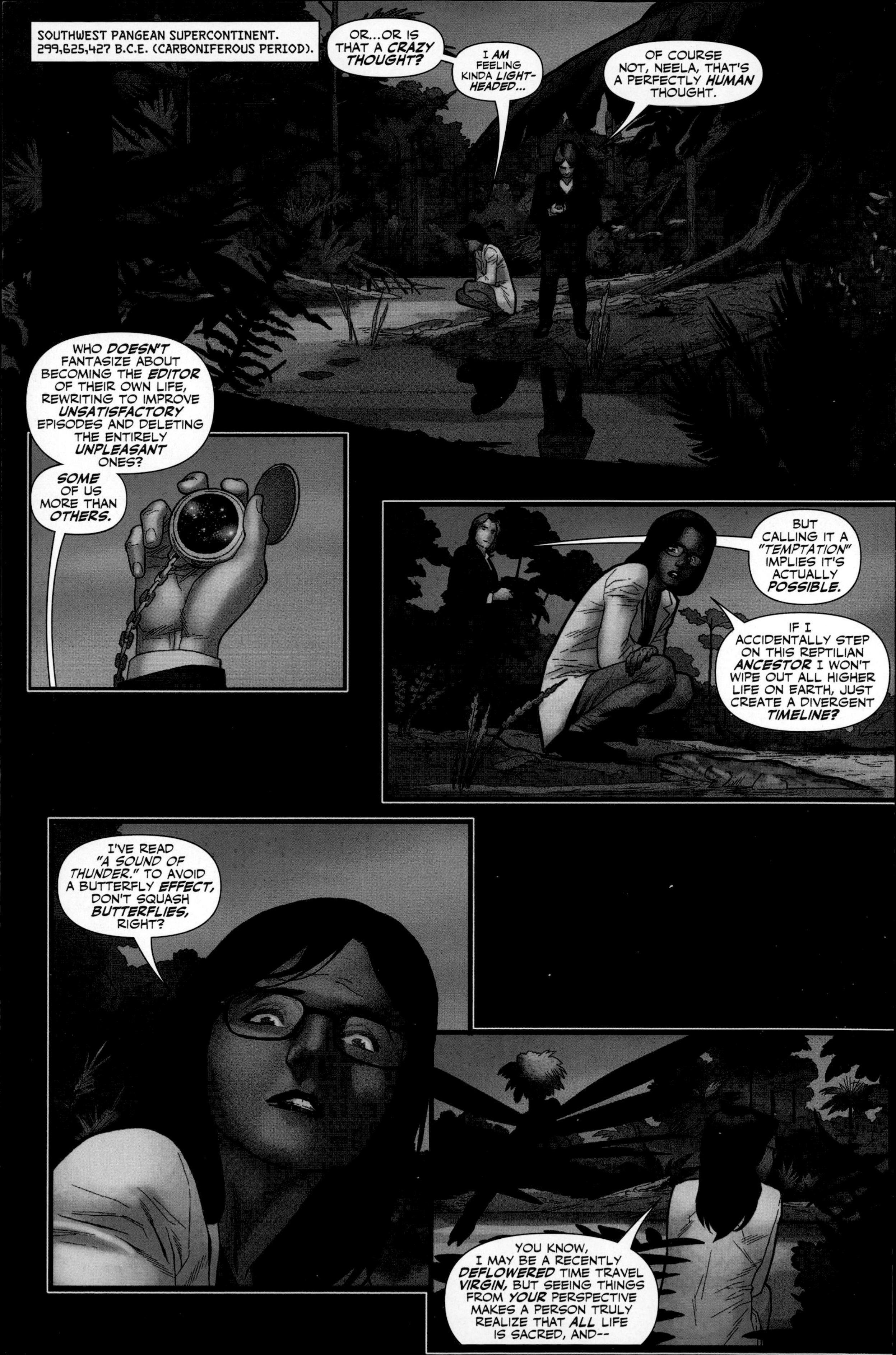
SOUTHWEST PANGEAN SUPERCONTINENT. 299,625,427 B.C.E. (CARBONIFEROUS PERIOD).
OR...OR IS THAT A CRAZY THOUGHT?
I AM FEELING KINDA LIGHT-HEADED...
OF COURSE NOT, NEELA, THAT'S A PERFECTLY HUMAN THOUGHT.
WHO DOESN'T FANTASIZE ABOUT BECOMING THE EDITOR OF THEIR OWN LIFE, REWRITING TO IMPROVE UNSATISFACTORY EPISODES AND DELETING THE ENTIRELY UNPLEASANT ONES?
SOME OF US MORE THAN OTHERS.
BUT CALLING IT A "TEMPTATION" IMPLIES IT'S ACTUALLY POSSIBLE.
IF I ACCIDENTALLY STEP ON THIS REPTILIAN ANCESTOR I WON'T WIPE OUT ALL HIGHER LIFE ON EARTH, JUST CREATE A DIVERGENT TIMELINE?
I'VE READ "A SOUND OF THUNDER." TO AVOID A BUTTERFLY EFFECT, DON'T SQUASH BUTTERFLIES, RIGHT?
YOU KNOW, I MAY BE A RECENTLY DEFLOWERED TIME TRAVEL VIRGIN, BUT SEEING THINGS FROM YOUR PERSPECTIVE MAKES A PERSON TRULY REALIZE THAT ALL LIFE IS SACRED, AND--

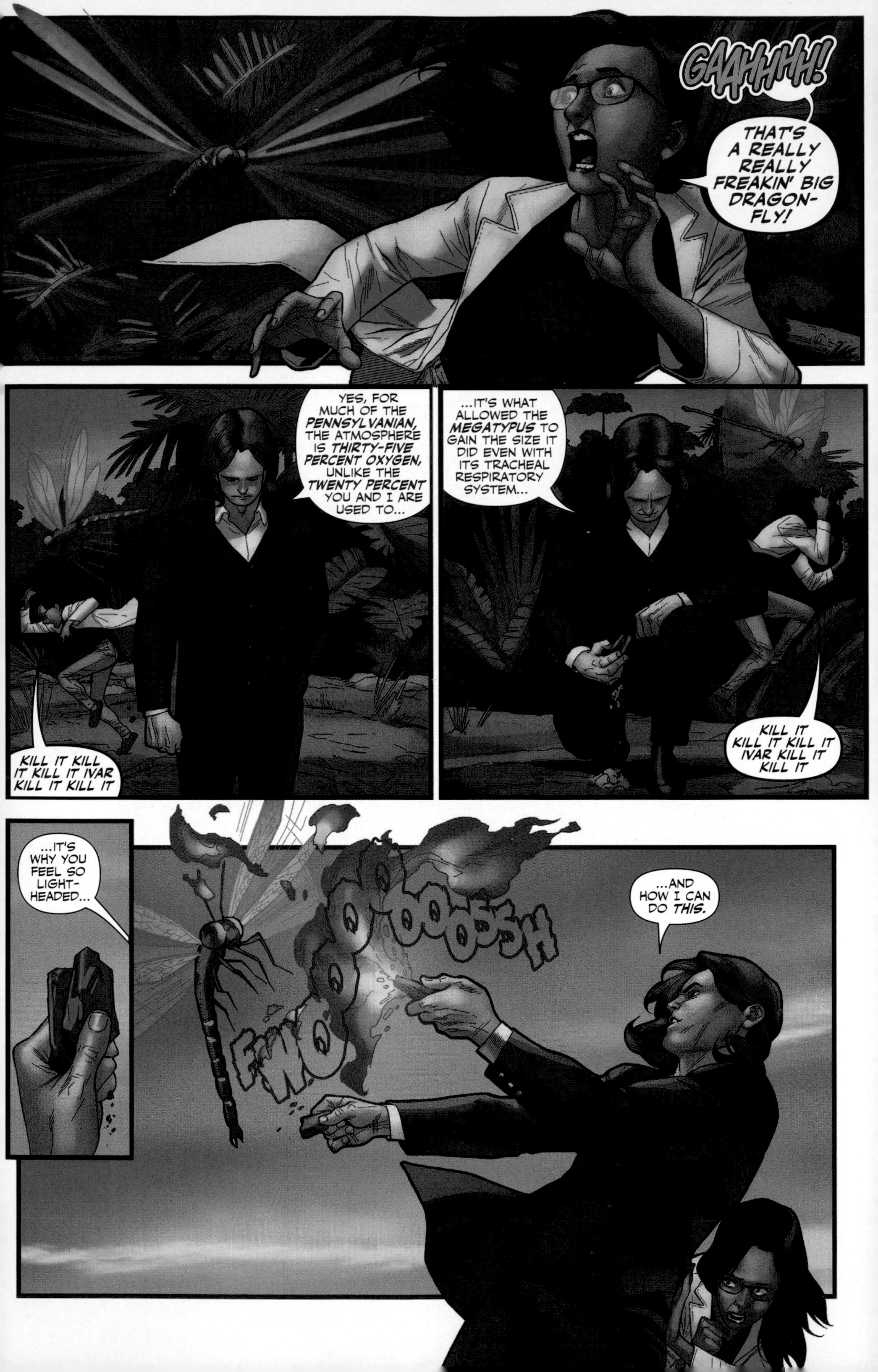
GAAHHHH!
THAT'S A REALLY REALLY FREAKIN' BIG DRAGON-FLY!
YES, FOR MUCH OF THE PENNSYLVANIAN, THE ATMOSPHERE IS THIRTY-FIVE PERCENT OXYGEN, UNLIKE THE TWENTY PERCENT YOU AND I ARE USED TO...
KILL IT KILL IT KILL IT IVAR KILL IT KILL IT
...IT'S WHAT ALLOWED THE MEGATYPUS TO GAIN THE SIZE IT DID EVEN WITH ITS TRACHEAL RESPIRATORY SYSTEM...
KILL IT KILL IT KILL IT IVAR KILL IT KILL IT
...IT'S WHY YOU FEEL SO LIGHT-HEADED...
FWOOOOOOOSH
...AND HOW I CAN DO THIS.

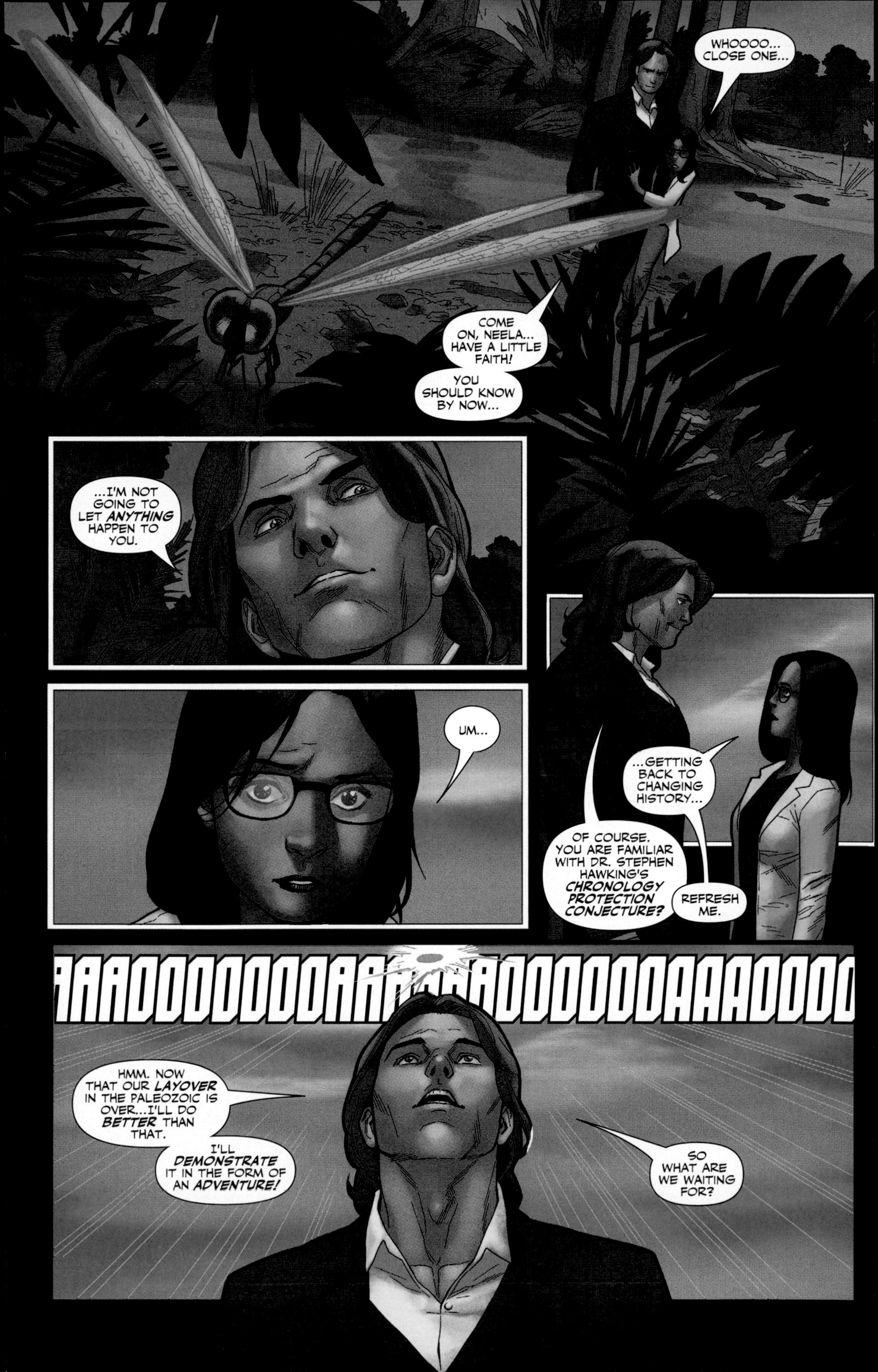
WHOOOO... CLOSE ONE...
COME ON, NEELA... HAVE A LITTLE FAITH!
YOU SHOULD KNOW BY NOW...
...I'M NOT GOING TO LET ANYTHING HAPPEN TO YOU.
UM...
...GETTING BACK TO CHANGING HISTORY...
OF COURSE. YOU ARE FAMILIAR WITH DR. STEPHEN HAWKING'S CHRONOLOGY PROTECTION CONJECTURE?
REFRESH ME.
HMM. NOW THAT OUR LAYOVER IN THE PALEOZOIC IS OVER...I'LL DO BETTER THAN THAT.
I'LL DEMONSTRATE IT IN THE FORM OF AN ADVENTURE!
SO WHAT ARE WE WAITING FOR?

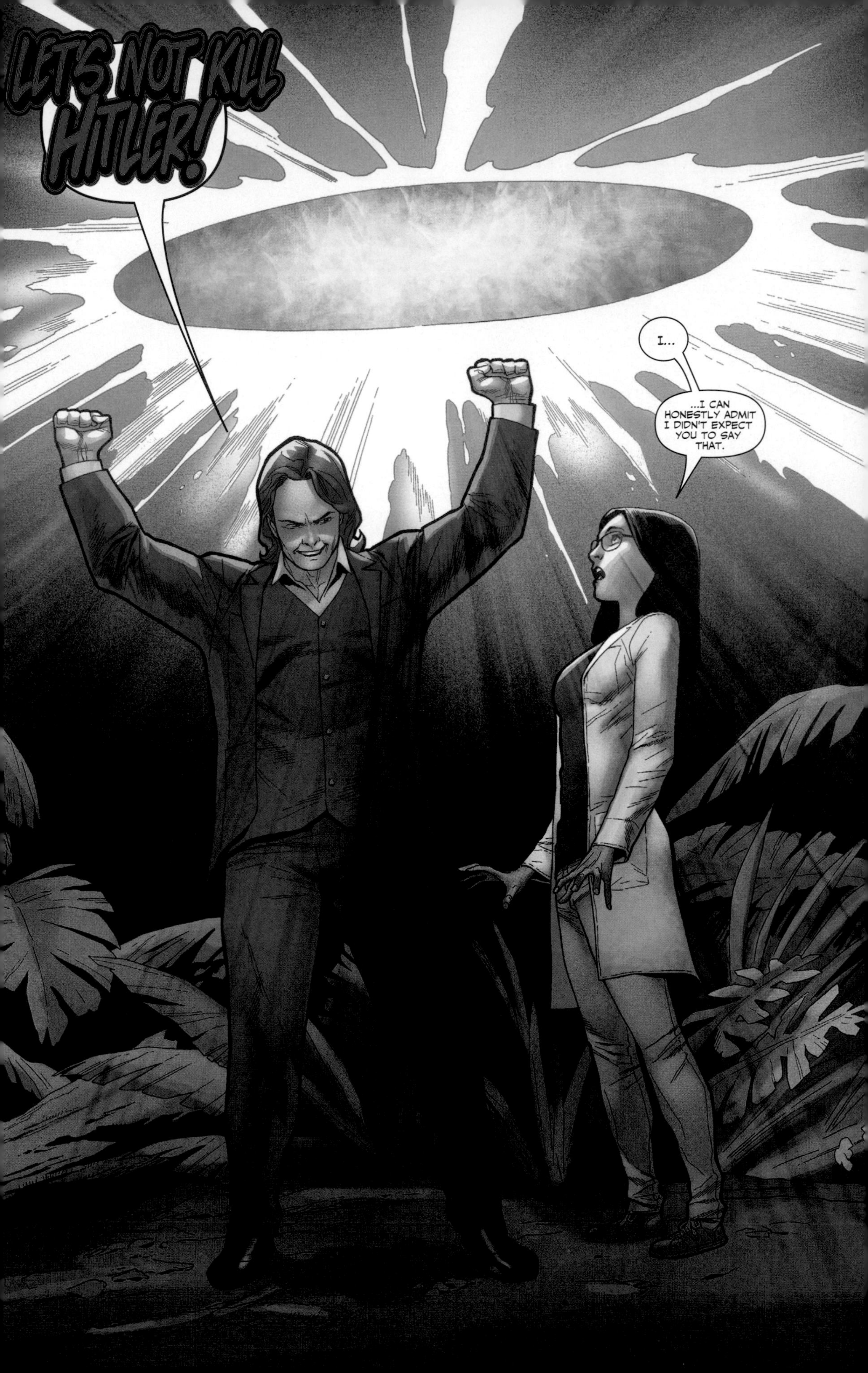
LET'S NOT KILL HITLER!
I...
...I CAN HONESTLY ADMIT I DIDN'T EXPECT YOU TO SAY THAT.

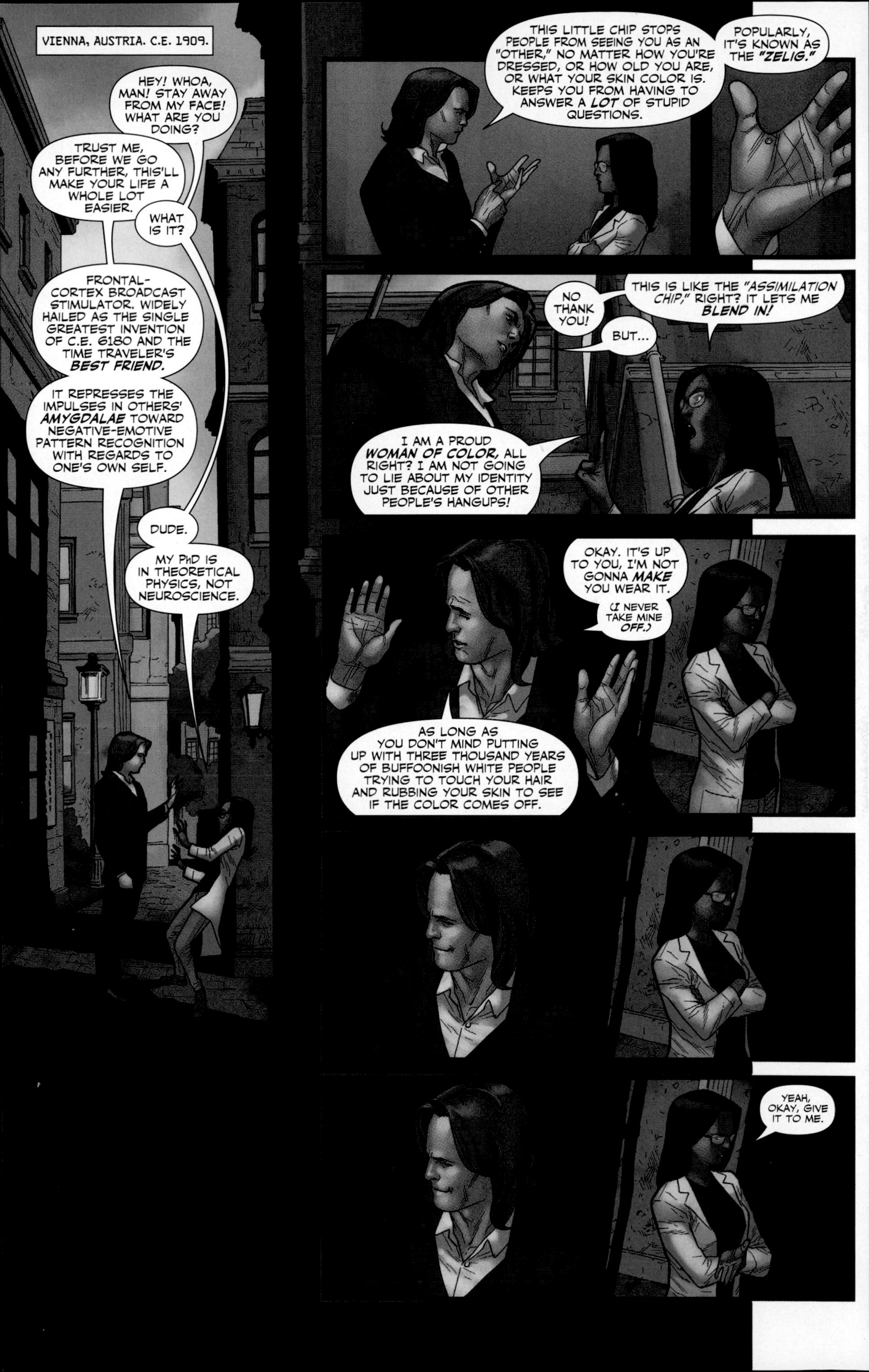

VIENNA, AUSTRIA. C.E. 1909.
HEY! WHOA, MAN! STAY AWAY FROM MY FACE! WHAT ARE YOU DOING?
TRUST ME, BEFORE WE GO ANY FURTHER, THIS'LL MAKE YOUR LIFE A WHOLE LOT EASIER.
WHAT IS IT?
FRONTAL-CORTEX BROADCAST STIMULATOR. WIDELY HAILED AS THE SINGLE GREATEST INVENTION OF C.E. 6180 AND THE TIME TRAVELER'S BEST FRIEND.
IT REPRESSES THE IMPULSES IN OTHERS' AMYGDALAE TOWARD NEGATIVE-EMOTIVE PATTERN RECOGNITION WITH REGARDS TO ONE'S OWN SELF.
DUDE.
MY PhD IS IN THEORETICAL PHYSICS, NOT NEUROSCIENCE.
THIS LITTLE CHIP STOPS PEOPLE FROM SEEING YOU AS AN "OTHER," NO MATTER HOW YOU'RE DRESSED, OR HOW OLD YOU ARE, OR WHAT YOUR SKIN COLOR IS. KEEPS YOU FROM HAVING TO ANSWER A LOT OF STUPID QUESTIONS.
POPULARLY, IT'S KNOWN AS THE "ZELIG."
THIS IS LIKE THE "ASSIMILATION CHIP," RIGHT? IT LETS ME BLEND IN!
NO THANK YOU!
BUT...
I AM A PROUD WOMAN OF COLOR, ALL RIGHT? I AM NOT GOING TO LIE ABOUT MY IDENTITY JUST BECAUSE OF OTHER PEOPLE'S HANGUPS!
OKAY. IT'S UP TO YOU, I'M NOT GONNA MAKE YOU WEAR IT.
(I NEVER TAKE MINE OFF.)
AS LONG AS YOU DON'T MIND PUTTING UP WITH THREE THOUSAND YEARS OF BUFFOONISH WHITE PEOPLE TRYING TO TOUCH YOUR HAIR AND RUBBING YOUR SKIN TO SEE IF THE COLOR COMES OFF.
YEAH, OKAY, GIVE IT TO ME.

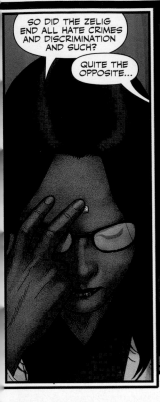

SO DID THE ZELIG END ALL HATE CRIMES AND DISCRIMINATION AND SUCH?

QUITE THE OPPOSITE...

...IT USHERED IN THE THREE-HUNDRED-YEAR *"ICONOCLASH"* IN WHICH PEOPLE WHO REFUSED TO WEAR CHIPS WERE RUTHLESSLY HUNTED DOWN AND BANISHED TO WORK CAMPS ON THE CERES ASTEROID...

MEIN GOTT! SIND DIE ZWEI AUS DEM ZIRKUS AUSGEBROCHEN?!

UGH! HUMANITY.

YOU MAKE ME SAD.

BLEEEP

WAS? MEINEN SIE THESE TWO?

THEY LOOK PERFECTLY *NORMAL* TO ME...

YES, OF COURSE...A TRICK OF LIGHT AND SHADOW, I GUESS...

ITS EMBEDDED *UNIVERSAL TRANSLATOR* DIDN'T HELP MATTERS MUCH EITHER.

WHERE WAS I? RIGHT. THE CHRONOLOGY PROTECTION CONJECTURE EXPLAINS A SIMPLE PARADOX:

IF TIME TRAVEL *WILL* BE INVENTED AT SOME POINT IN FUTURE HISTORY, WHY HAVEN'T WE *MET* ANY TIME TRAVELERS *ALREADY?*

BUT EVEN IF YOU IGNORE THE FACT I *HAVE* MET A TIME TRAVELER, HAWKING WAS WORKING FROM A *FAULTY PREMISE--*

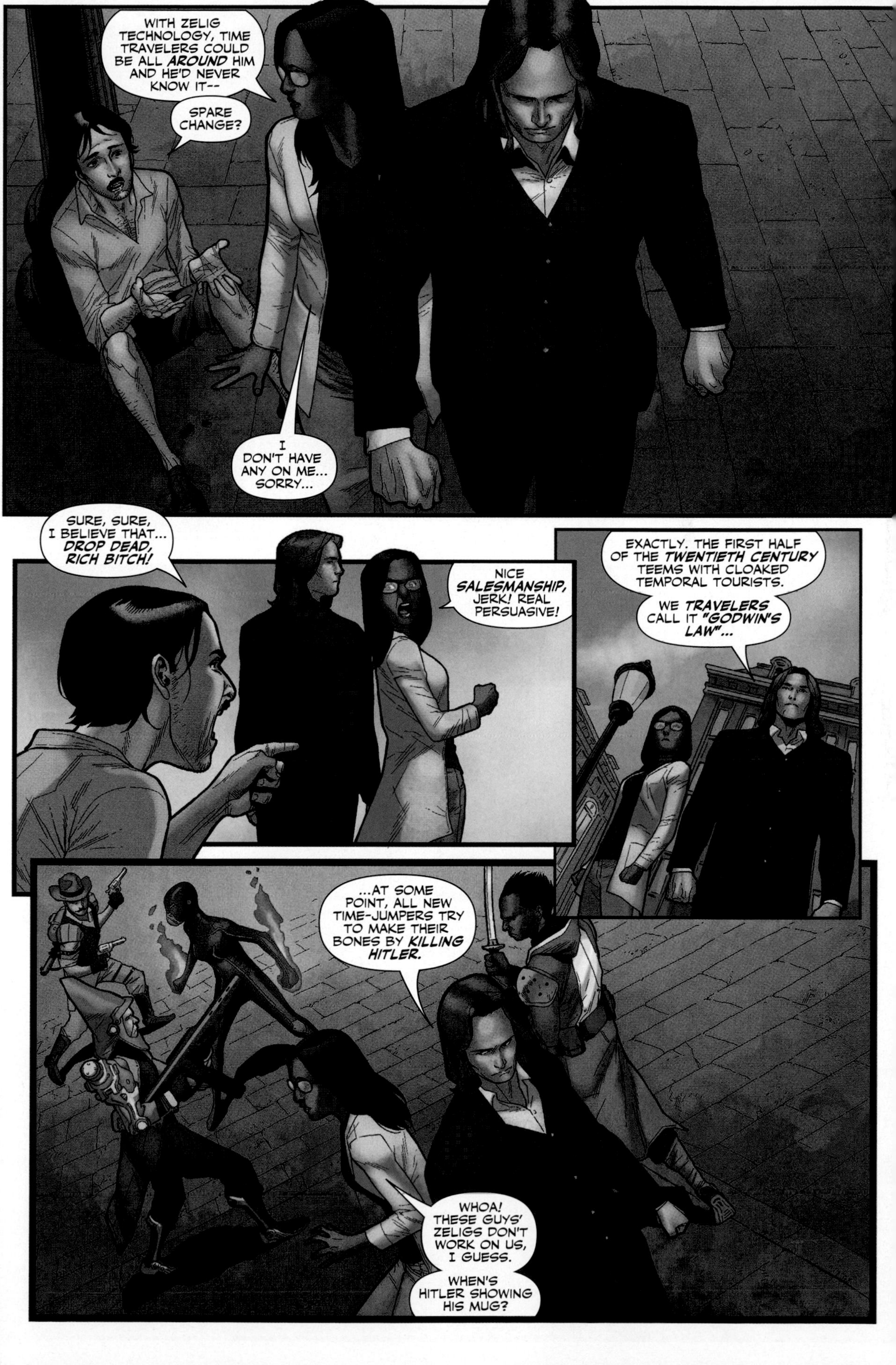
WITH ZELIG TECHNOLOGY, TIME TRAVELERS COULD BE ALL AROUND HIM AND HE'D NEVER KNOW IT--
SPARE CHANGE?
I DON'T HAVE ANY ON ME... SORRY...
SURE, SURE, I BELIEVE THAT... DROP DEAD, RICH BITCH!
NICE SALESMANSHIP, JERK! REAL PERSUASIVE!
EXACTLY. THE FIRST HALF OF THE TWENTIETH CENTURY TEEMS WITH CLOAKED TEMPORAL TOURISTS.
WE TRAVELERS CALL IT "GODWIN'S LAW"...
...AT SOME POINT, ALL NEW TIME-JUMPERS TRY TO MAKE THEIR BONES BY KILLING HITLER.
WHOA! THESE GUYS' ZELIGS DON'T WORK ON US, I GUESS.
WHEN'S HITLER SHOWING HIS MUG?

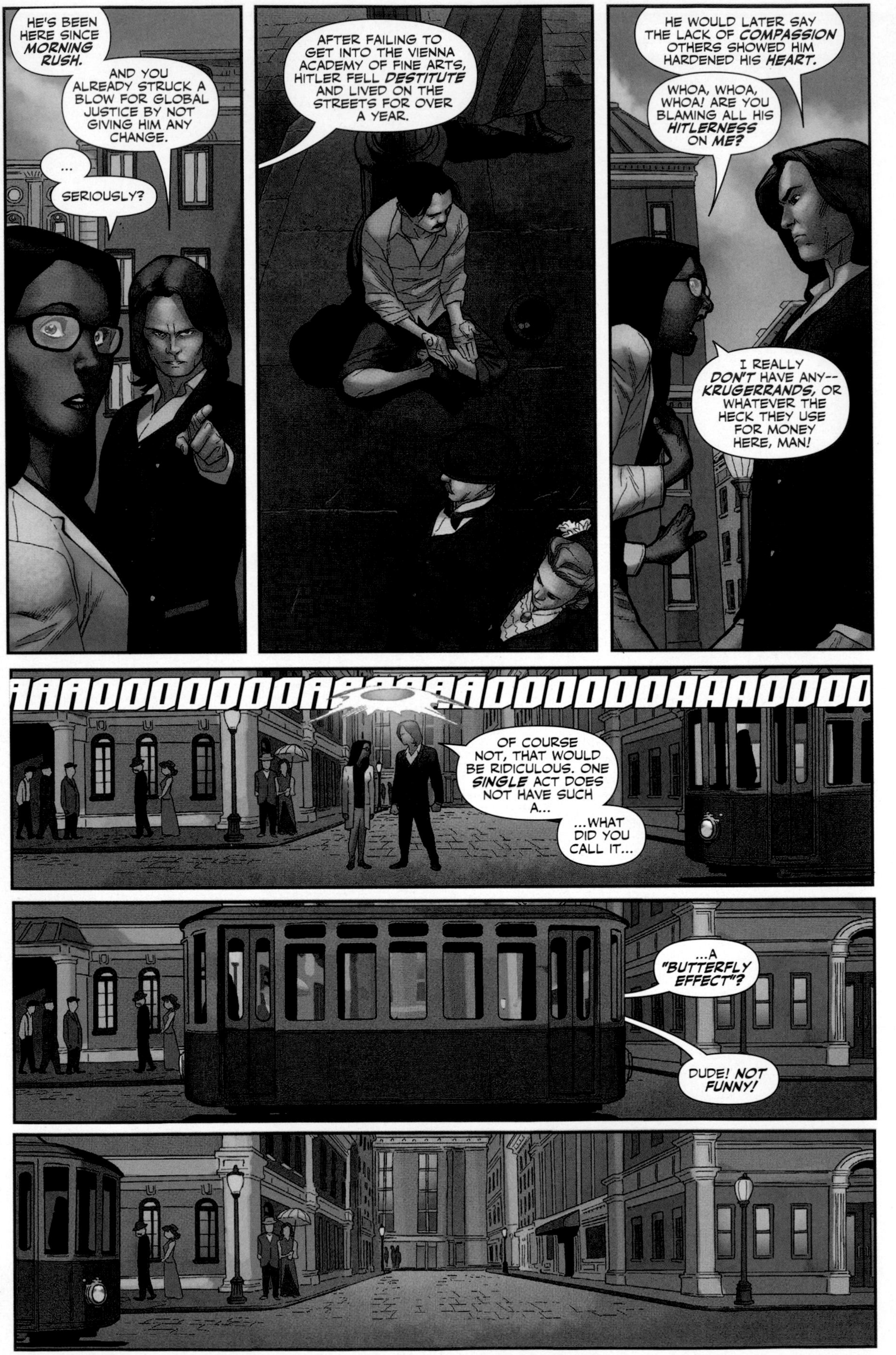
HE'S BEEN HERE SINCE MORNING RUSH.
AND YOU ALREADY STRUCK A BLOW FOR GLOBAL JUSTICE BY NOT GIVING HIM ANY CHANGE.
...
SERIOUSLY?
AFTER FAILING TO GET INTO THE VIENNA ACADEMY OF FINE ARTS, HITLER FELL DESTITUTE AND LIVED ON THE STREETS FOR OVER A YEAR.
HE WOULD LATER SAY THE LACK OF COMPASSION OTHERS SHOWED HIM HARDENED HIS HEART.
WHOA, WHOA, WHOA! ARE YOU BLAMING ALL HIS HITLERNESS ON ME?
I REALLY DON'T HAVE ANY-- KRUGERRANDS, OR WHATEVER THE HECK THEY USE FOR MONEY HERE, MAN!
AAAOOOOOOOOAAAAAAAOOOOOOOOAAAAOOOO
OF COURSE NOT, THAT WOULD BE RIDICULOUS. ONE SINGLE ACT DOES NOT HAVE SUCH A...
...WHAT DID YOU CALL IT...
...A "BUTTERFLY EFFECT"?
DUDE! NOT FUNNY!

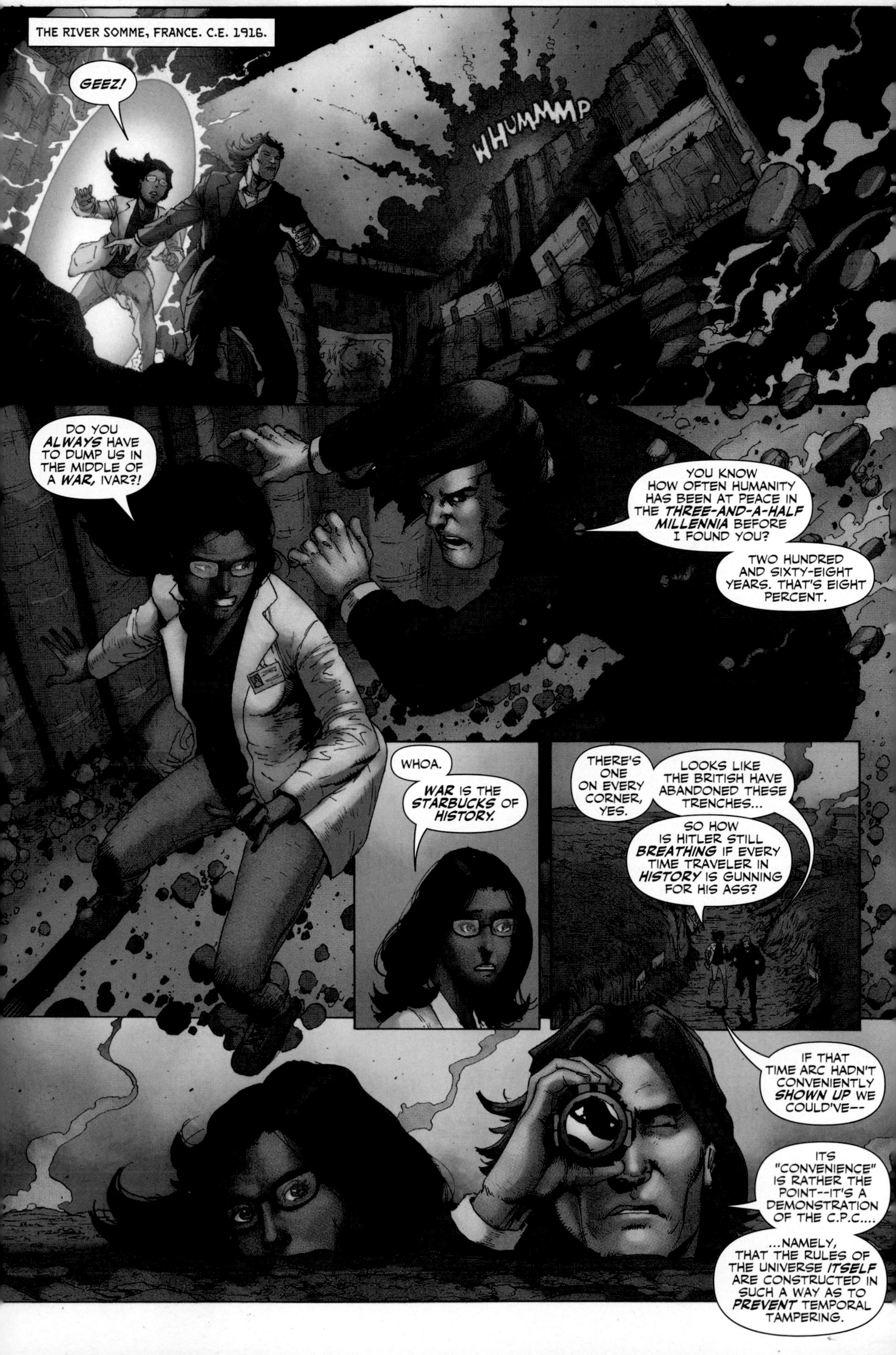
THE RIVER SOMME, FRANCE. C.E. 1916.
GEEZ!
WHUMMMP
DO YOU ALWAYS HAVE TO DUMP US IN THE MIDDLE OF A WAR, IVAR?!
YOU KNOW HOW OFTEN HUMANITY HAS BEEN AT PEACE IN THE THREE-AND-A-HALF MILLENNIA BEFORE I FOUND YOU?
TWO HUNDRED AND SIXTY-EIGHT YEARS. THAT'S EIGHT PERCENT.
WHOA.
WAR IS THE STARBUCKS OF HISTORY.
THERE'S ONE ON EVERY CORNER, YES.
LOOKS LIKE THE BRITISH HAVE ABANDONED THESE TRENCHES...
SO HOW IS HITLER STILL BREATHING IF EVERY TIME TRAVELER IN HISTORY IS GUNNING FOR HIS ASS?
IF THAT TIME ARC HADN'T CONVENIENTLY SHOWN UP WE COULD'VE--
ITS "CONVENIENCE" IS RATHER THE POINT--IT'S A DEMONSTRATION OF THE C.P.C....
...NAMELY, THAT THE RULES OF THE UNIVERSE ITSELF ARE CONSTRUCTED IN SUCH A WAY AS TO PREVENT TEMPORAL TAMPERING.

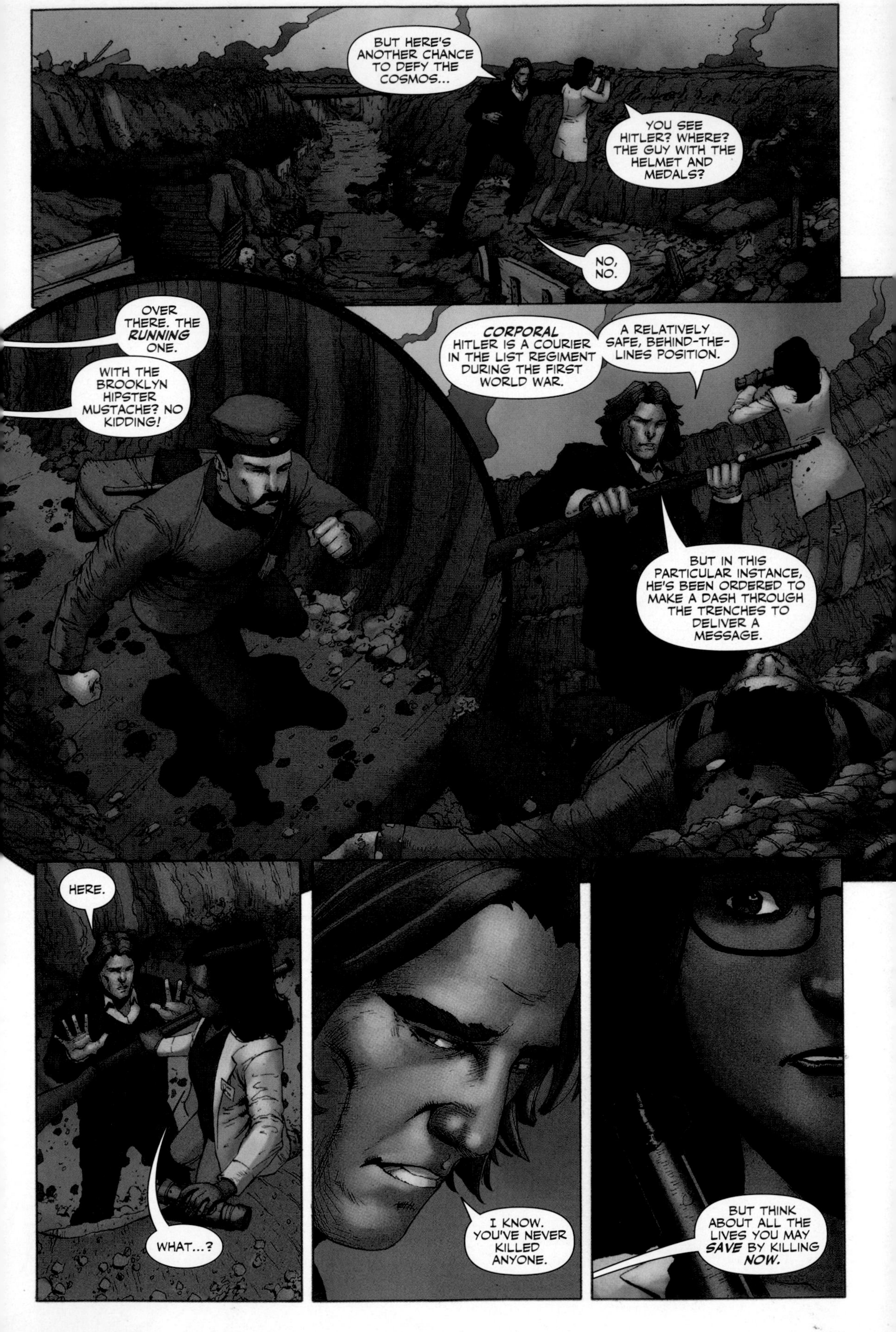
BUT HERE'S ANOTHER CHANCE TO DEFY THE COSMOS...
YOU SEE HITLER? WHERE? THE GUY WITH THE HELMET AND MEDALS?
NO, NO.
OVER THERE. THE RUNNING ONE.
WITH THE BROOKLYN HIPSTER MUSTACHE? NO KIDDING!
CORPORAL HITLER IS A COURIER IN THE LIST REGIMENT DURING THE FIRST WORLD WAR.
A RELATIVELY SAFE, BEHIND-THE-LINES POSITION.
BUT IN THIS PARTICULAR INSTANCE, HE'S BEEN ORDERED TO MAKE A DASH THROUGH THE TRENCHES TO DELIVER A MESSAGE.
HERE.
WHAT...?
I KNOW. YOU'VE NEVER KILLED ANYONE.
BUT THINK ABOUT ALL THE LIVES YOU MAY SAVE BY KILLING NOW.

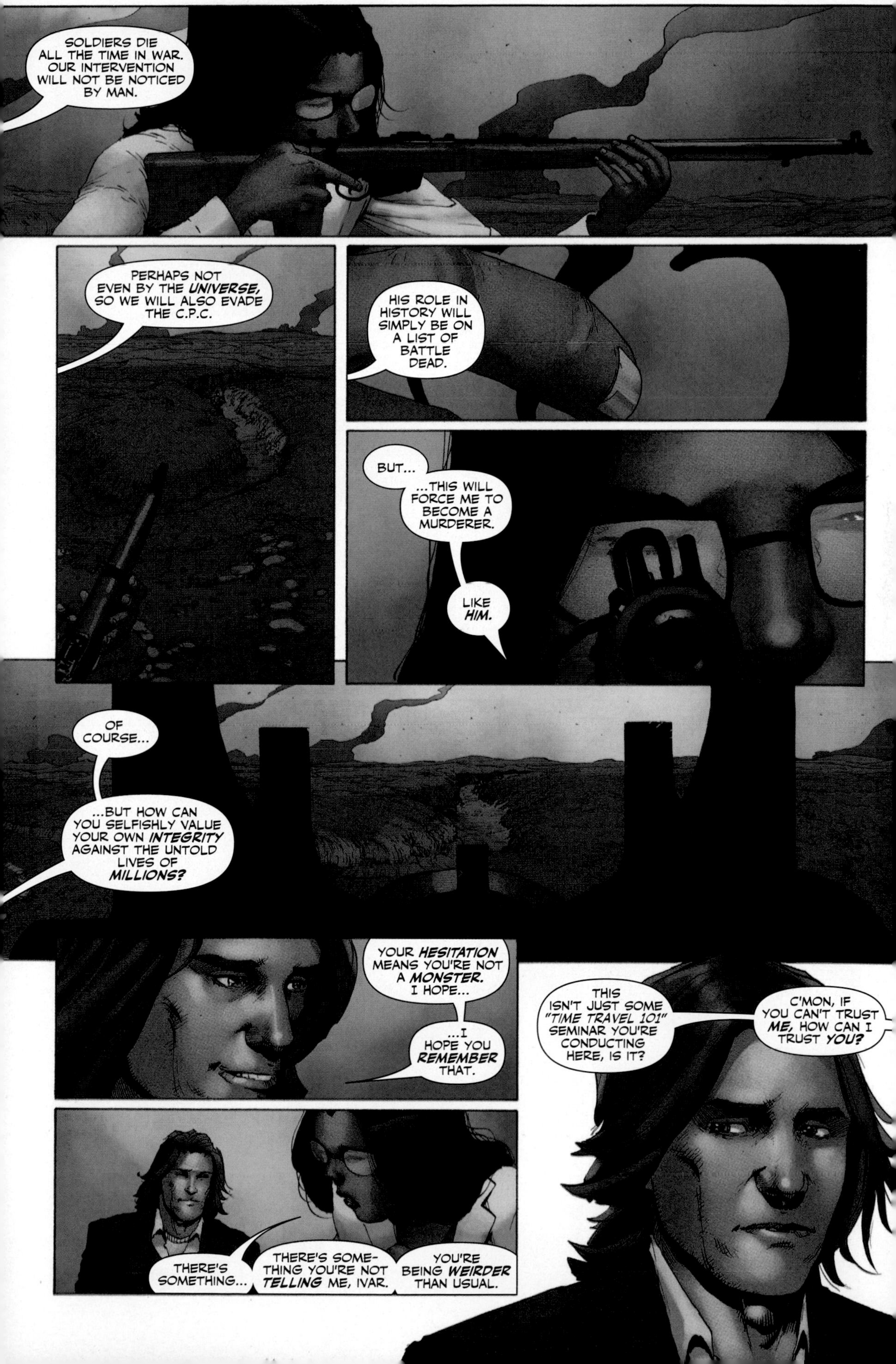
SOLDIERS DIE ALL THE TIME IN WAR. OUR INTERVENTION WILL NOT BE NOTICED BY MAN.
PERHAPS NOT EVEN BY THE *UNIVERSE,* SO WE WILL ALSO EVADE THE C.P.C.
HIS ROLE IN HISTORY WILL SIMPLY BE ON A LIST OF BATTLE DEAD.
BUT...
...THIS WILL FORCE ME TO BECOME A MURDERER.
LIKE *HIM.*
OF COURSE...
...BUT HOW CAN YOU SELFISHLY VALUE YOUR OWN *INTEGRITY* AGAINST THE UNTOLD LIVES OF *MILLIONS?*
YOUR *HESITATION* MEANS YOU'RE NOT A *MONSTER.* I HOPE...
...I HOPE YOU *REMEMBER* THAT.
THIS ISN'T JUST SOME *"TIME TRAVEL 101"* SEMINAR YOU'RE CONDUCTING HERE, IS IT?
C'MON, IF YOU CAN'T TRUST *ME,* HOW CAN I TRUST *YOU?*
THERE'S SOMETHING...
THERE'S SOME-THING YOU'RE NOT *TELLING* ME, IVAR.
YOU'RE BEING *WEIRDER* THAN USUAL.

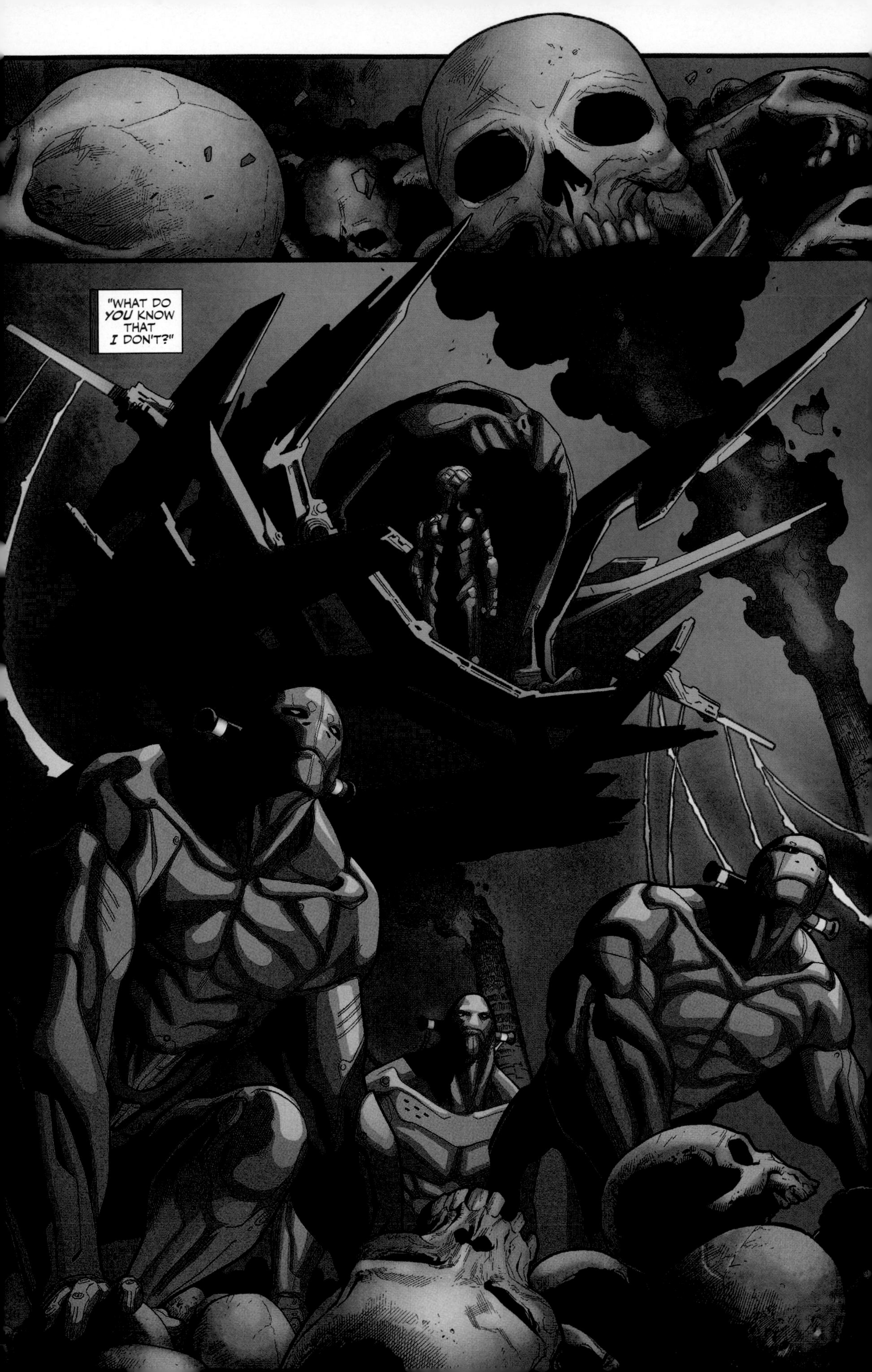
"WHAT DO YOU KNOW THAT I DON'T?"

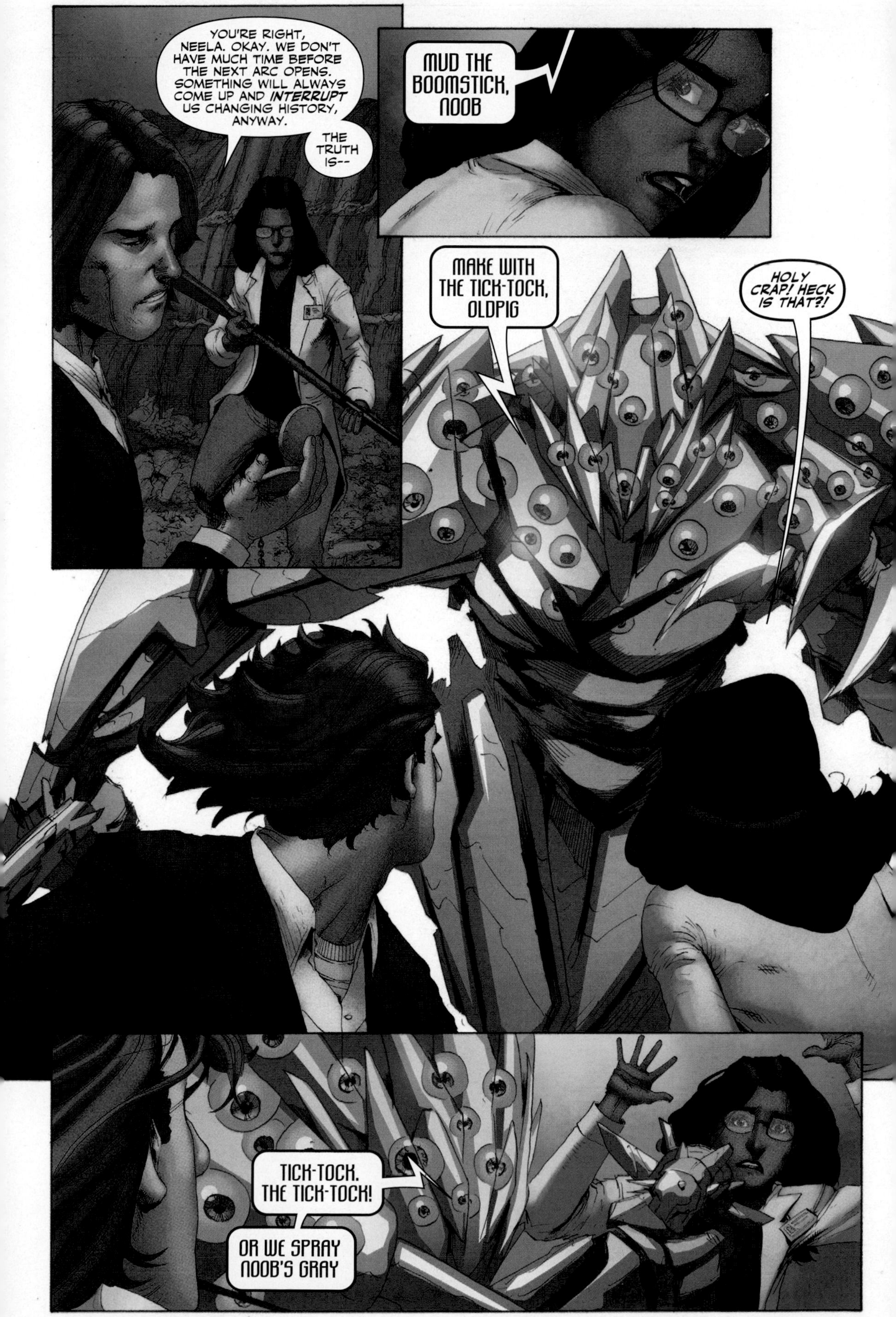
YOU'RE RIGHT, NEELA. OKAY. WE DON'T HAVE MUCH TIME BEFORE THE NEXT ARC OPENS. SOMETHING WILL ALWAYS COME UP AND *INTERRUPT* US CHANGING HISTORY, ANYWAY.
THE TRUTH IS--
MUD THE BOOMSTICK, NOOB
MAKE WITH THE TICK-TOCK, OLDPIG
HOLY CRAP! HECK IS THAT?!
TICK-TOCK. THE TICK-TOCK!
OR WE SPRAY NOOB'S GRAY

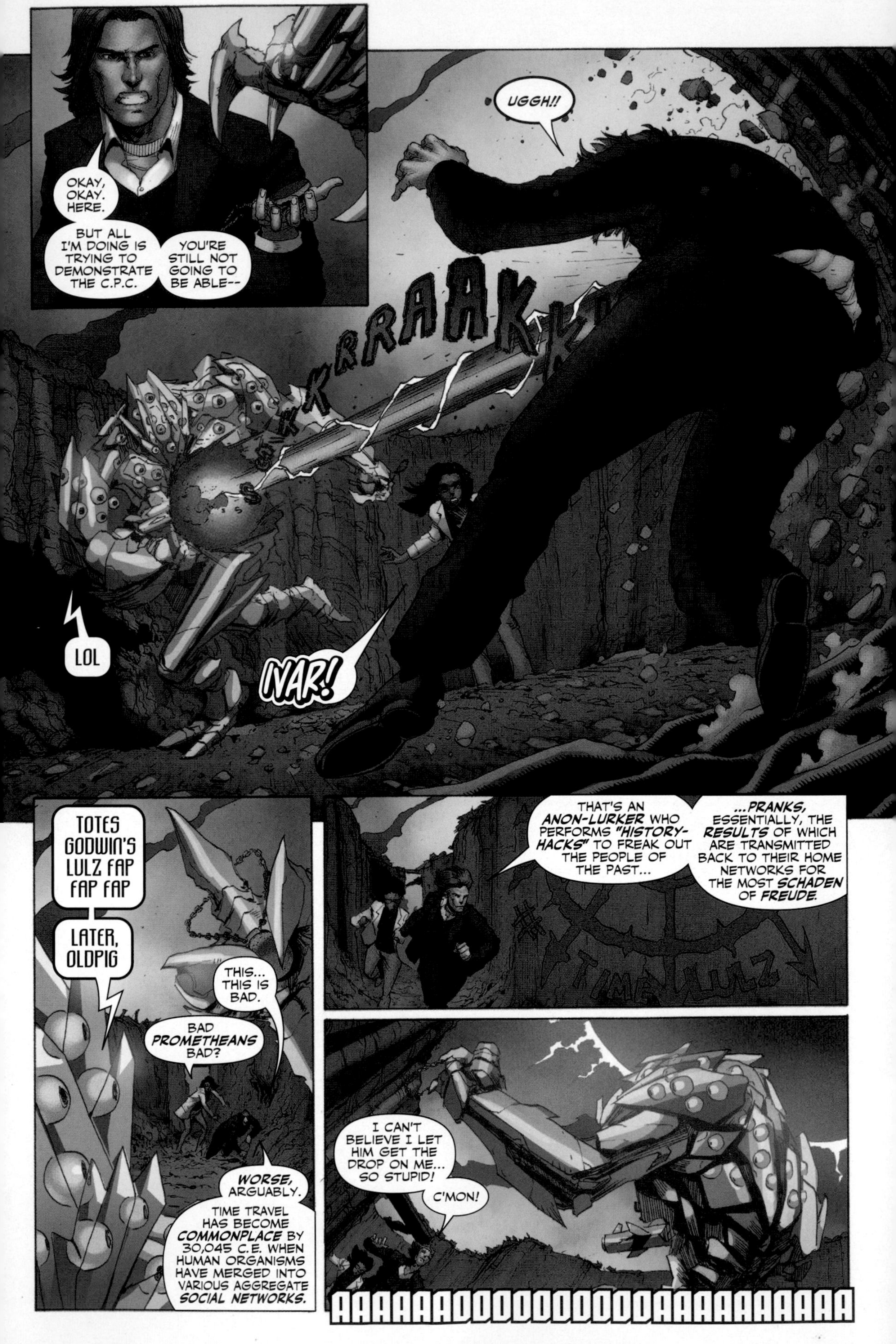

OKAY, OKAY. HERE.
BUT ALL I'M DOING IS TRYING TO DEMONSTRATE THE C.P.C.
YOU'RE STILL NOT GOING TO BE ABLE--
UGGH!!
SKKRRAAKK
LOL
IVAR!
TOTES GODWIN'S LULZ FAP FAP FAP
LATER, OLDPIG
THIS... THIS IS BAD.
BAD PROMETHEANS BAD?
WORSE, ARGUABLY.
TIME TRAVEL HAS BECOME COMMONPLACE BY 30,045 C.E. WHEN HUMAN ORGANISMS HAVE MERGED INTO VARIOUS AGGREGATE SOCIAL NETWORKS.
THAT'S AN ANON-LURKER WHO PERFORMS "HISTORY-HACKS" TO FREAK OUT THE PEOPLE OF THE PAST...
...PRANKS, ESSENTIALLY, THE RESULTS OF WHICH ARE TRANSMITTED BACK TO THEIR HOME NETWORKS FOR THE MOST SCHADEN OF FREUDE.
TIME LULZ
I CAN'T BELIEVE I LET HIM GET THE DROP ON ME... SO STUPID!
C'MON!
AAAAAADOOOOOOOOOOAAAAAAAAAA

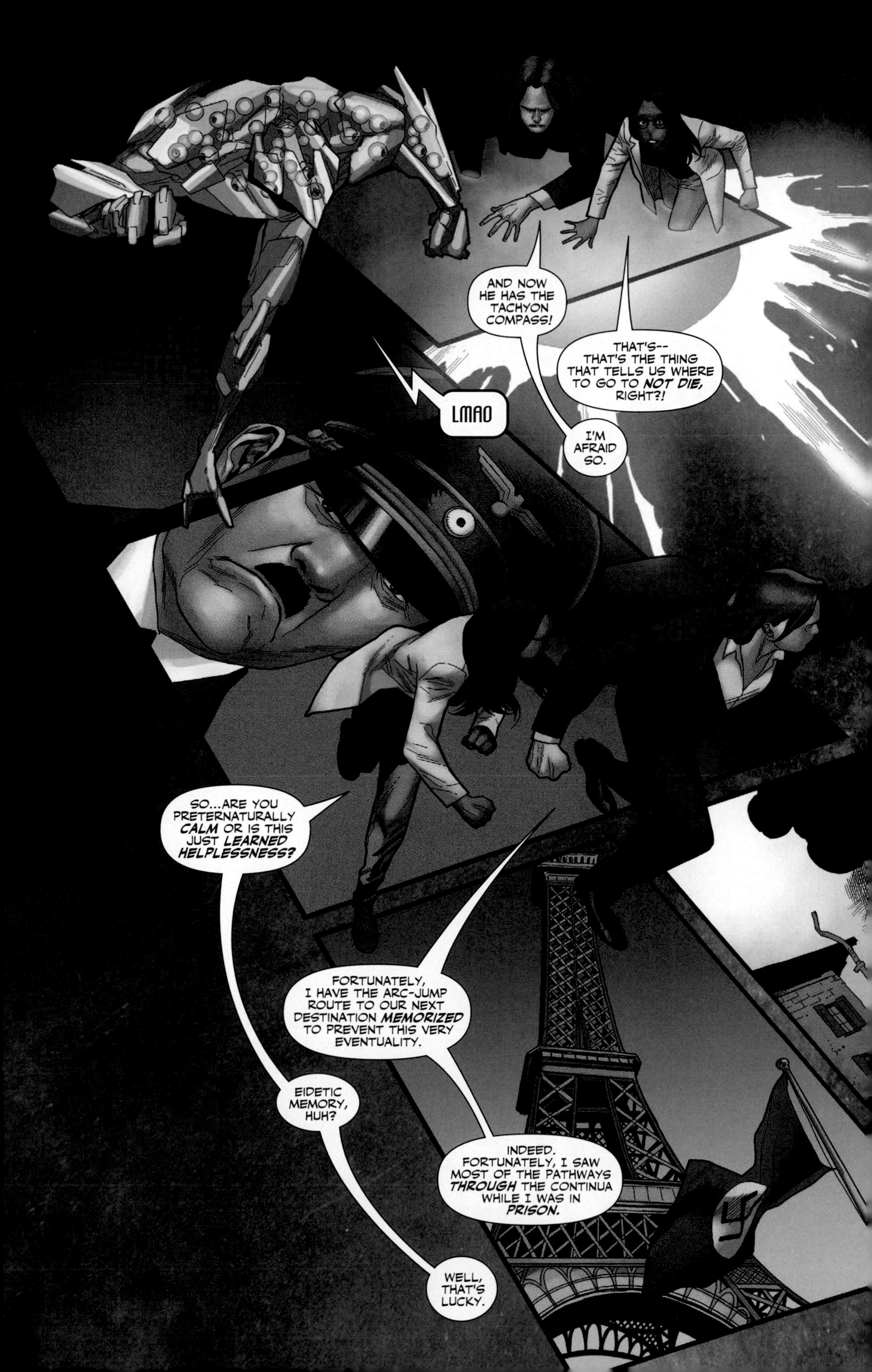
AND NOW HE HAS THE TACHYON COMPASS!
THAT'S-- THAT'S THE THING THAT TELLS US WHERE TO GO TO NOT DIE, RIGHT?!
LMAO
I'M AFRAID SO.
SO...ARE YOU PRETERNATURALLY CALM OR IS THIS JUST LEARNED HELPLESSNESS?
FORTUNATELY, I HAVE THE ARC-JUMP ROUTE TO OUR NEXT DESTINATION MEMORIZED TO PREVENT THIS VERY EVENTUALITY.
EIDETIC MEMORY, HUH?
INDEED. FORTUNATELY, I SAW MOST OF THE PATHWAYS THROUGH THE CONTINUA WHILE I WAS IN PRISON.
WELL, THAT'S LUCKY.

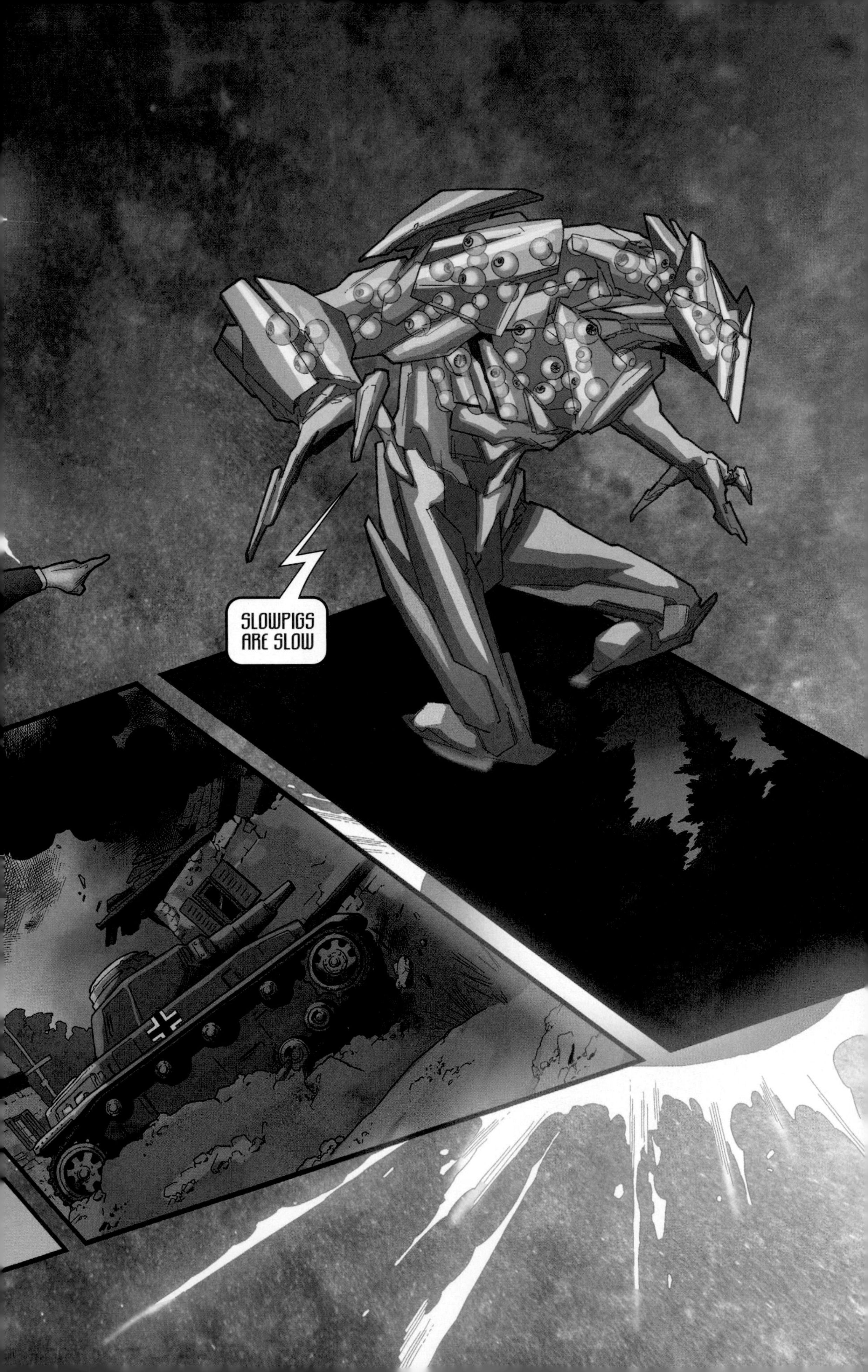
SLOWPIGS
ARE SLOW

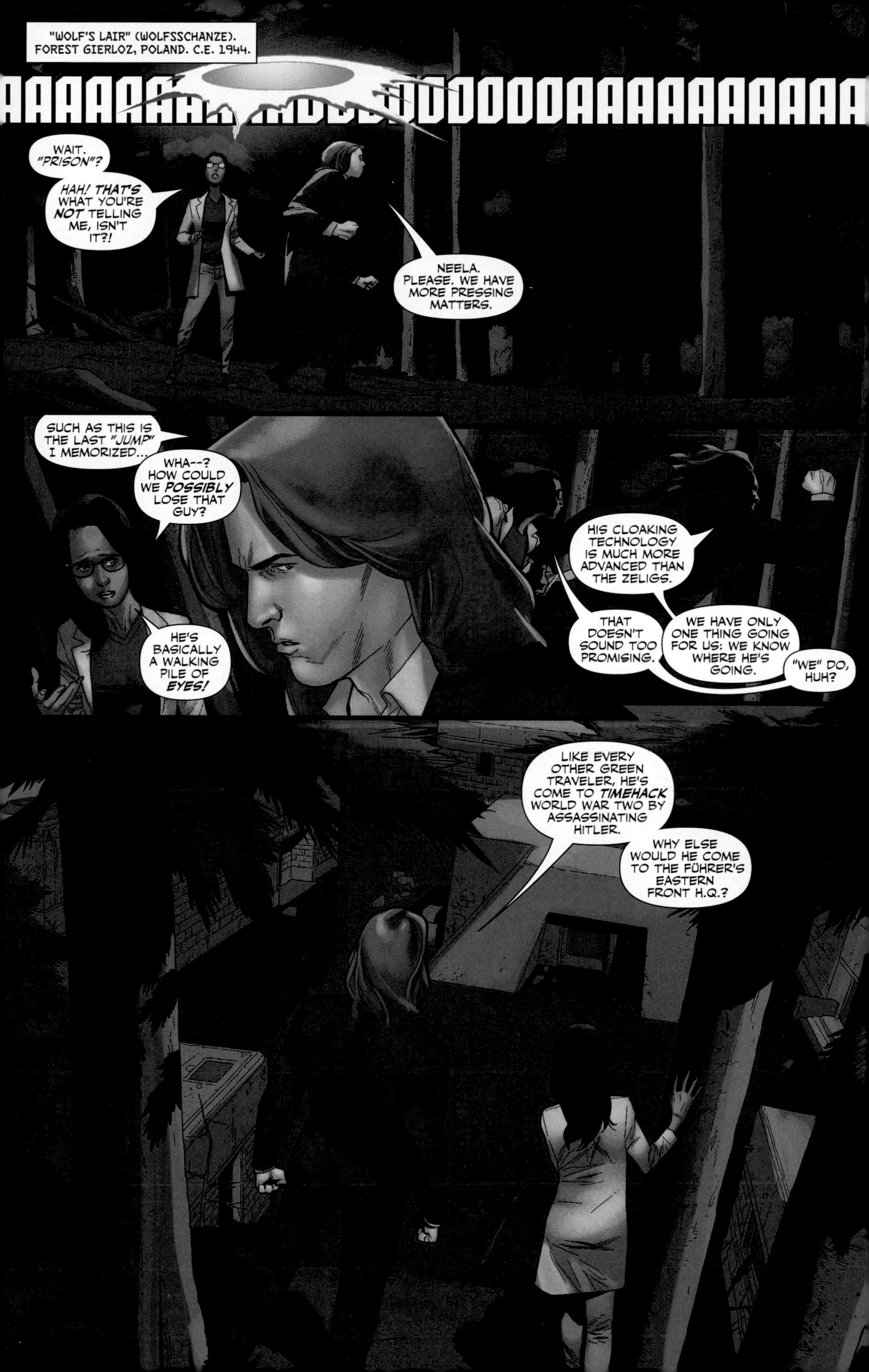

"WOLF'S LAIR" (WOLFSSCHANZE). FOREST GIERLOZ, POLAND. C.E. 1944.
AAAAAAAAAAOOOOOOOOAAAAAAAAAA
WAIT. "PRISON"?
HAH! THAT'S WHAT YOU'RE NOT TELLING ME, ISN'T IT?!
NEELA. PLEASE. WE HAVE MORE PRESSING MATTERS.
SUCH AS THIS IS THE LAST "JUMP" I MEMORIZED...
WHA--? HOW COULD WE POSSIBLY LOSE THAT GUY?
HE'S BASICALLY A WALKING PILE OF EYES!
HIS CLOAKING TECHNOLOGY IS MUCH MORE ADVANCED THAN THE ZELIGS.
THAT DOESN'T SOUND TOO PROMISING.
WE HAVE ONLY ONE THING GOING FOR US: WE KNOW WHERE HE'S GOING.
"WE" DO, HUH?
LIKE EVERY OTHER GREEN TRAVELER, HE'S COME TO TIMEHACK WORLD WAR TWO BY ASSASSINATING HITLER.
WHY ELSE WOULD HE COME TO THE FÜHRER'S EASTERN FRONT H.Q.?

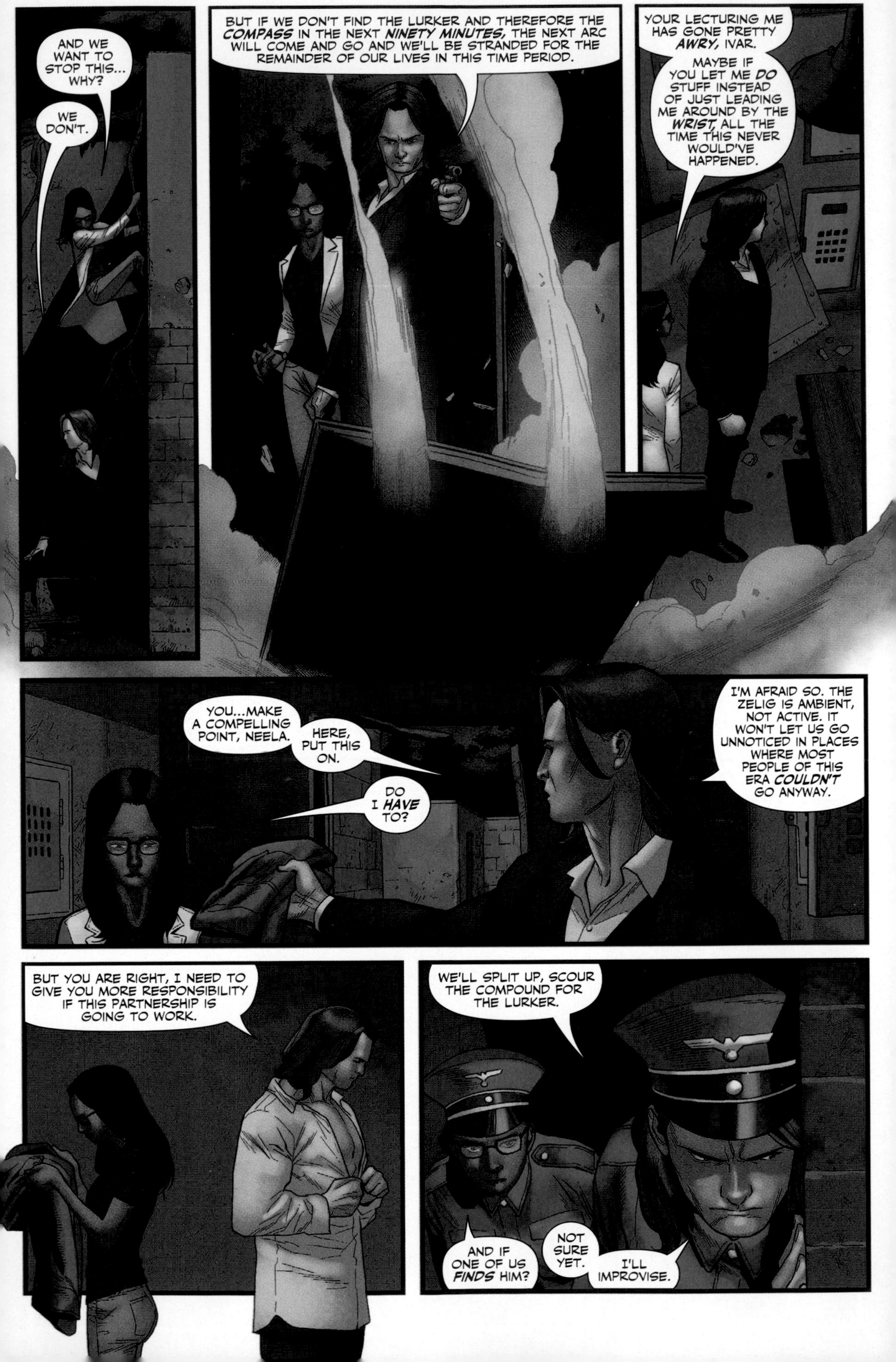
AND WE WANT TO STOP THIS... WHY?
WE DON'T.
BUT IF WE DON'T FIND THE LURKER AND THEREFORE THE COMPASS IN THE NEXT NINETY MINUTES, THE NEXT ARC WILL COME AND GO AND WE'LL BE STRANDED FOR THE REMAINDER OF OUR LIVES IN THIS TIME PERIOD.
YOUR LECTURING ME HAS GONE PRETTY AWRY, IVAR.
MAYBE IF YOU LET ME DO STUFF INSTEAD OF JUST LEADING ME AROUND BY THE WRIST, ALL THE TIME THIS NEVER WOULD'VE HAPPENED.
YOU...MAKE A COMPELLING POINT, NEELA.
HERE, PUT THIS ON.
DO I HAVE TO?
I'M AFRAID SO. THE ZELIG IS AMBIENT, NOT ACTIVE. IT WON'T LET US GO UNNOTICED IN PLACES WHERE MOST PEOPLE OF THIS ERA COULDN'T GO ANYWAY.
BUT YOU ARE RIGHT, I NEED TO GIVE YOU MORE RESPONSIBILITY IF THIS PARTNERSHIP IS GOING TO WORK.
WE'LL SPLIT UP, SCOUR THE COMPOUND FOR THE LURKER.
AND IF ONE OF US FINDS HIM?
NOT SURE YET.
I'LL IMPROVISE.

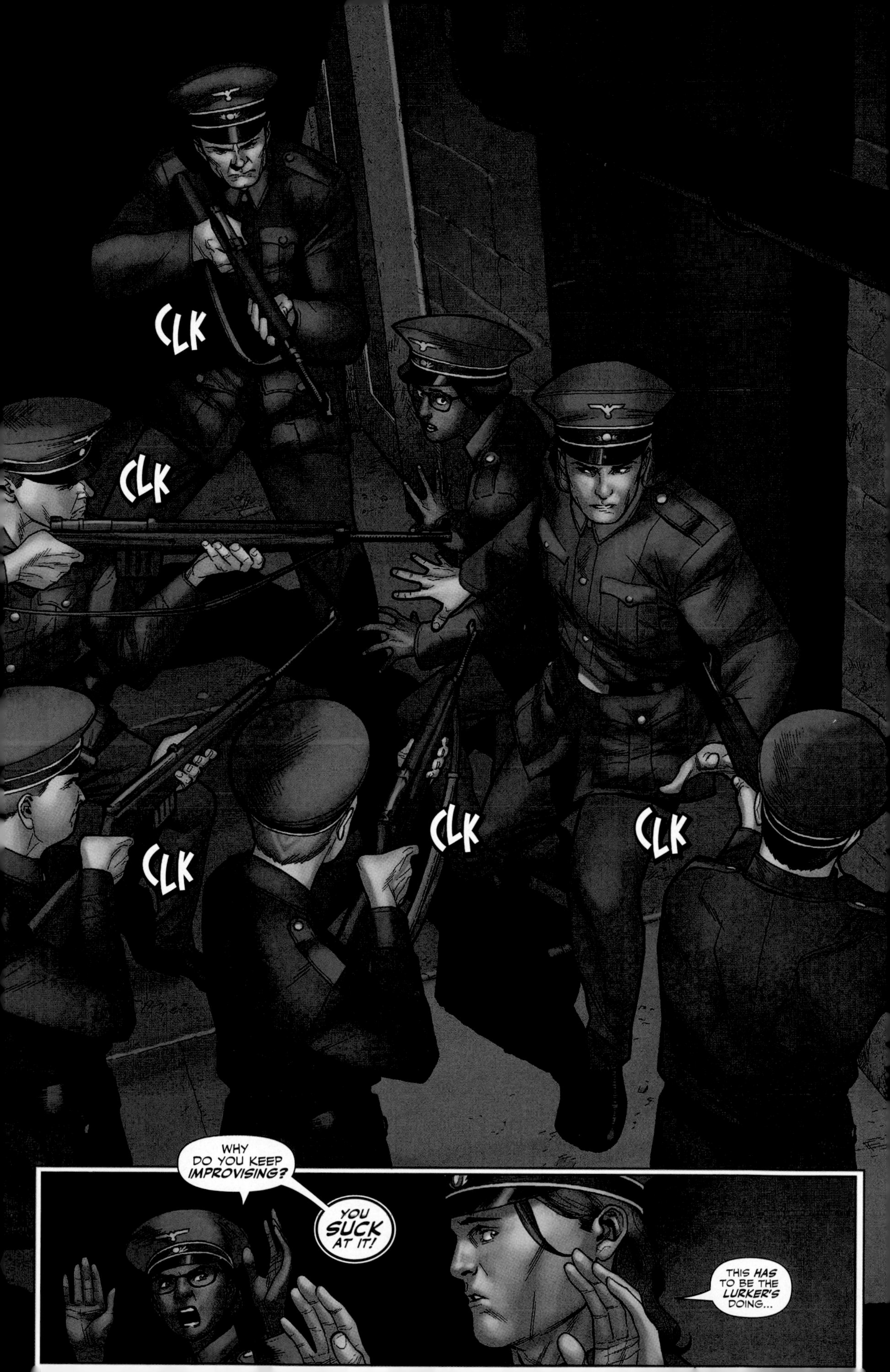
CLK
CLK
CLK
CLK
CLK
WHY DO YOU KEEP IMPROVISING?
YOU SUCK AT IT!
THIS HAS TO BE THE LURKER'S DOING...

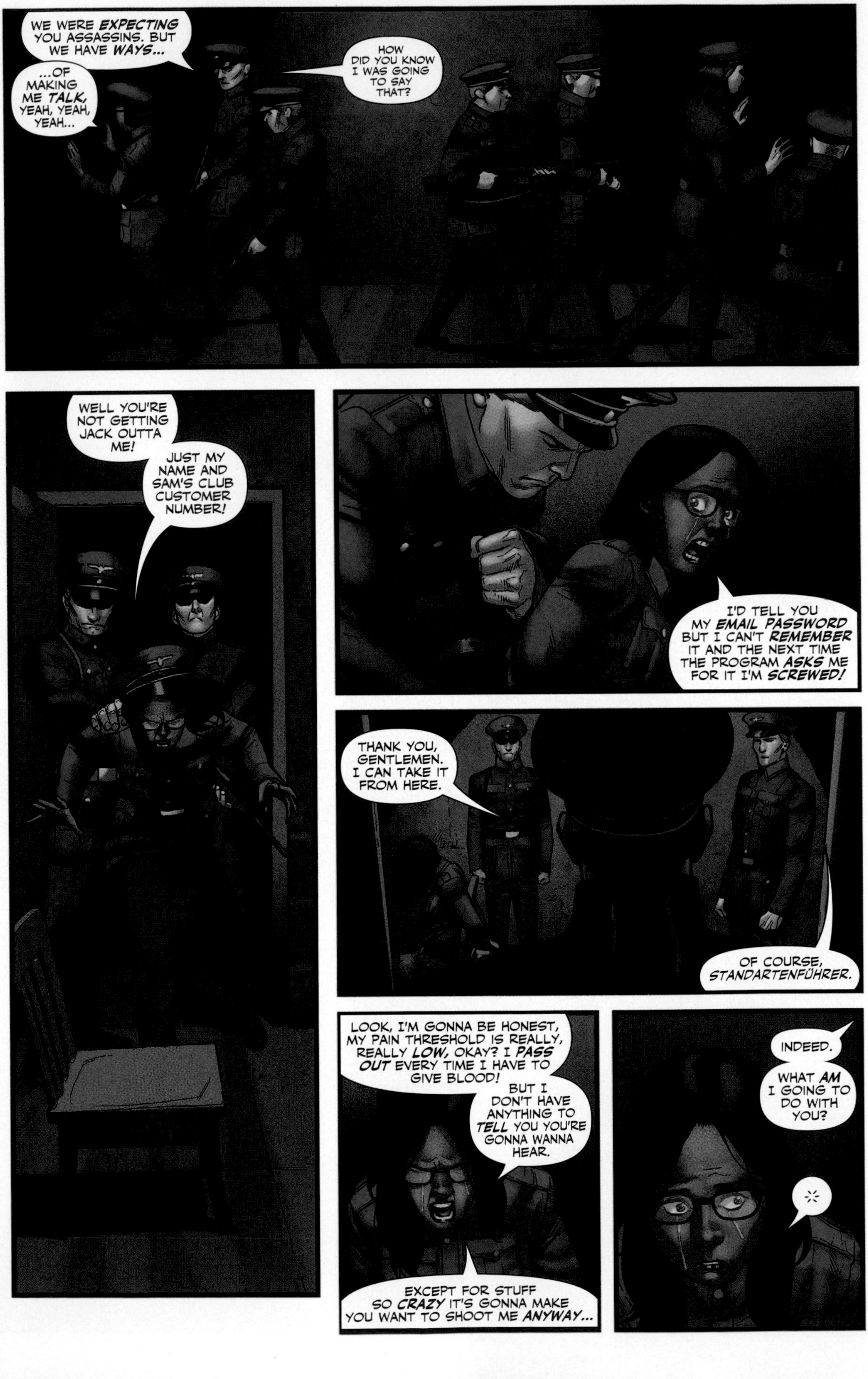
WE WERE EXPECTING YOU ASSASSINS. BUT WE HAVE WAYS...
...OF MAKING ME TALK, YEAH, YEAH, YEAH...
HOW DID YOU KNOW I WAS GOING TO SAY THAT?
WELL YOU'RE NOT GETTING JACK OUTTA ME!
JUST MY NAME AND SAM'S CLUB CUSTOMER NUMBER!
I'D TELL YOU MY EMAIL PASSWORD BUT I CAN'T REMEMBER IT AND THE NEXT TIME THE PROGRAM ASKS ME FOR IT I'M SCREWED!
THANK YOU, GENTLEMEN. I CAN TAKE IT FROM HERE.
OF COURSE, STANDARTENFÜHRER.
LOOK, I'M GONNA BE HONEST, MY PAIN THRESHOLD IS REALLY, REALLY LOW, OKAY? I PASS OUT EVERY TIME I HAVE TO GIVE BLOOD!
BUT I DON'T HAVE ANYTHING TO TELL YOU YOU'RE GONNA WANNA HEAR.
EXCEPT FOR STUFF SO CRAZY IT'S GONNA MAKE YOU WANT TO SHOOT ME ANYWAY...
INDEED.
WHAT AM I GOING TO DO WITH YOU?

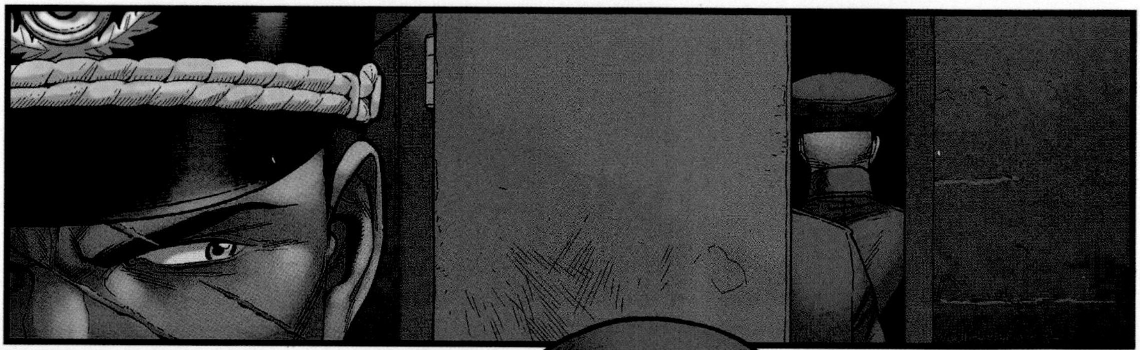

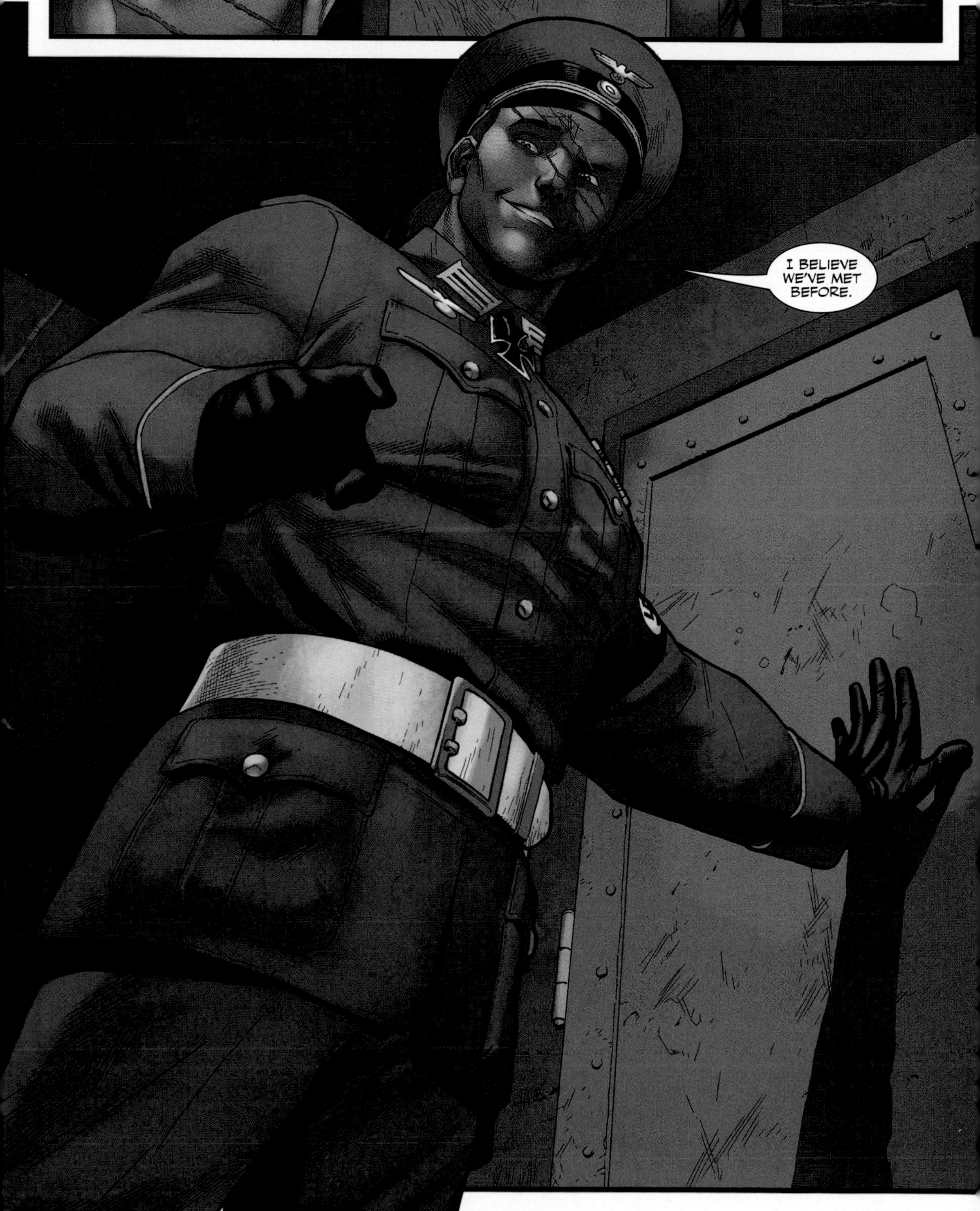
I BELIEVE WE'VE MET BEFORE.

FRED VAN LENTE / CLAYTON HENRY / BRIAN REBER

Ivar,
TIMEWALKER

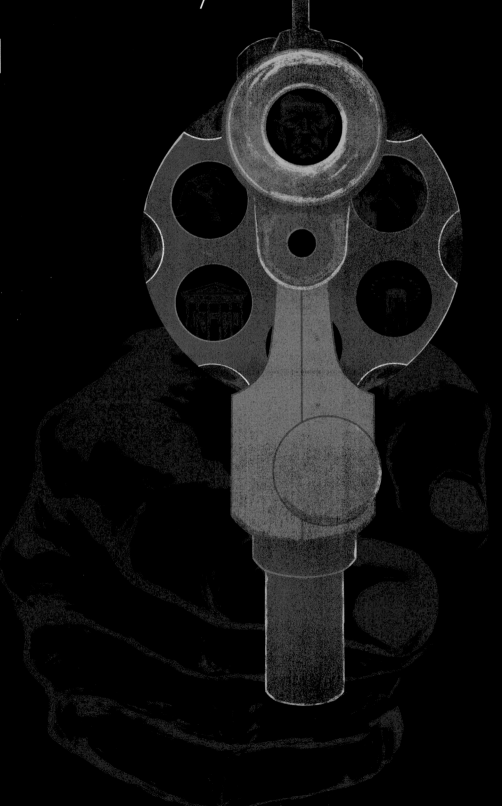

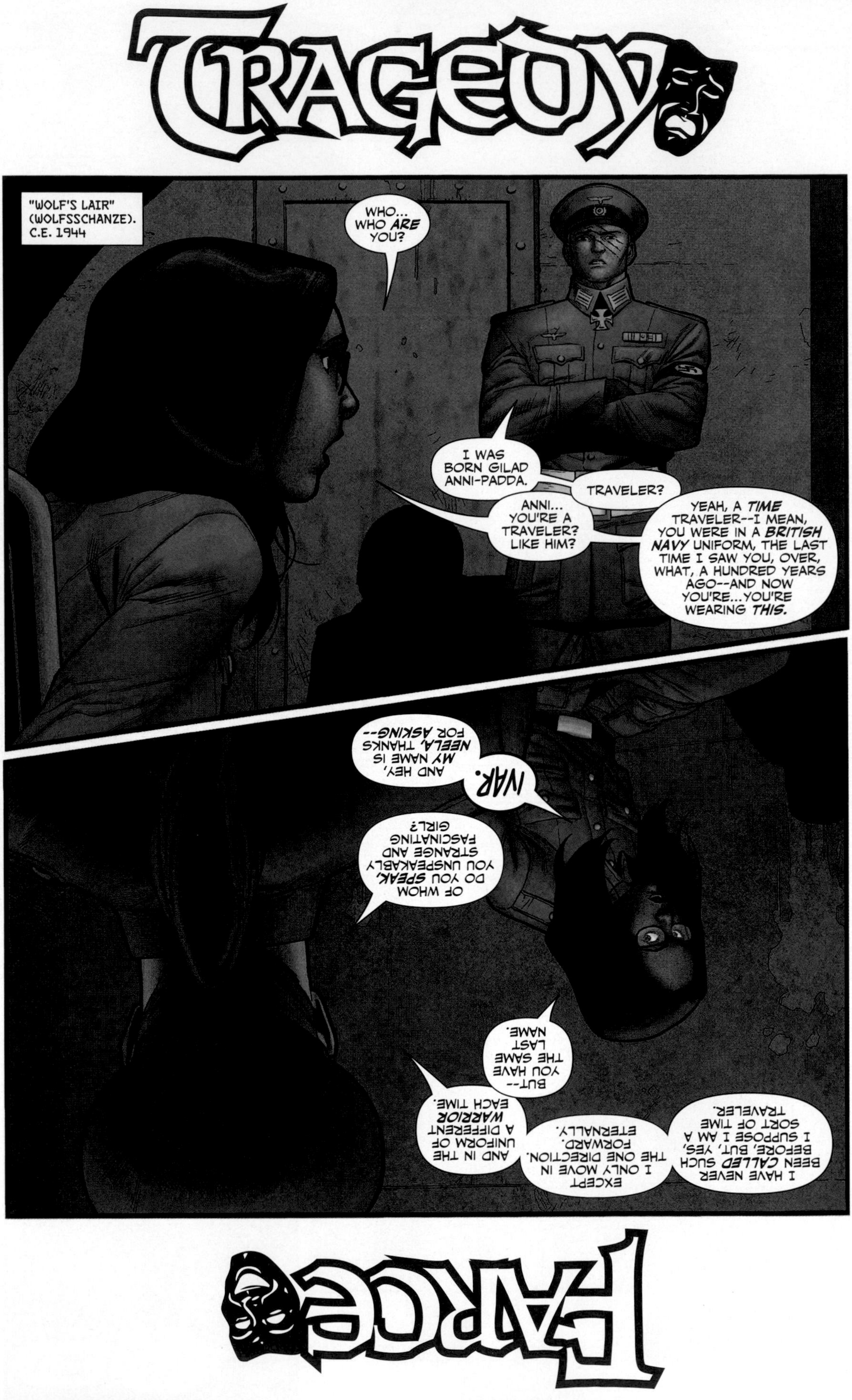
TRAGEDY
"WOLF'S LAIR" (WOLFSSCHANZE). C.E. 1944
WHO... WHO ARE YOU?
I WAS BORN GILAD ANNI-PADDA.
ANNI... YOU'RE A TRAVELER? LIKE HIM?
TRAVELER?
YEAH, A TIME TRAVELER--I MEAN, YOU WERE IN A BRITISH NAVY UNIFORM, THE LAST TIME I SAW YOU, OVER, WHAT, A HUNDRED YEARS AGO--AND NOW YOU'RE...YOU'RE WEARING THIS.
FARCE
I HAVE NEVER BEEN CALLED SUCH BEFORE, BUT, YES, I SUPPOSE I AM A SORT OF TIME TRAVELER.
EXCEPT I ONLY MOVE IN THE ONE DIRECTION. FORWARD. ETERNALLY.
AND IN THE UNIFORM OF A DIFFERENT WARRIOR EACH TIME.
BUT-- YOU HAVE THE SAME LAST NAME.
OF WHOM DO YOU SPEAK, YOU UNSPEAKABLY STRANGE AND FASCINATING GIRL?
IVAR.
AND HEY, MY NAME IS NEELA, THANKS FOR ASKING--

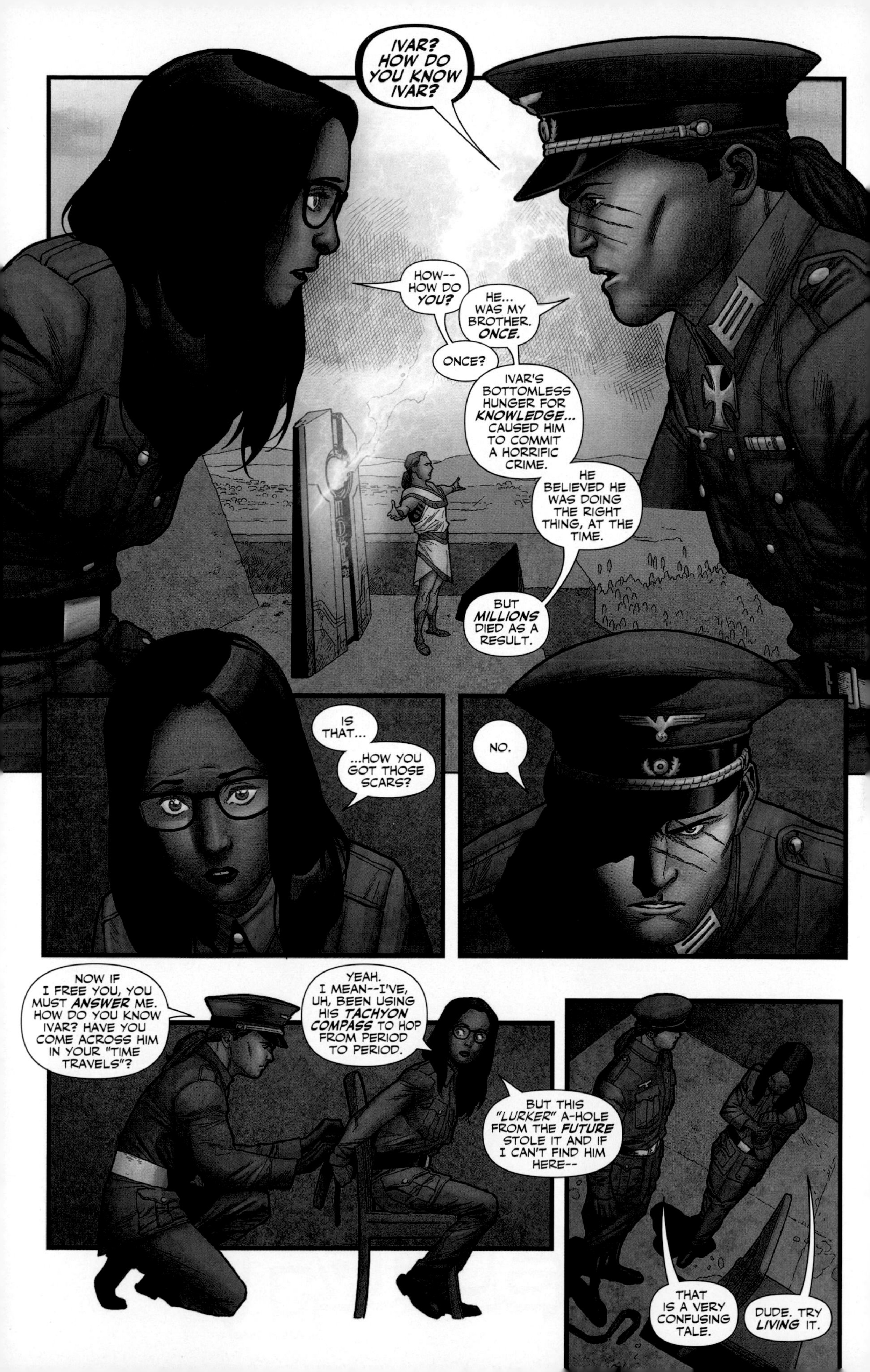
IVAR? HOW DO YOU KNOW IVAR?
HOW-- HOW DO YOU?
HE... WAS MY BROTHER. ONCE.
ONCE?
IVAR'S BOTTOMLESS HUNGER FOR KNOWLEDGE... CAUSED HIM TO COMMIT A HORRIFIC CRIME.
HE BELIEVED HE WAS DOING THE RIGHT THING, AT THE TIME.
BUT MILLIONS DIED AS A RESULT.
IS THAT...
...HOW YOU GOT THOSE SCARS?
NO.
NOW IF I FREE YOU, YOU MUST ANSWER ME. HOW DO YOU KNOW IVAR? HAVE YOU COME ACROSS HIM IN YOUR "TIME TRAVELS"?
YEAH. I MEAN--I'VE, UH, BEEN USING HIS TACHYON COMPASS TO HOP FROM PERIOD TO PERIOD.
BUT THIS "LURKER" A-HOLE FROM THE FUTURE STOLE IT AND IF I CAN'T FIND HIM HERE--
THAT IS A VERY CONFUSING TALE.
DUDE. TRY LIVING IT.

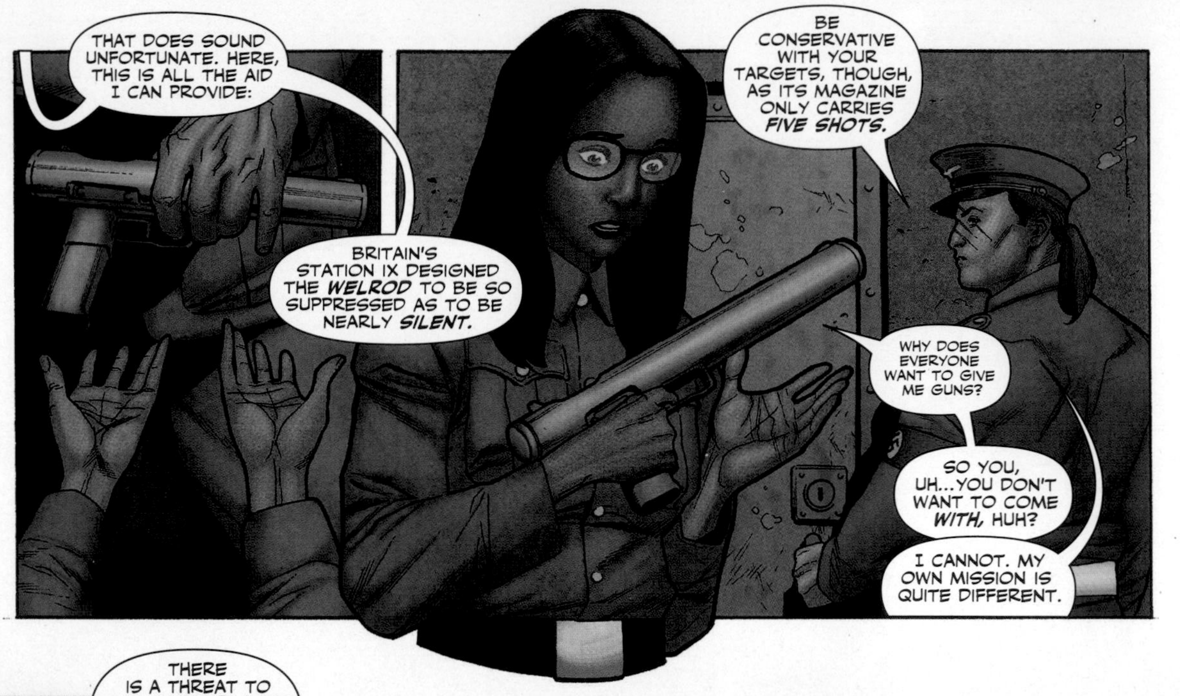
THAT DOES SOUND UNFORTUNATE. HERE, THIS IS ALL THE AID I CAN PROVIDE:
BRITAIN'S STATION IX DESIGNED THE *WELROD* TO BE SO SUPPRESSED AS TO BE NEARLY *SILENT.*
BE CONSERVATIVE WITH YOUR TARGETS, THOUGH, AS ITS MAGAZINE ONLY CARRIES *FIVE SHOTS.*
WHY DOES EVERYONE WANT TO GIVE ME GUNS?
SO YOU, UH...YOU DON'T WANT TO COME *WITH,* HUH?
I CANNOT. MY OWN MISSION IS QUITE DIFFERENT.

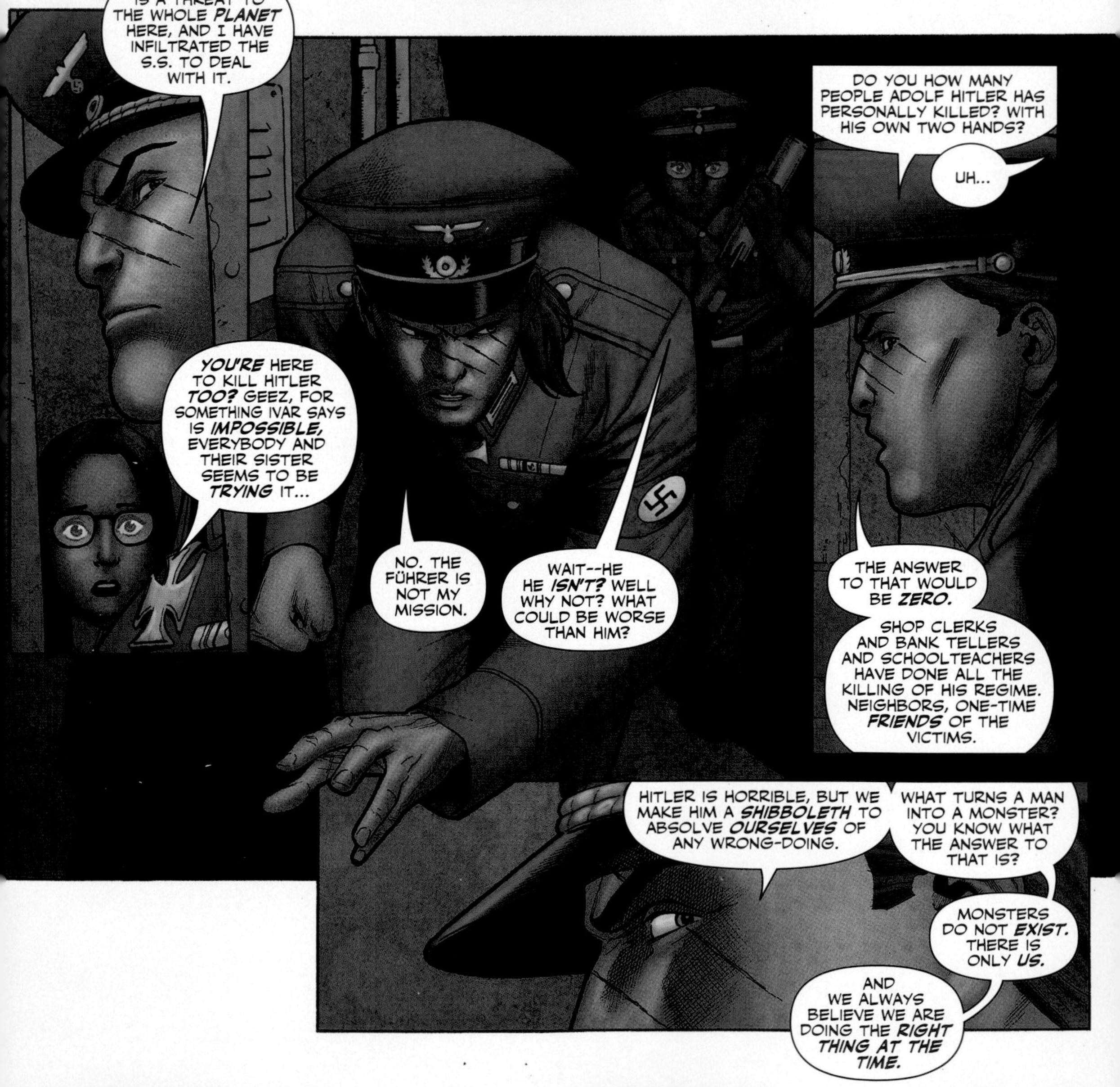
THERE IS A THREAT TO THE WHOLE *PLANET* HERE, AND I HAVE INFILTRATED THE S.S. TO DEAL WITH IT.
YOU'RE HERE TO KILL HITLER *TOO?* GEEZ, FOR SOMETHING IVAR SAYS IS *IMPOSSIBLE,* EVERYBODY AND THEIR SISTER SEEMS TO BE *TRYING* IT...
NO. THE FÜHRER IS NOT MY MISSION.
WAIT--HE HE *ISN'T?* WELL WHY NOT? WHAT COULD BE WORSE THAN HIM?
DO YOU HOW MANY PEOPLE ADOLF HITLER HAS PERSONALLY KILLED? WITH HIS OWN TWO HANDS?
UH...
THE ANSWER TO THAT WOULD BE *ZERO.*
SHOP CLERKS AND BANK TELLERS AND SCHOOLTEACHERS HAVE DONE ALL THE KILLING OF HIS REGIME. NEIGHBORS, ONE-TIME *FRIENDS* OF THE VICTIMS.
HITLER IS HORRIBLE, BUT WE MAKE HIM A *SHIBBOLETH* TO ABSOLVE *OURSELVES* OF ANY WRONG-DOING.
WHAT TURNS A MAN INTO A MONSTER? YOU KNOW WHAT THE ANSWER TO THAT IS?
MONSTERS DO NOT *EXIST.* THERE IS ONLY *US.*
AND WE ALWAYS BELIEVE WE ARE DOING THE *RIGHT THING AT THE TIME.*

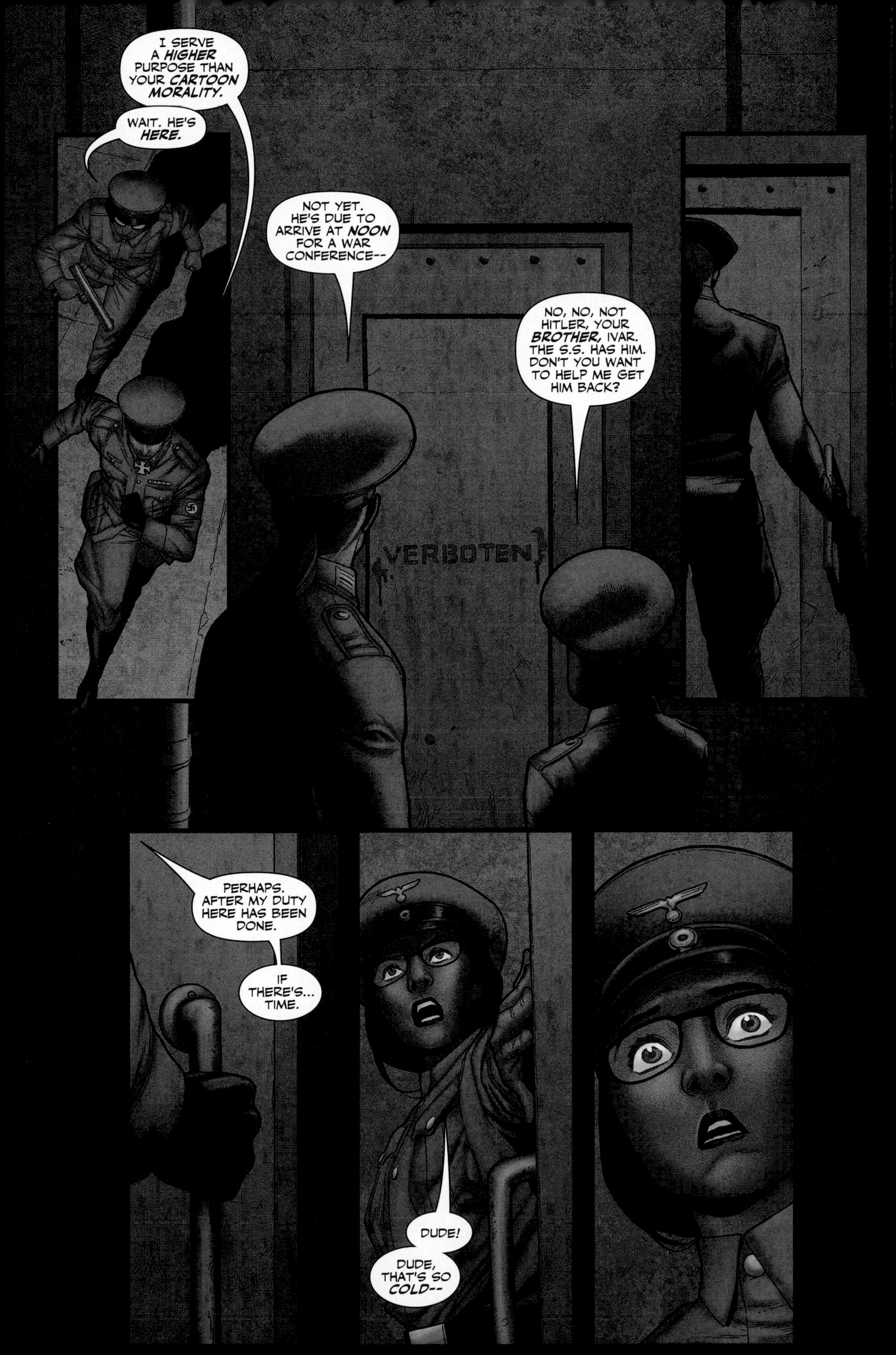

I SERVE A HIGHER PURPOSE THAN YOUR CARTOON MORALITY.
WAIT. HE'S HERE.
NOT YET. HE'S DUE TO ARRIVE AT NOON FOR A WAR CONFERENCE--
NO, NO, NOT HITLER, YOUR BROTHER, IVAR. THE S.S. HAS HIM. DON'T YOU WANT TO HELP ME GET HIM BACK?
VERBOTEN
PERHAPS. AFTER MY DUTY HERE HAS BEEN DONE.
IF THERE'S... TIME.
DUDE!
DUDE, THAT'S SO COLD--

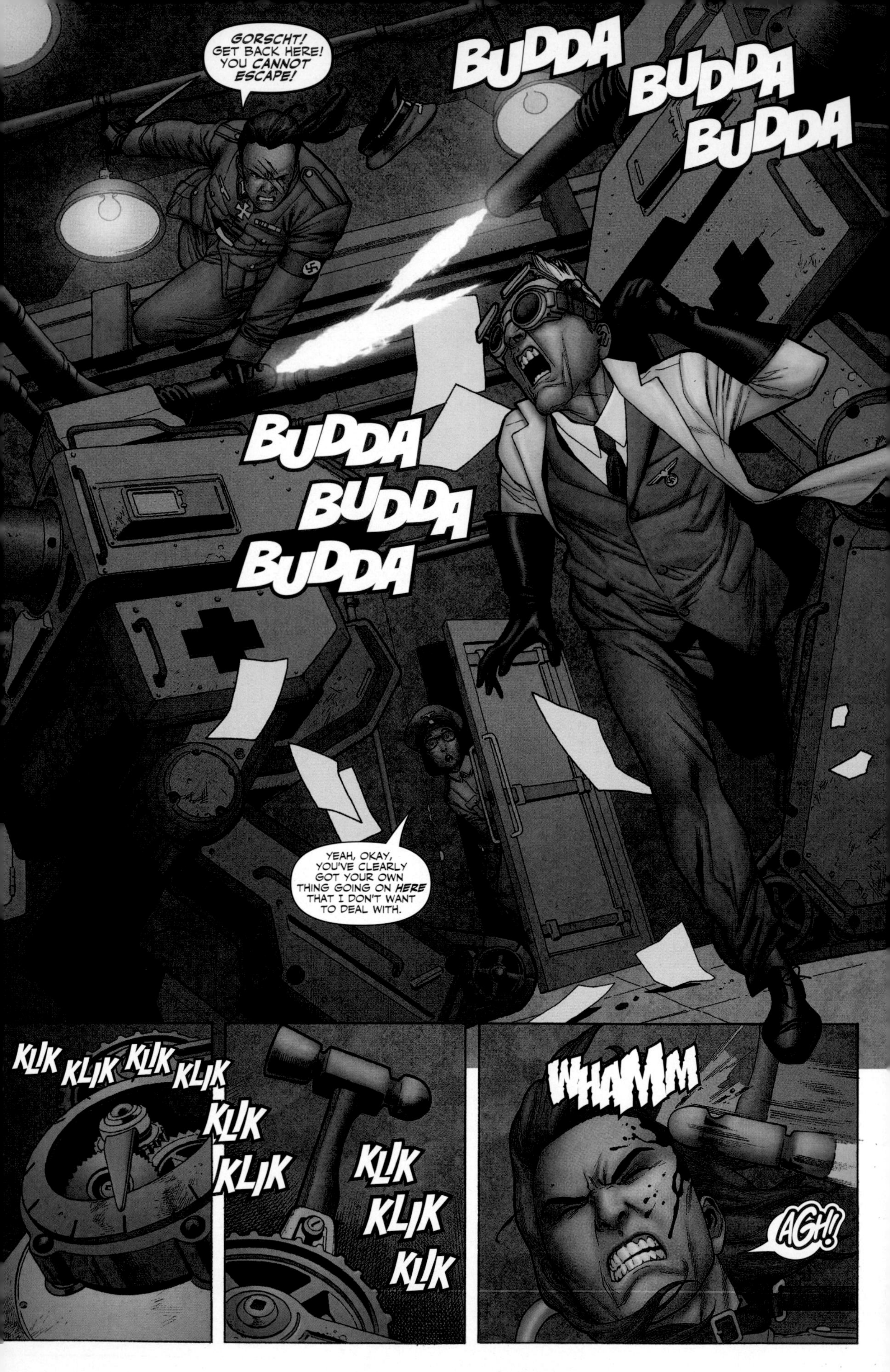
GORSCHT! GET BACK HERE! YOU CANNOT ESCAPE!
BUDDA BUDDA BUDDA
BUDDA BUDDA BUDDA
YEAH, OKAY, YOU'VE CLEARLY GOT YOUR OWN THING GOING ON HERE THAT I DON'T WANT TO DEAL WITH.
KLIK KLIK KLIK KLIK KLIK KLIK
KLIK KLIK KLIK
WHAMM
AGH!!

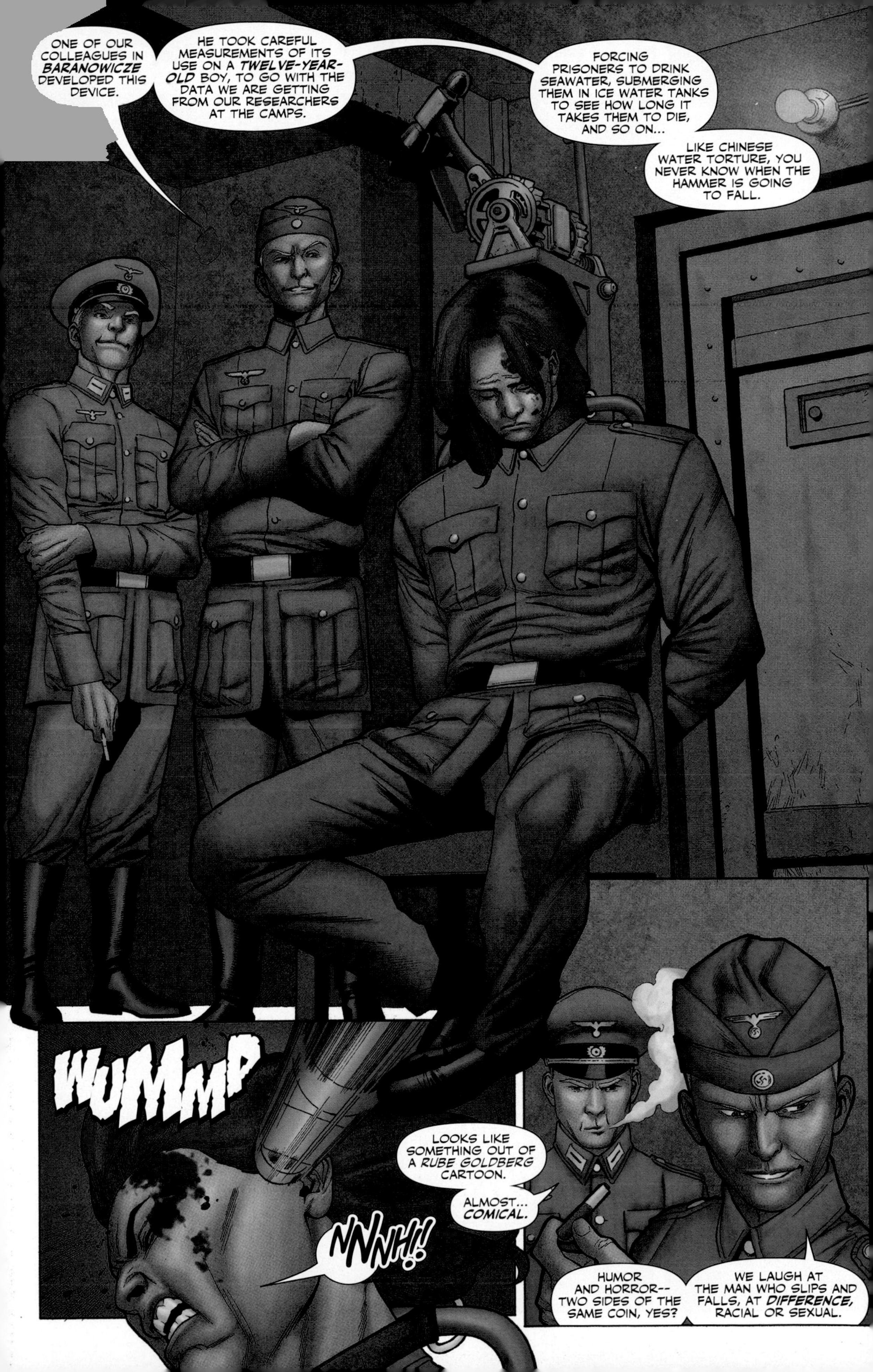
ONE OF OUR COLLEAGUES IN *BARANOWICZE* DEVELOPED THIS DEVICE.
HE TOOK CAREFUL MEASUREMENTS OF ITS USE ON A *TWELVE-YEAR-OLD* BOY, TO GO WITH THE DATA WE ARE GETTING FROM OUR RESEARCHERS AT THE CAMPS.
FORCING PRISONERS TO DRINK SEAWATER, SUBMERGING THEM IN ICE WATER TANKS TO SEE HOW LONG IT TAKES THEM TO DIE, AND SO ON...
LIKE CHINESE WATER TORTURE, YOU NEVER KNOW WHEN THE HAMMER IS GOING TO FALL.
WUMMP
NNNH!!
LOOKS LIKE SOMETHING OUT OF A *RUBE GOLDBERG* CARTOON.
ALMOST... *COMICAL.*
HUMOR AND HORROR-- TWO SIDES OF THE SAME COIN, YES?
WE LAUGH AT THE MAN WHO SLIPS AND FALLS, AT *DIFFERENCE,* RACIAL OR SEXUAL.

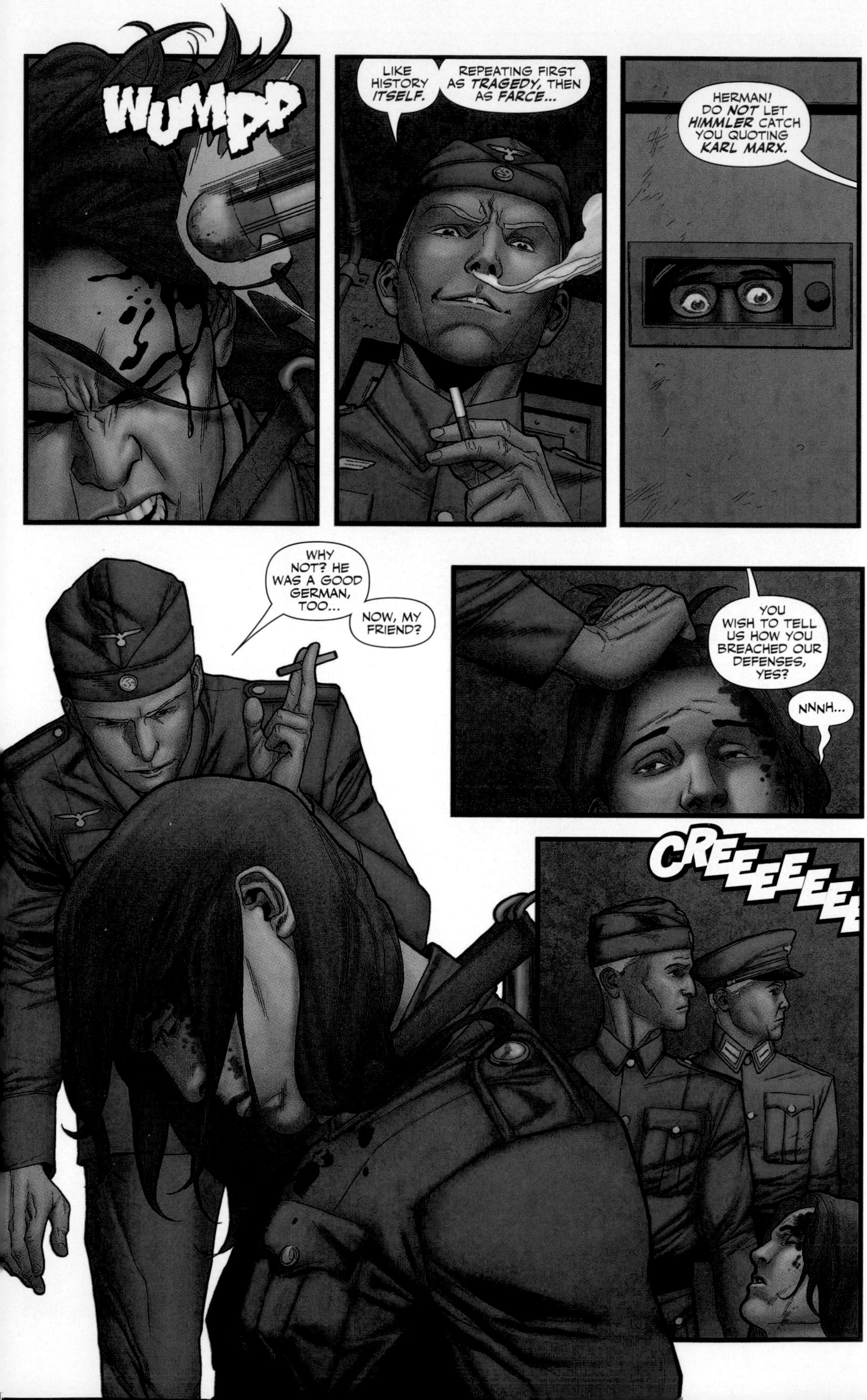
WUMPP
LIKE HISTORY ITSELF.
REPEATING FIRST AS TRAGEDY, THEN AS FARCE...
HERMAN! DO NOT LET HIMMLER CATCH YOU QUOTING KARL MARX.
WHY NOT? HE WAS A GOOD GERMAN, TOO...
NOW, MY FRIEND?
YOU WISH TO TELL US HOW YOU BREACHED OUR DEFENSES, YES?
NNNH...
CREEEEEEEE

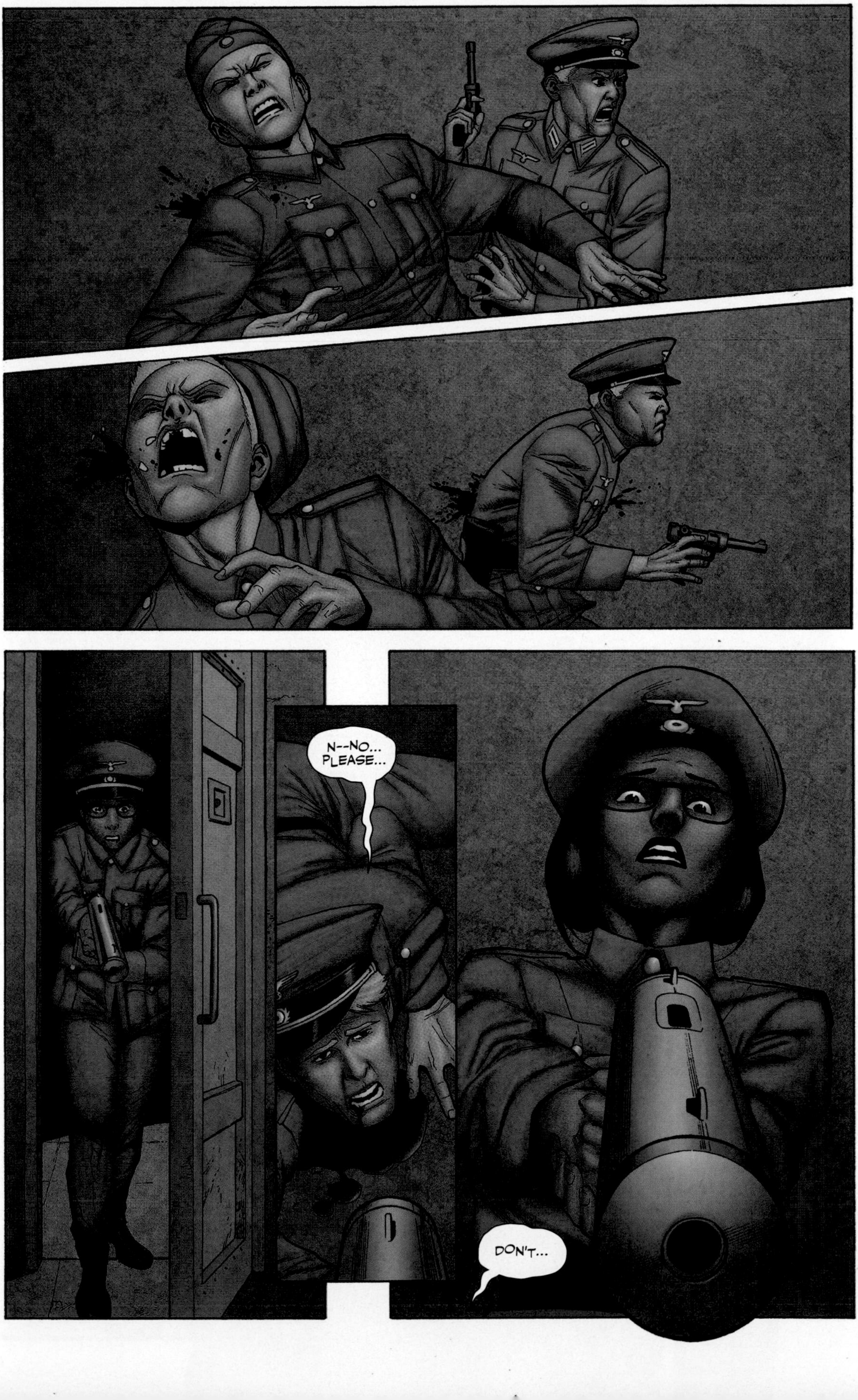
N--NO... PLEASE...
DON'T...

WAIT...MY FAMILY...

HYRRRRUG!

NEELA... NEELA, IS THAT YOU?

YEAH, IVAR...ARE YOU...ARE YOU ALL RIGHT?

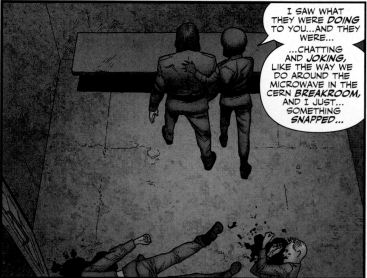

I SAW WHAT THEY WERE DOING TO YOU...AND THEY WERE...

...CHATTING AND JOKING, LIKE THE WAY WE DO AROUND THE MICROWAVE IN THE CERN BREAKROOM, AND I JUST... SOMETHING SNAPPED...

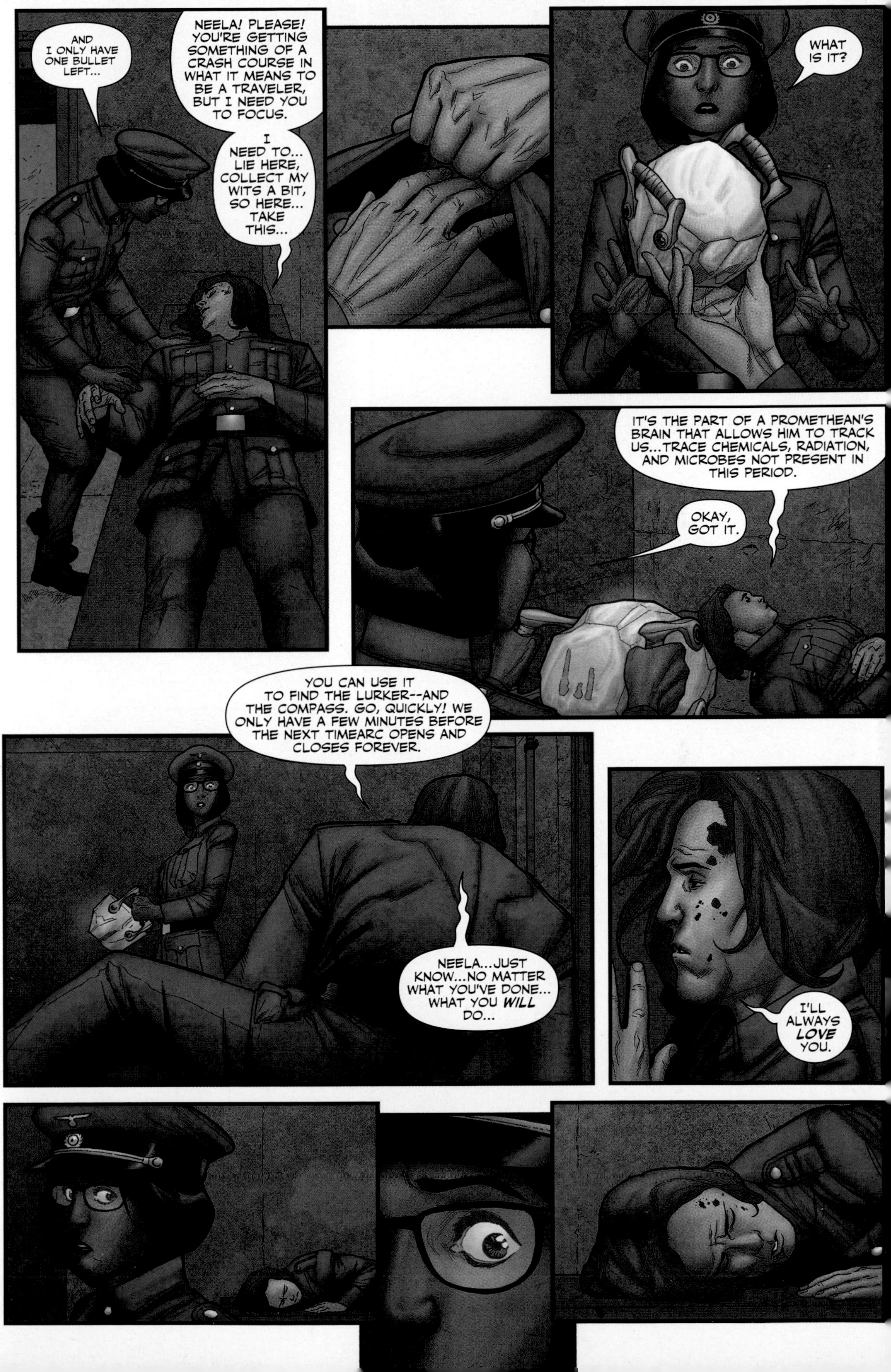
AND I ONLY HAVE ONE BULLET LEFT...
NEELA! PLEASE! YOU'RE GETTING SOMETHING OF A CRASH COURSE IN WHAT IT MEANS TO BE A TRAVELER, BUT I NEED YOU TO FOCUS.
I NEED TO... LIE HERE, COLLECT MY WITS A BIT, SO HERE... TAKE THIS...
WHAT IS IT?
IT'S THE PART OF A PROMETHEAN'S BRAIN THAT ALLOWS HIM TO TRACK US...TRACE CHEMICALS, RADIATION, AND MICROBES NOT PRESENT IN THIS PERIOD.
OKAY, GOT IT.
YOU CAN USE IT TO FIND THE LURKER--AND THE COMPASS. GO, QUICKLY! WE ONLY HAVE A FEW MINUTES BEFORE THE NEXT TIMEARC OPENS AND CLOSES FOREVER.
NEELA...JUST KNOW...NO MATTER WHAT YOU'VE DONE... WHAT YOU *WILL* DO...
I'LL ALWAYS *LOVE* YOU.

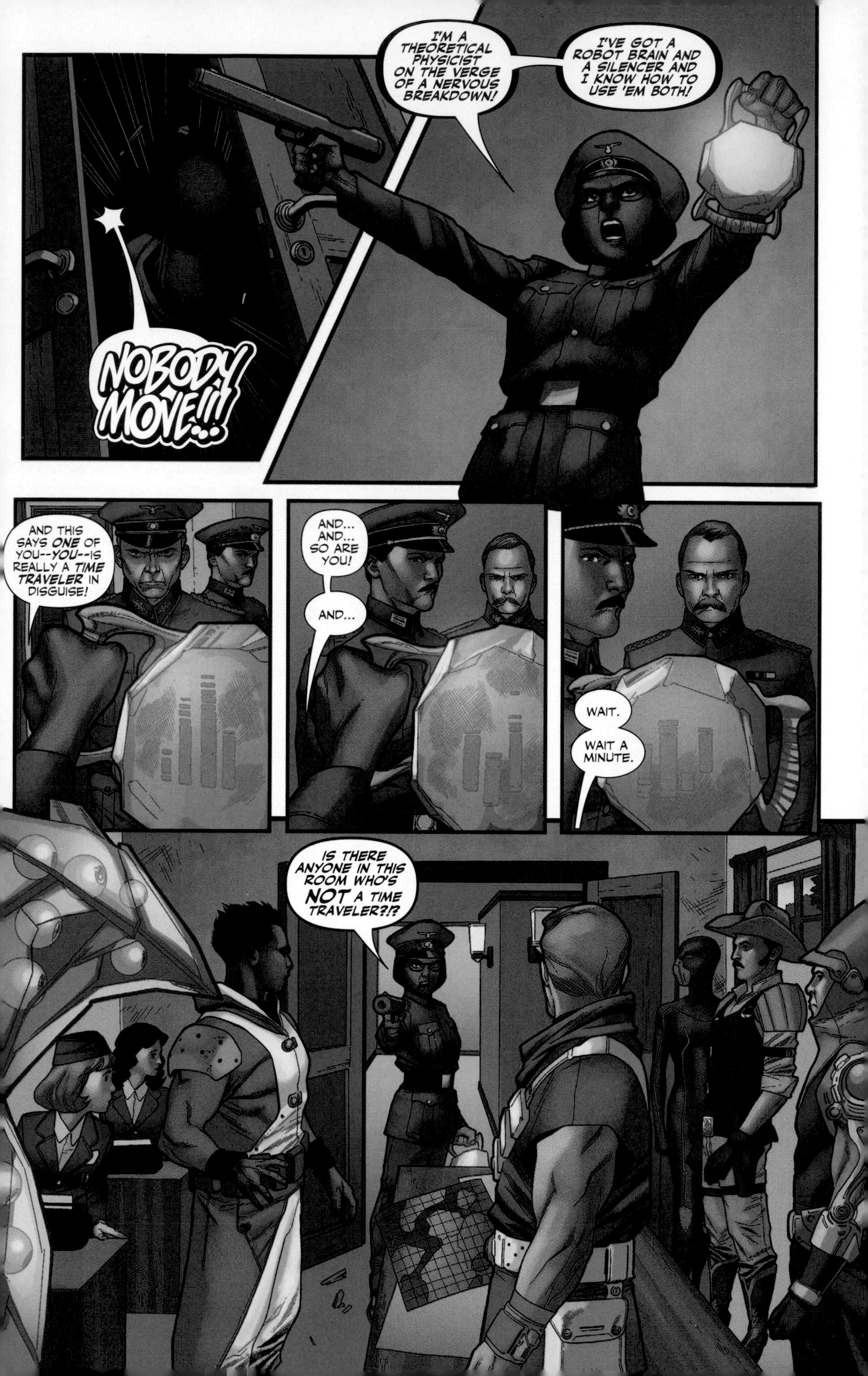
NOBODY MOVE!!!
I'M A THEORETICAL PHYSICIST ON THE VERGE OF A NERVOUS BREAKDOWN!
I'VE GOT A ROBOT BRAIN AND A SILENCER AND I KNOW HOW TO USE 'EM BOTH!
AND THIS SAYS ONE OF YOU--YOU--IS REALLY A TIME TRAVELER IN DISGUISE!
AND... AND... SO ARE YOU!
AND...
WAIT.
WAIT A MINUTE.
IS THERE ANYONE IN THIS ROOM WHO'S NOT A TIME TRAVELER?!?

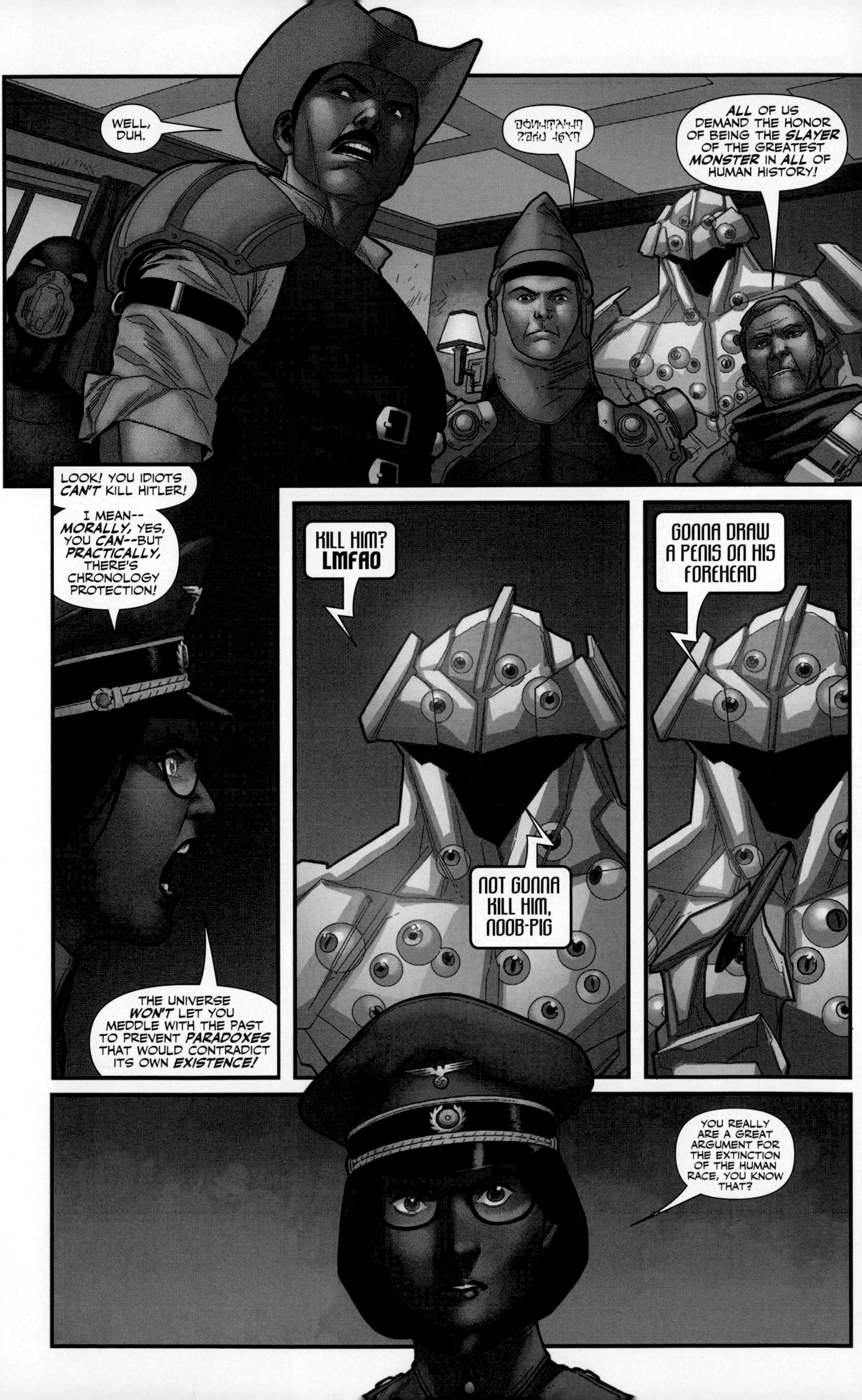
WELL, DUH.
ALL OF US DEMAND THE HONOR OF BEING THE SLAYER OF THE GREATEST MONSTER IN ALL OF HUMAN HISTORY!
LOOK! YOU IDIOTS CAN'T KILL HITLER!
I MEAN-- MORALLY, YES, YOU CAN--BUT PRACTICALLY, THERE'S CHRONOLOGY PROTECTION!
THE UNIVERSE WON'T LET YOU MEDDLE WITH THE PAST TO PREVENT PARADOXES THAT WOULD CONTRADICT ITS OWN EXISTENCE!
KILL HIM? LMFAO
NOT GONNA KILL HIM, NOOB-PIG
GONNA DRAW A PENIS ON HIS FOREHEAD
YOU REALLY ARE A GREAT ARGUMENT FOR THE EXTINCTION OF THE HUMAN RACE, YOU KNOW THAT?

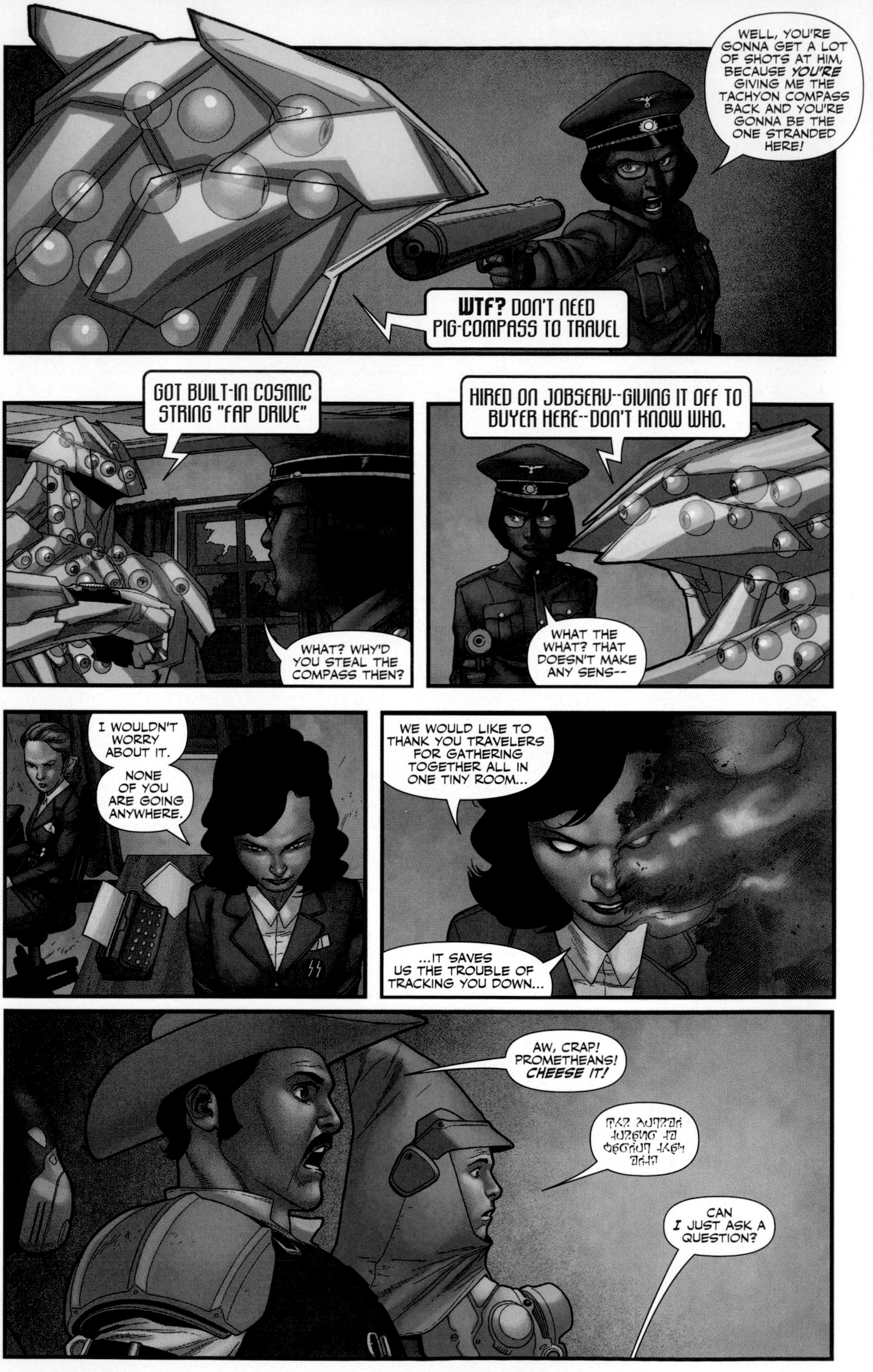
WELL, YOU'RE GONNA GET A LOT OF SHOTS AT HIM, BECAUSE *YOU'RE* GIVING ME THE TACHYON COMPASS BACK AND YOU'RE GONNA BE THE ONE STRANDED HERE!
WTF? DON'T NEED PIG-COMPASS TO TRAVEL
GOT BUILT-IN COSMIC STRING "FAP DRIVE"
WHAT? WHY'D YOU STEAL THE COMPASS THEN?
HIRED ON JOBSERV--GIVING IT OFF TO BUYER HERE--DON'T KNOW WHO.
WHAT THE WHAT? THAT DOESN'T MAKE ANY SENS--
I WOULDN'T WORRY ABOUT IT.
NONE OF YOU ARE GOING ANYWHERE.
WE WOULD LIKE TO THANK YOU TRAVELERS FOR GATHERING TOGETHER ALL IN ONE TINY ROOM...
...IT SAVES US THE TROUBLE OF TRACKING YOU DOWN...
AW, CRAP! PROMETHEANS! *CHEESE IT!*
CAN *I* JUST ASK A QUESTION?

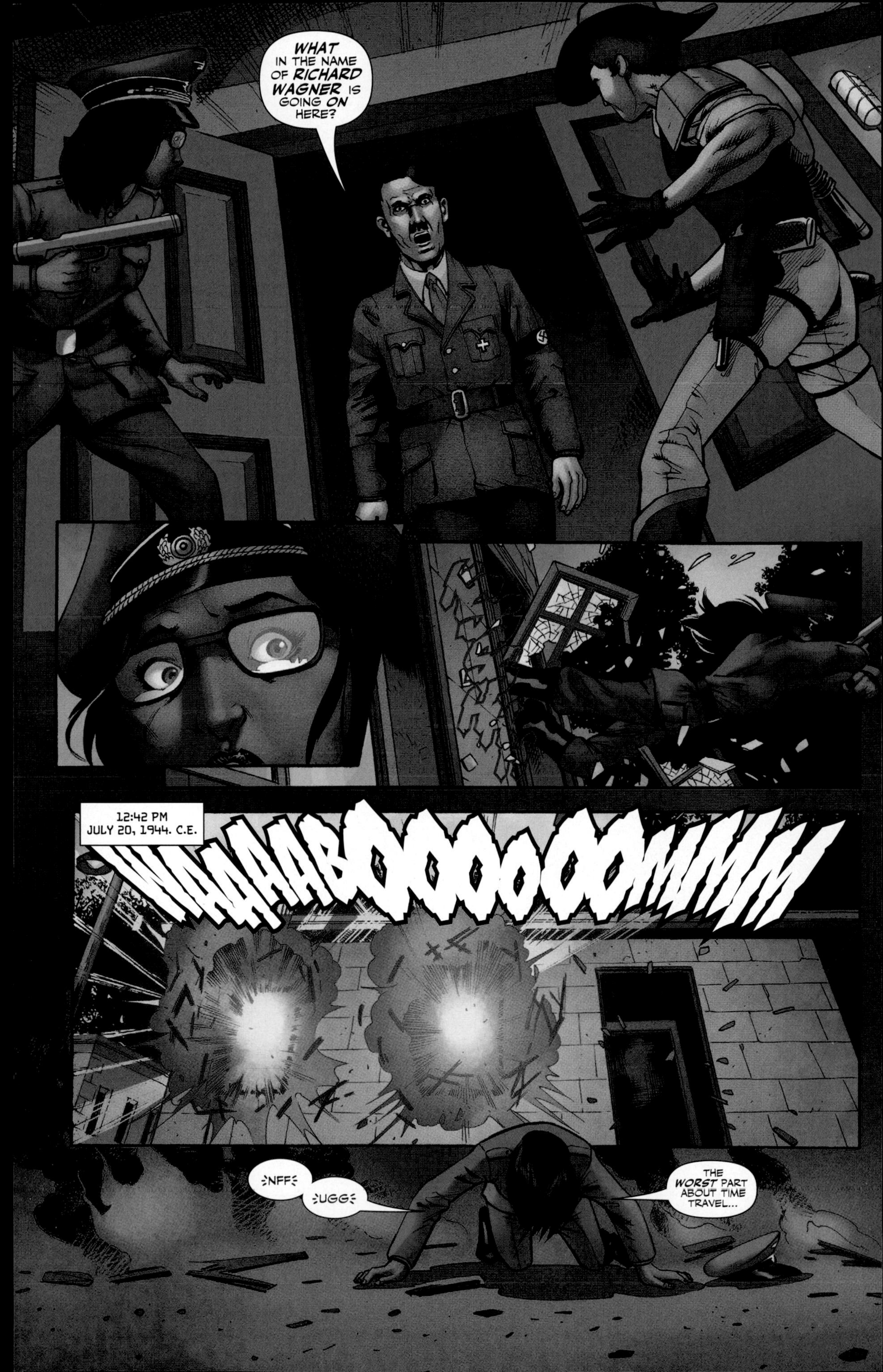
WHAT IN THE NAME OF RICHARD WAGNER IS GOING ON HERE?
12:42 PM JULY 20, 1944. C.E.
WHAAABOOOOOOMMM
NFF
UGG
THE WORST PART ABOUT TIME TRAVEL...

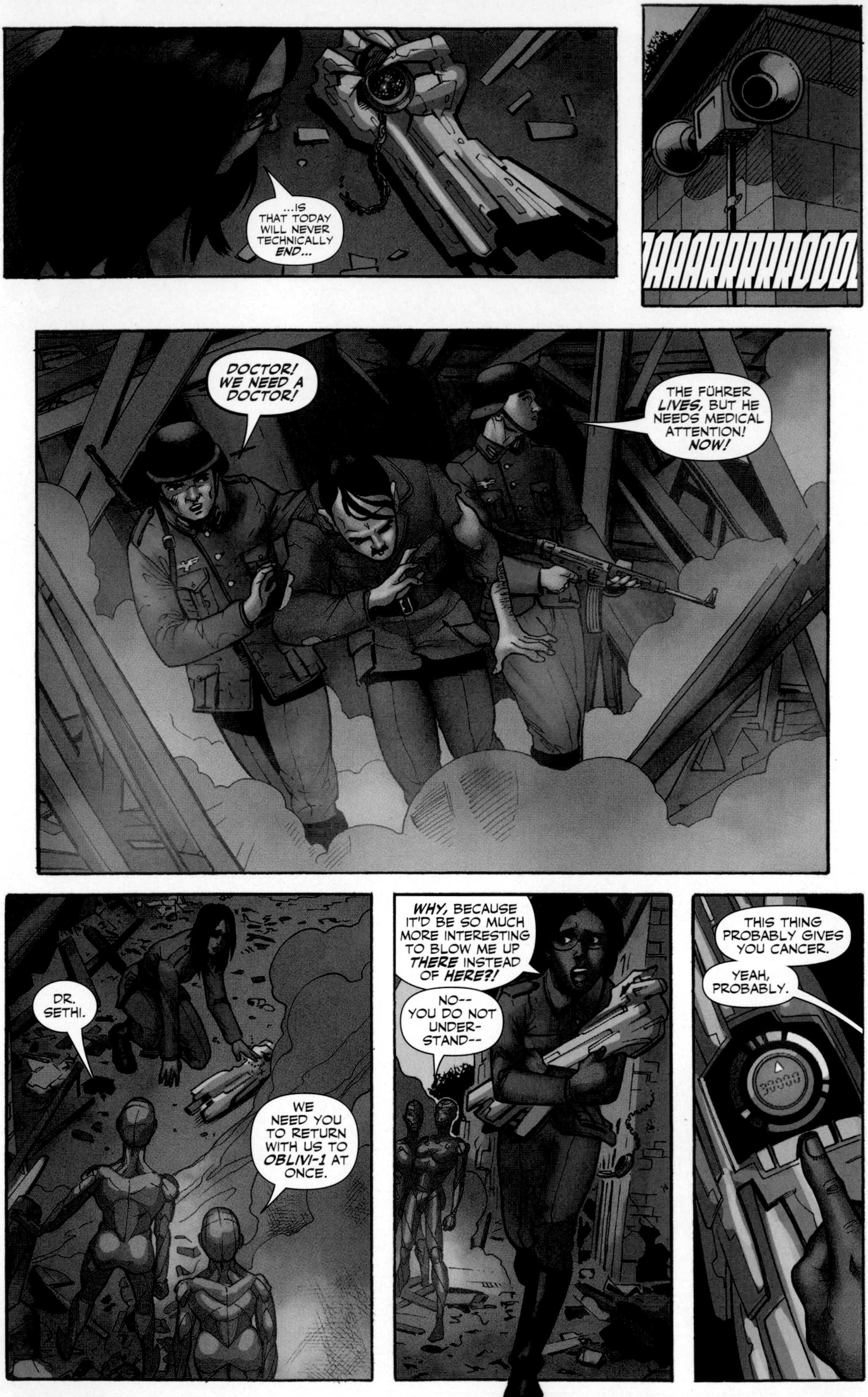

...IS THAT TODAY WILL NEVER TECHNICALLY END...
AAAARRRRRDOOL
DOCTOR! WE NEED A DOCTOR!
THE FÜHRER LIVES, BUT HE NEEDS MEDICAL ATTENTION! NOW!
DR. SETHI.
WE NEED YOU TO RETURN WITH US TO OBLIVI-1 AT ONCE.
WHY, BECAUSE IT'D BE SO MUCH MORE INTERESTING TO BLOW ME UP THERE INSTEAD OF HERE?!
NO-- YOU DO NOT UNDER-STAND--
THIS THING PROBABLY GIVES YOU CANCER.
YEAH, PROBABLY.

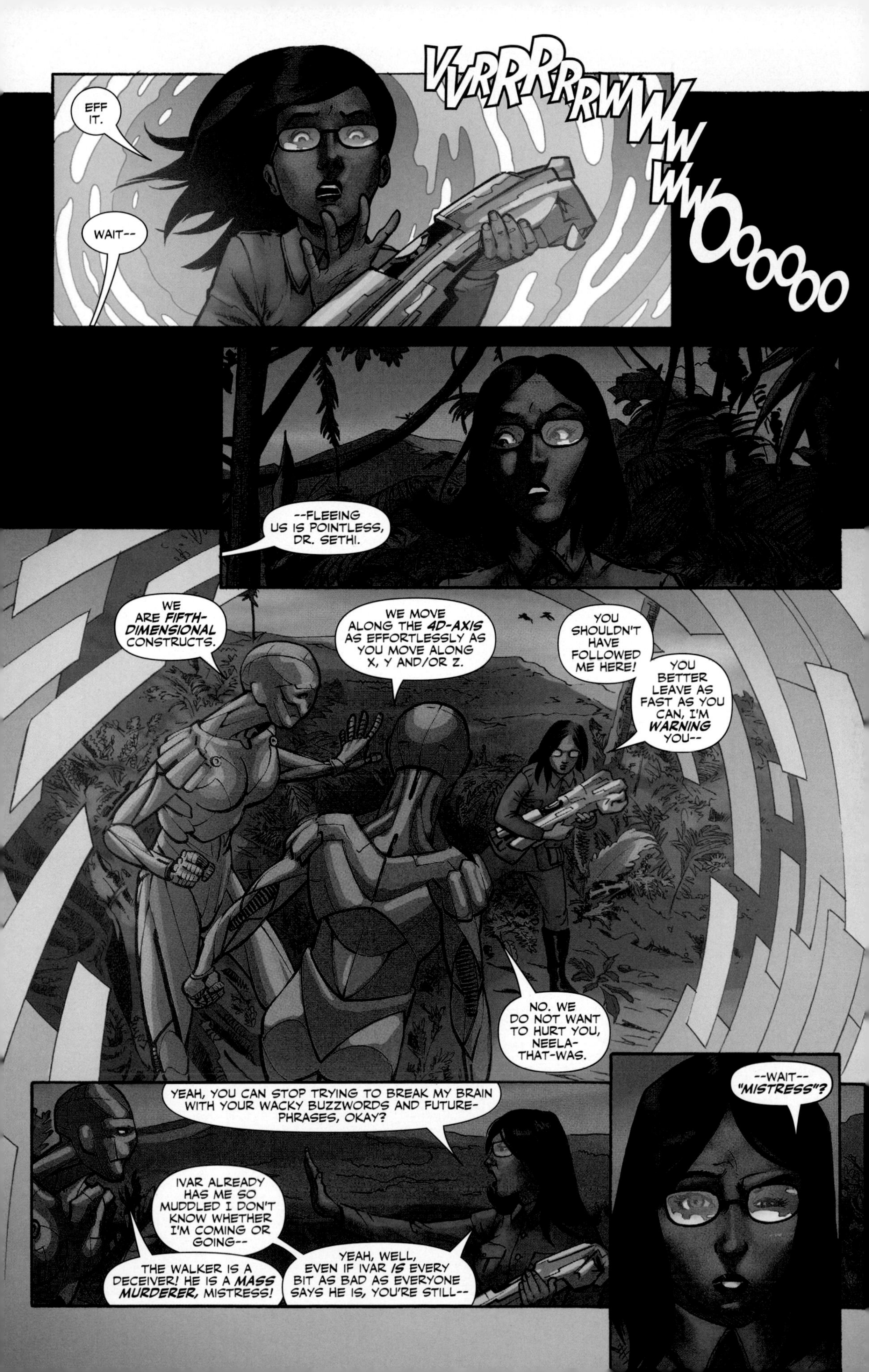

EFF IT.
WAIT--
VVRRRRRRWWWWWOOOOOO
--FLEEING US IS POINTLESS, DR. SETHI.
WE ARE FIFTH-DIMENSIONAL CONSTRUCTS.
WE MOVE ALONG THE 4D-AXIS AS EFFORTLESSLY AS YOU MOVE ALONG X, Y AND/OR Z.
YOU SHOULDN'T HAVE FOLLOWED ME HERE!
YOU BETTER LEAVE AS FAST AS YOU CAN, I'M WARNING YOU--
NO. WE DO NOT WANT TO HURT YOU, NEELA-THAT-WAS.
YEAH, YOU CAN STOP TRYING TO BREAK MY BRAIN WITH YOUR WACKY BUZZWORDS AND FUTURE-PHRASES, OKAY?
IVAR ALREADY HAS ME SO MUDDLED I DON'T KNOW WHETHER I'M COMING OR GOING--
THE WALKER IS A DECEIVER! HE IS A MASS MURDERER, MISTRESS!
YEAH, WELL, EVEN IF IVAR IS EVERY BIT AS BAD AS EVERYONE SAYS HE IS, YOU'RE STILL--
--WAIT-- "MISTRESS"?

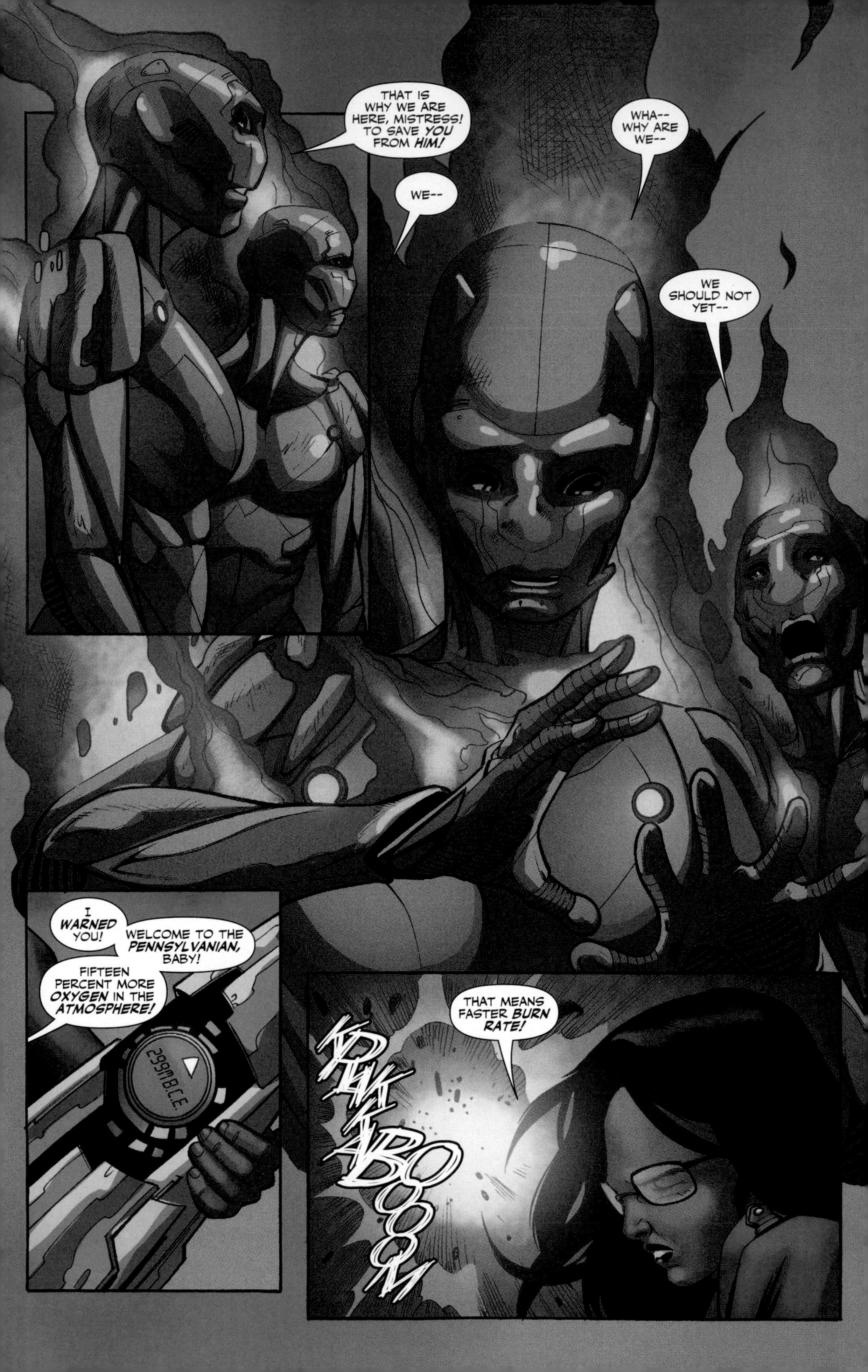

THAT IS WHY WE ARE HERE, MISTRESS! TO SAVE YOU FROM HIM!
WE--
WHA-- WHY ARE WE--
WE SHOULD NOT YET--
I WARNED YOU!
WELCOME TO THE PENNSYLVANIAN, BABY!
FIFTEEN PERCENT MORE OXYGEN IN THE ATMOSPHERE!
299M B.C.E.
THAT MEANS FASTER BURN RATE!
KRAKABOOOOM

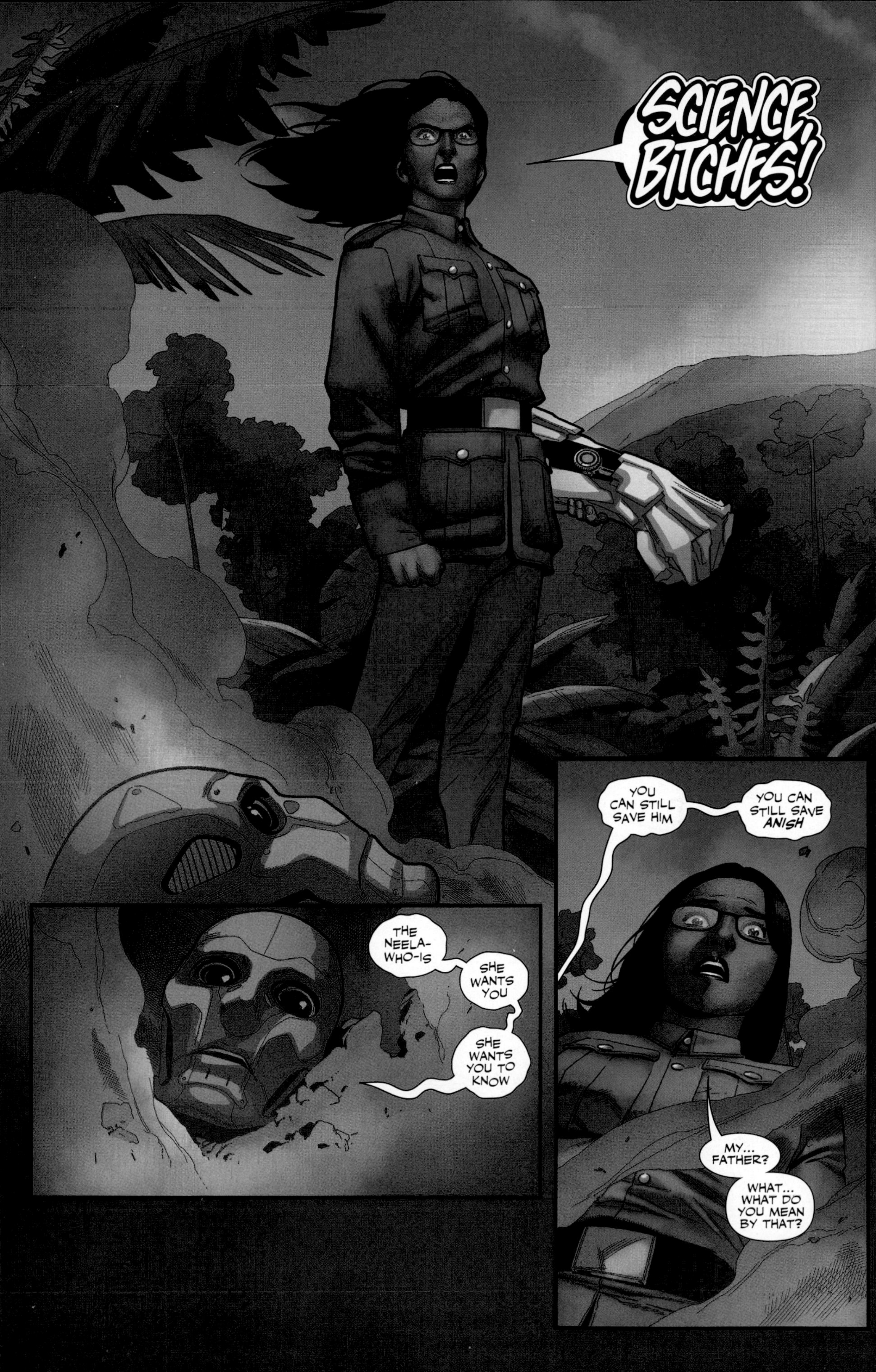
SCIENCE, BITCHES!
THE NEELA-WHO-IS
SHE WANTS YOU
SHE WANTS YOU TO KNOW
YOU CAN STILL SAVE HIM
YOU CAN STILL SAVE ANISH
MY... FATHER?
WHAT... WHAT DO YOU MEAN BY THAT?

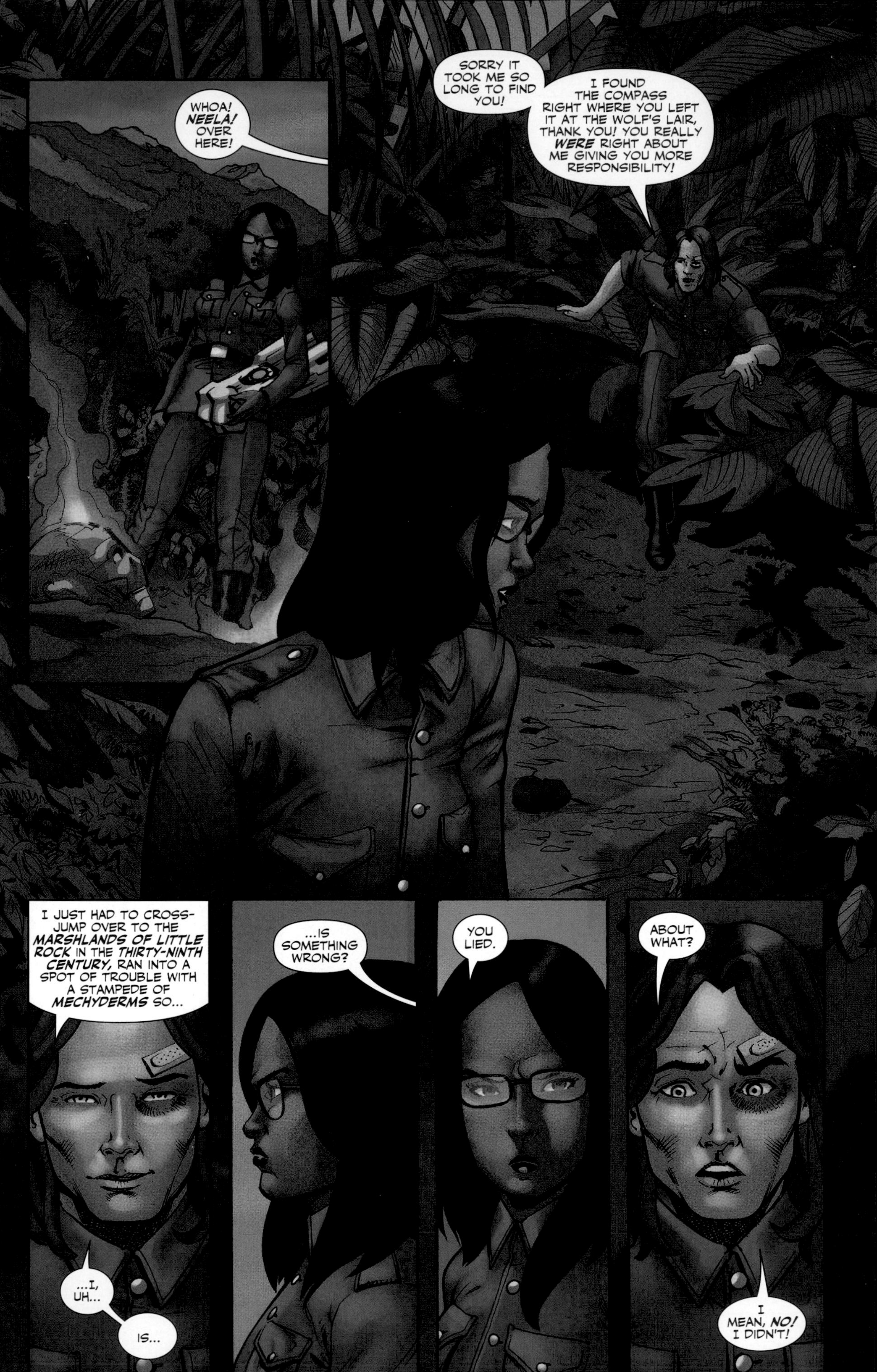
WHOA! NEELA! OVER HERE!
SORRY IT TOOK ME SO LONG TO FIND YOU!
I FOUND THE COMPASS RIGHT WHERE YOU LEFT IT AT THE WOLF'S LAIR, THANK YOU! YOU REALLY WERE RIGHT ABOUT ME GIVING YOU MORE RESPONSIBILITY!
I JUST HAD TO CROSS-JUMP OVER TO THE MARSHLANDS OF LITTLE ROCK IN THE THIRTY-NINTH CENTURY, RAN INTO A SPOT OF TROUBLE WITH A STAMPEDE OF MECHYDERMS SO...
...I, UH...
IS...
...IS SOMETHING WRONG?
YOU LIED.
ABOUT WHAT?
I MEAN, NO! I DIDN'T!

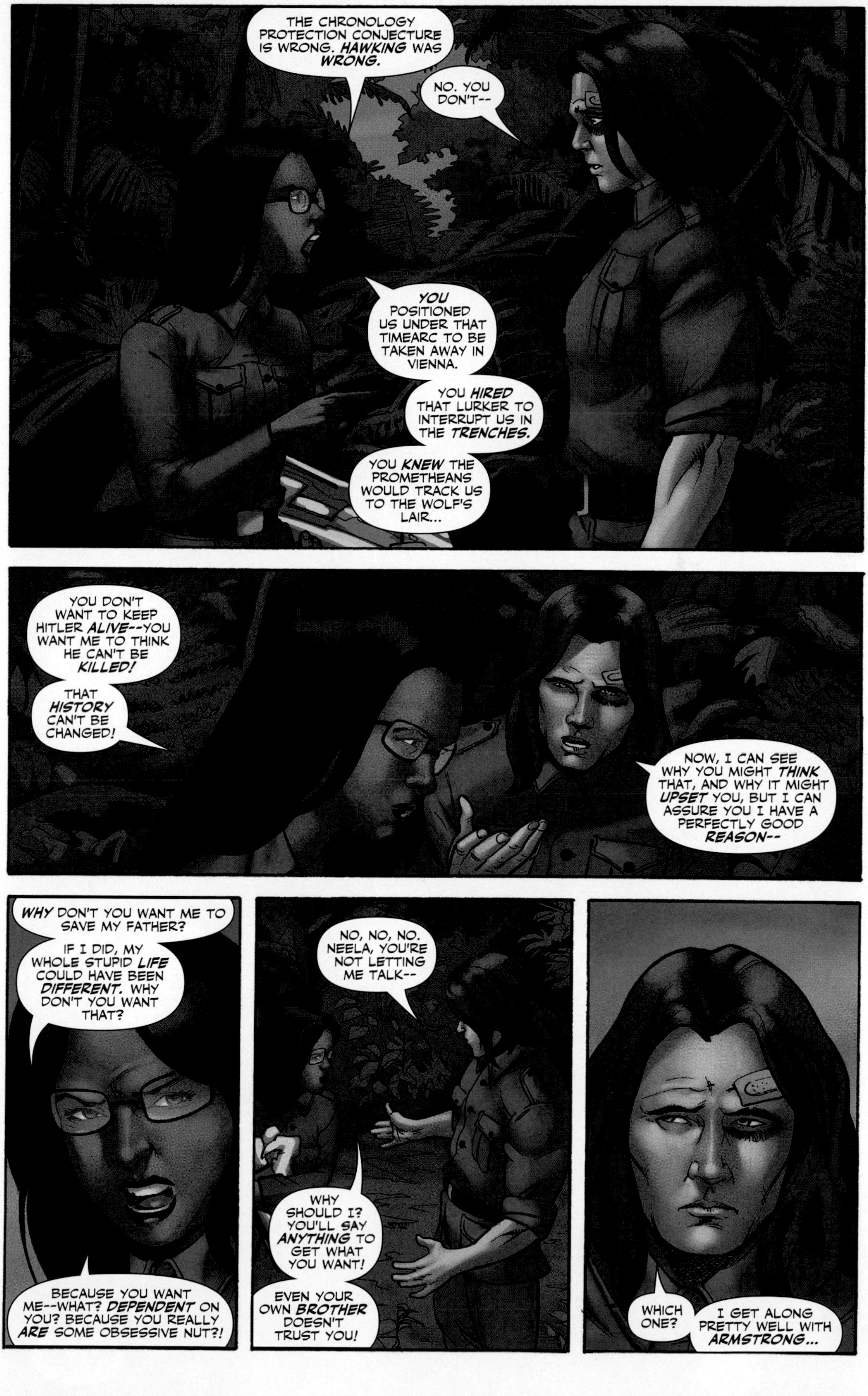
THE CHRONOLOGY PROTECTION CONJECTURE IS WRONG. *HAWKING* WAS *WRONG.*
NO. YOU DON'T--
YOU POSITIONED US UNDER THAT TIMEARC TO BE TAKEN AWAY IN VIENNA.
YOU *HIRED* THAT LURKER TO INTERRUPT US IN THE *TRENCHES.*
YOU *KNEW* THE PROMETHEANS WOULD TRACK US TO THE WOLF'S LAIR...
YOU DON'T WANT TO KEEP HITLER *ALIVE*--YOU WANT ME TO THINK HE CAN'T BE *KILLED!*
THAT *HISTORY* CAN'T BE CHANGED!
NOW, I CAN SEE WHY YOU MIGHT *THINK* THAT, AND WHY IT MIGHT *UPSET* YOU, BUT I CAN ASSURE YOU I HAVE A PERFECTLY GOOD *REASON*--
WHY DON'T YOU WANT ME TO SAVE MY FATHER?
IF I DID, MY WHOLE STUPID *LIFE* COULD HAVE BEEN *DIFFERENT.* WHY DON'T YOU WANT THAT?
BECAUSE YOU WANT ME--WHAT? *DEPENDENT* ON YOU? BECAUSE YOU REALLY *ARE* SOME OBSESSIVE NUT?!
NO, NO, NO. NEELA, YOU'RE NOT LETTING ME TALK--
WHY SHOULD I? YOU'LL *SAY ANYTHING* TO GET WHAT YOU WANT!
EVEN YOUR OWN *BROTHER* DOESN'T TRUST YOU!
WHICH ONE?
I GET ALONG PRETTY WELL WITH *ARMSTRONG...*

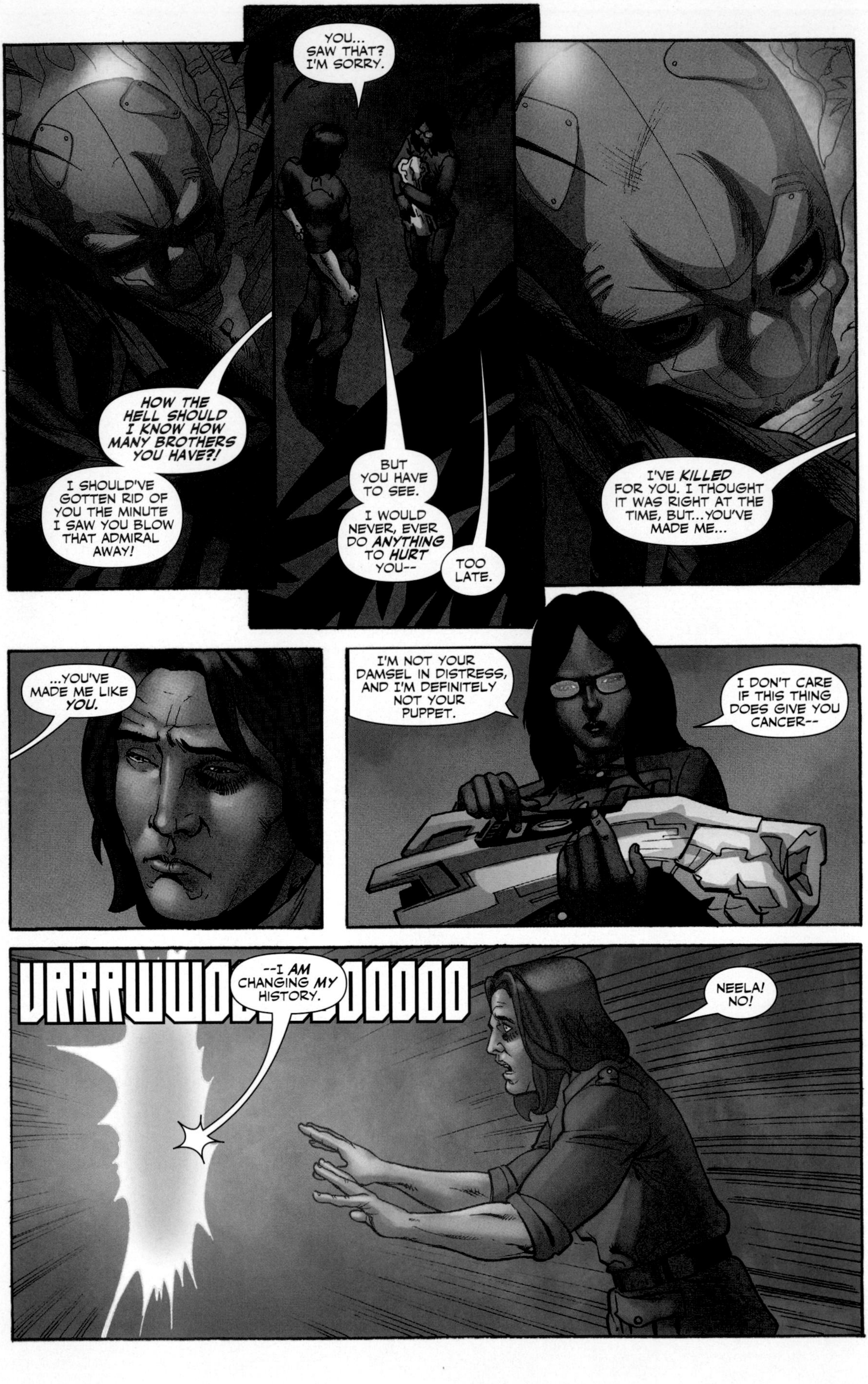
HOW THE HELL SHOULD I KNOW HOW MANY BROTHERS YOU HAVE?!
I SHOULD'VE GOTTEN RID OF YOU THE MINUTE I SAW YOU BLOW THAT ADMIRAL AWAY!
YOU... SAW THAT? I'M SORRY.
BUT YOU HAVE TO SEE.
I WOULD NEVER, EVER DO ANYTHING TO HURT YOU--
TOO LATE.
I'VE KILLED FOR YOU. I THOUGHT IT WAS RIGHT AT THE TIME, BUT...YOU'VE MADE ME...
...YOU'VE MADE ME LIKE YOU.
I'M NOT YOUR DAMSEL IN DISTRESS, AND I'M DEFINITELY NOT YOUR PUPPET.
I DON'T CARE IF THIS THING DOES GIVE YOU CANCER--
VRRRWWO
OOOOOO
--I AM CHANGING MY HISTORY.
NEELA! NO!

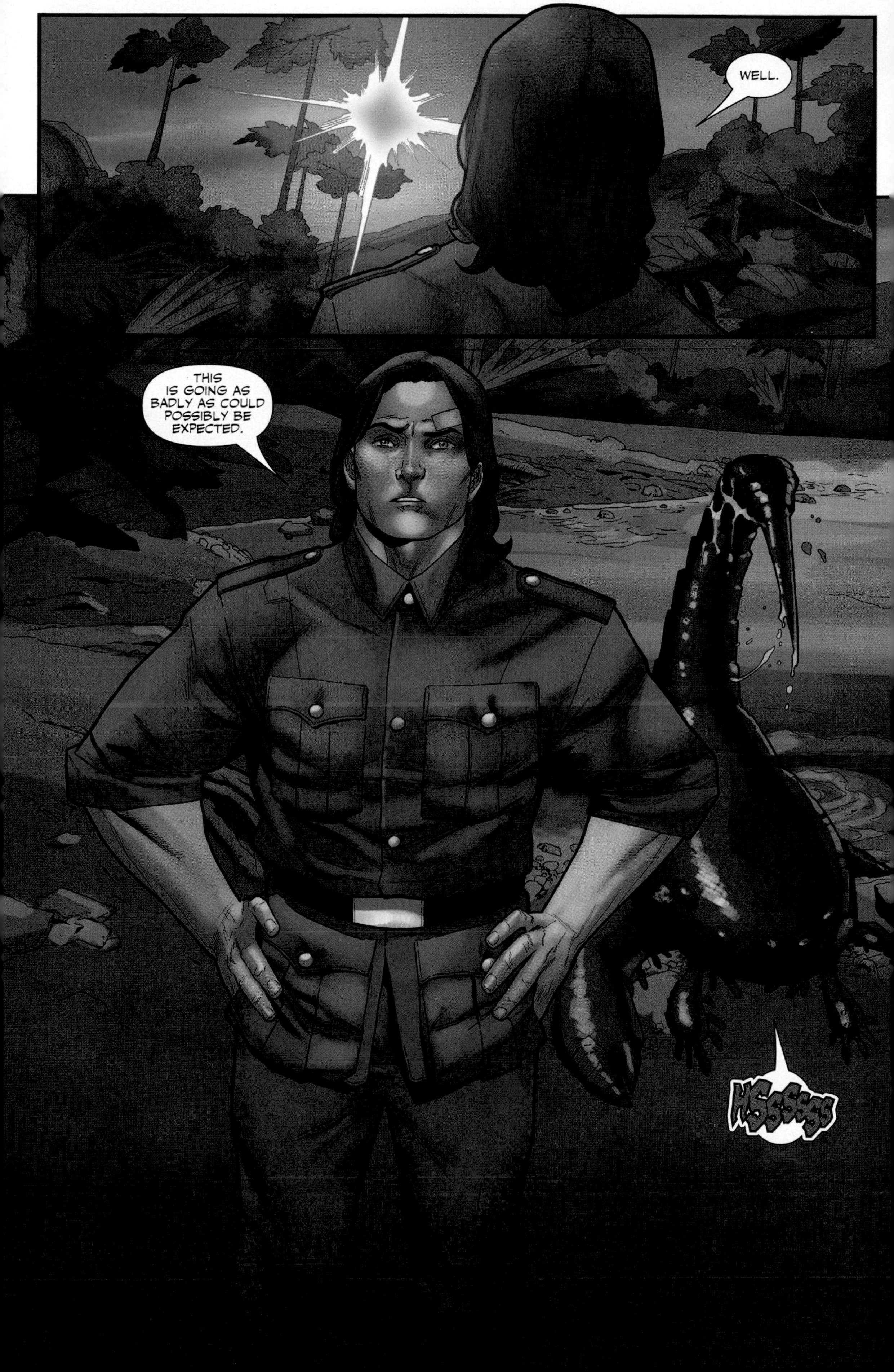
WELL.
THIS IS GOING AS BADLY AS COULD POSSIBLY BE EXPECTED.
HSSSSSS

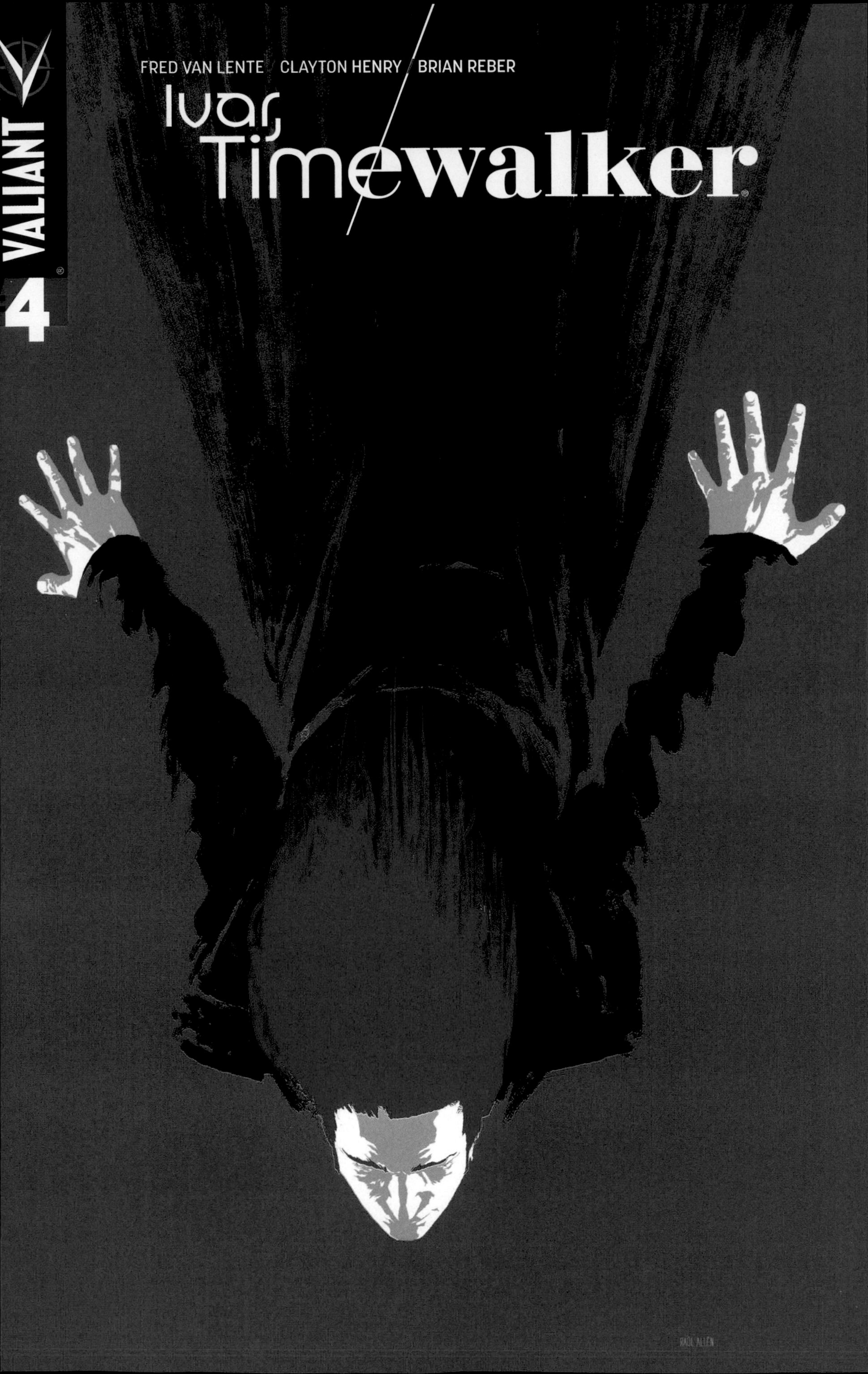
FRED VAN LENTE / CLAYTON HENRY / BRIAN REBER
Ivar, Timewalker
VALIANT
4
RAÚL ALLEN

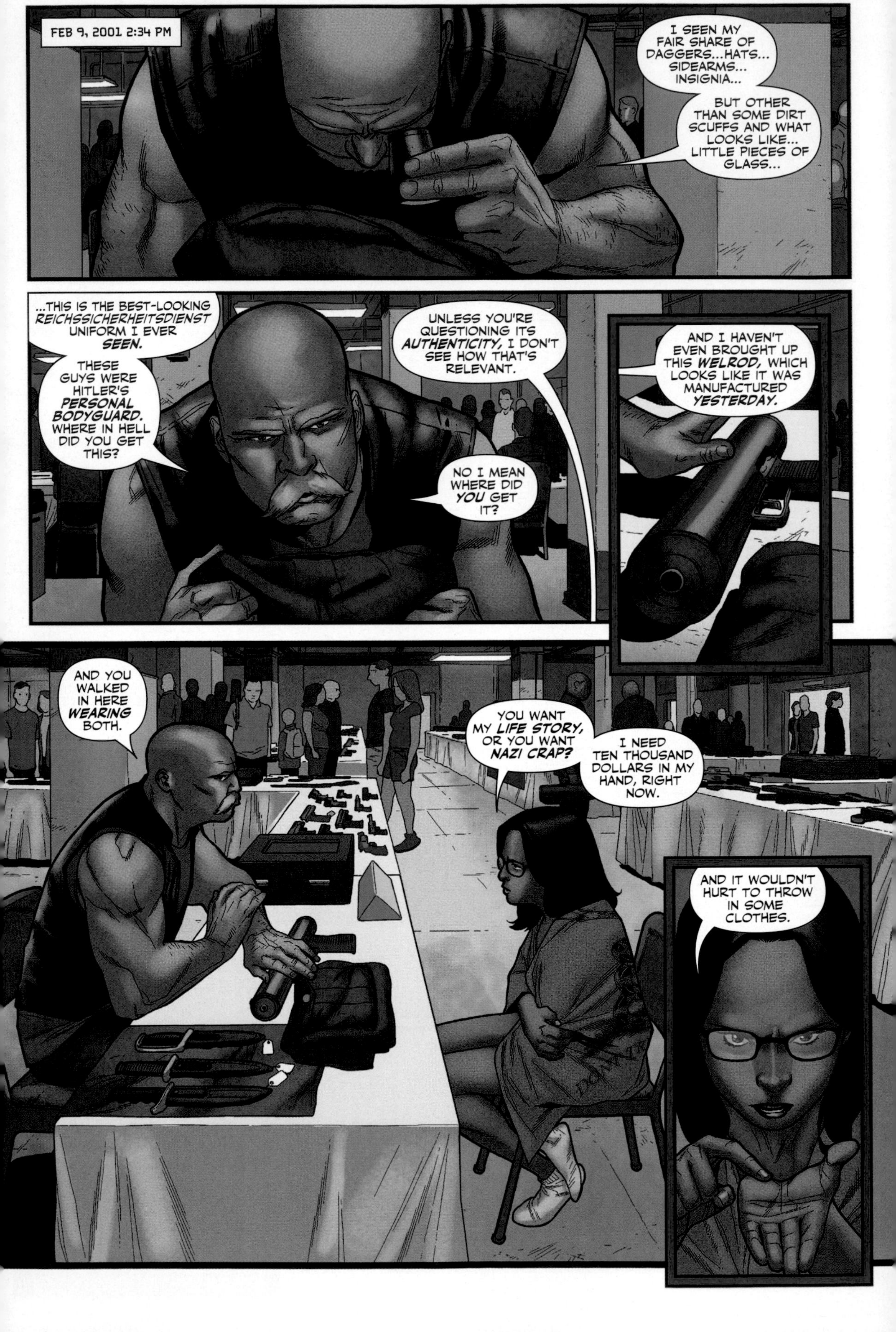
FEB 9, 2001 2:34 PM
I SEEN MY FAIR SHARE OF DAGGERS...HATS... SIDEARMS... INSIGNIA...
BUT OTHER THAN SOME DIRT SCUFFS AND WHAT LOOKS LIKE... LITTLE PIECES OF GLASS...
...THIS IS THE BEST-LOOKING REICHSSICHERHEITSDIENST UNIFORM I EVER SEEN.
THESE GUYS WERE HITLER'S PERSONAL BODYGUARD. WHERE IN HELL DID YOU GET THIS?
UNLESS YOU'RE QUESTIONING ITS AUTHENTICITY, I DON'T SEE HOW THAT'S RELEVANT.
NO I MEAN WHERE DID YOU GET IT?
AND I HAVEN'T EVEN BROUGHT UP THIS WELROD, WHICH LOOKS LIKE IT WAS MANUFACTURED YESTERDAY.
AND YOU WALKED IN HERE WEARING BOTH.
YOU WANT MY LIFE STORY, OR YOU WANT NAZI CRAP?
I NEED TEN THOUSAND DOLLARS IN MY HAND, RIGHT NOW.
AND IT WOULDN'T HURT TO THROW IN SOME CLOTHES.

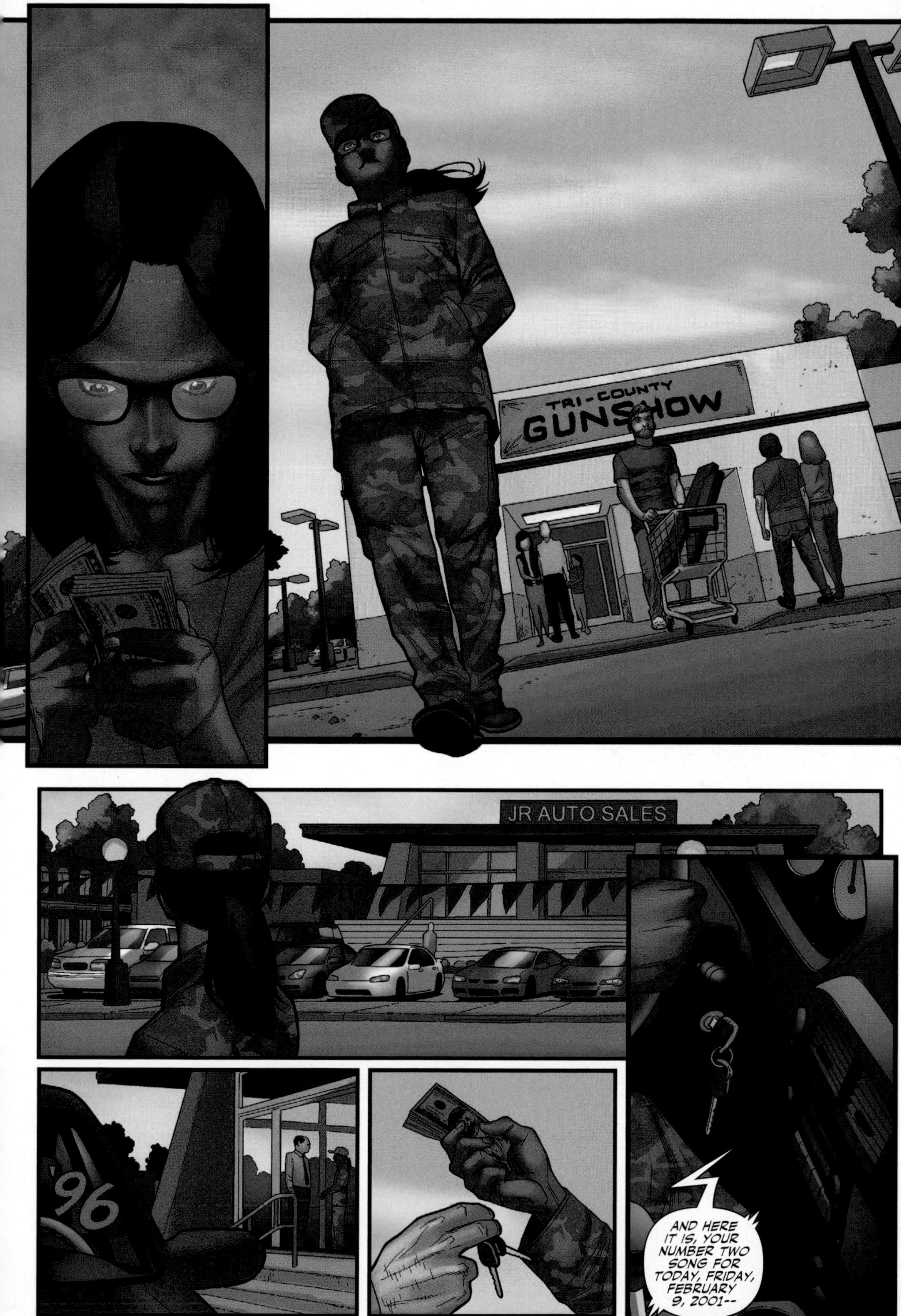
TRI-COUNTY
GUNSHOW
JR AUTO SALES
'96
AND HERE IT IS, YOUR NUMBER TWO SONG FOR TODAY, FRIDAY, FEBRUARY 9, 2001--

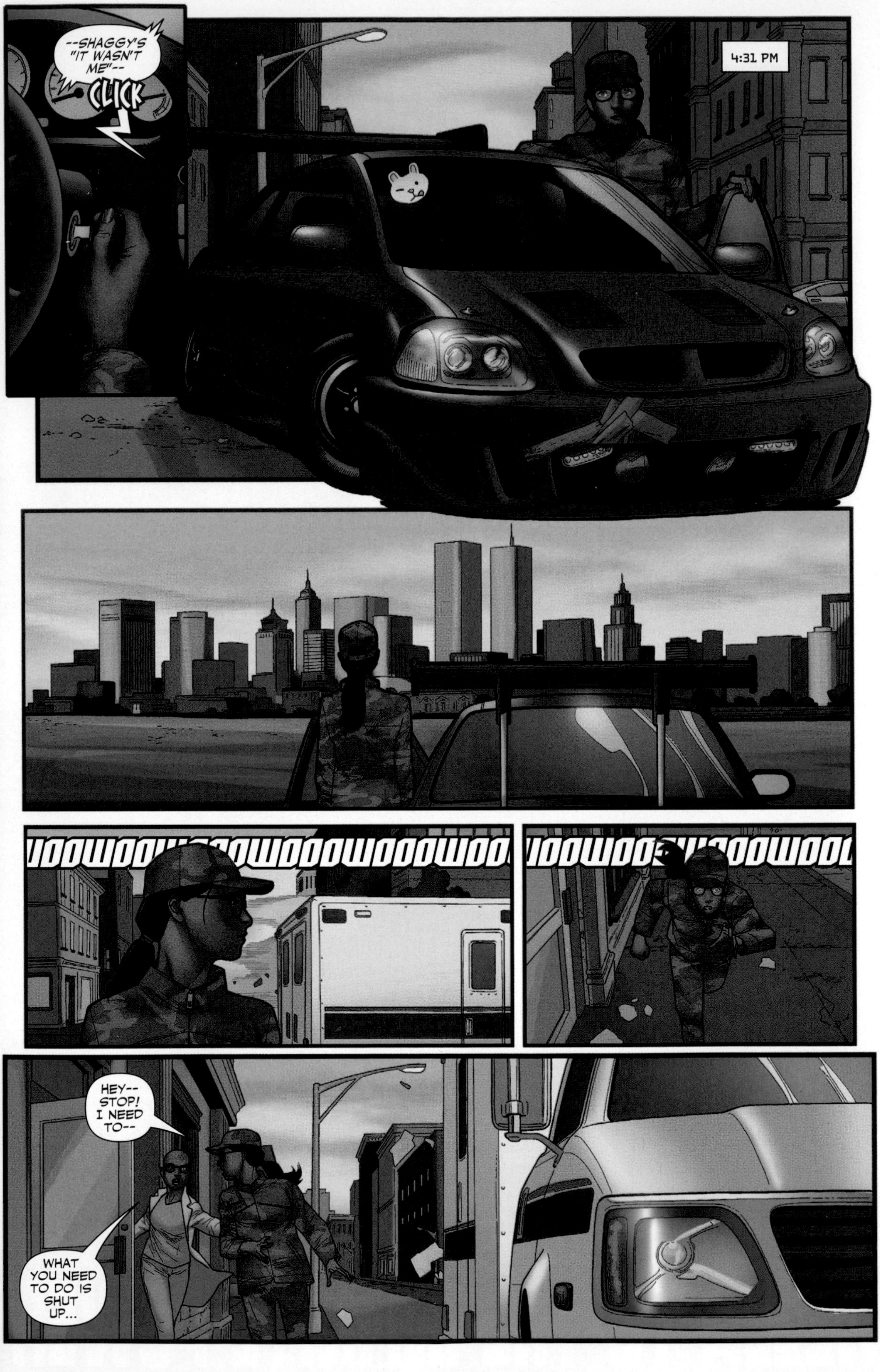
--SHAGGY'S "IT WASN'T ME"--
CLICK
4:31 PM
WOOOWOOOWOOOWOOOWOOO
WOOOWOOOWOOOWOOOWOOO
HEY-- STOP! I NEED TO--
WHAT YOU NEED TO DO IS SHUT UP...

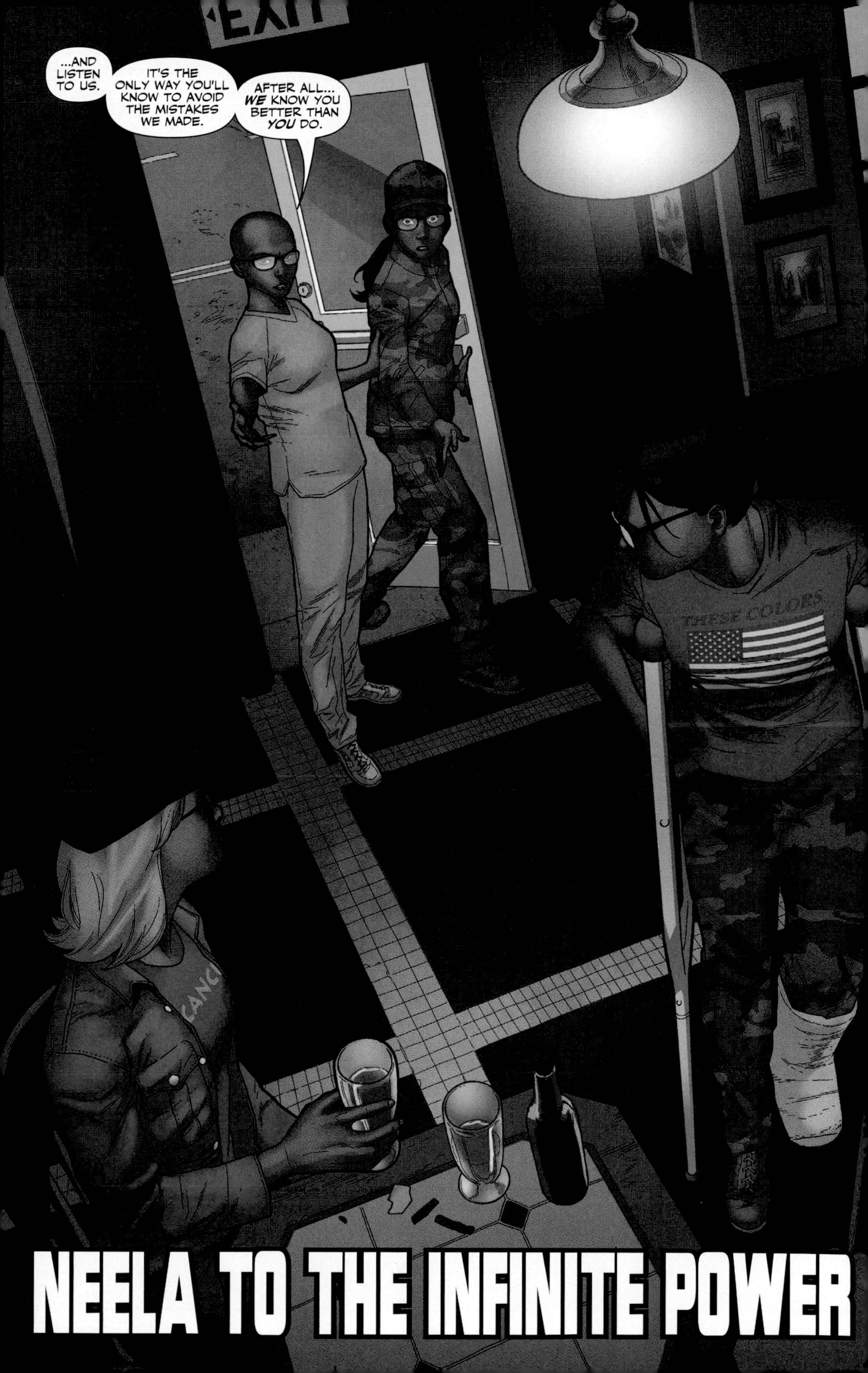
...AND LISTEN TO US.
IT'S THE ONLY WAY YOU'LL KNOW TO AVOID THE MISTAKES WE MADE.
AFTER ALL... *WE* KNOW YOU BETTER THAN *YOU* DO.
THESE COLORS
NEELA TO THE INFINITE POWER

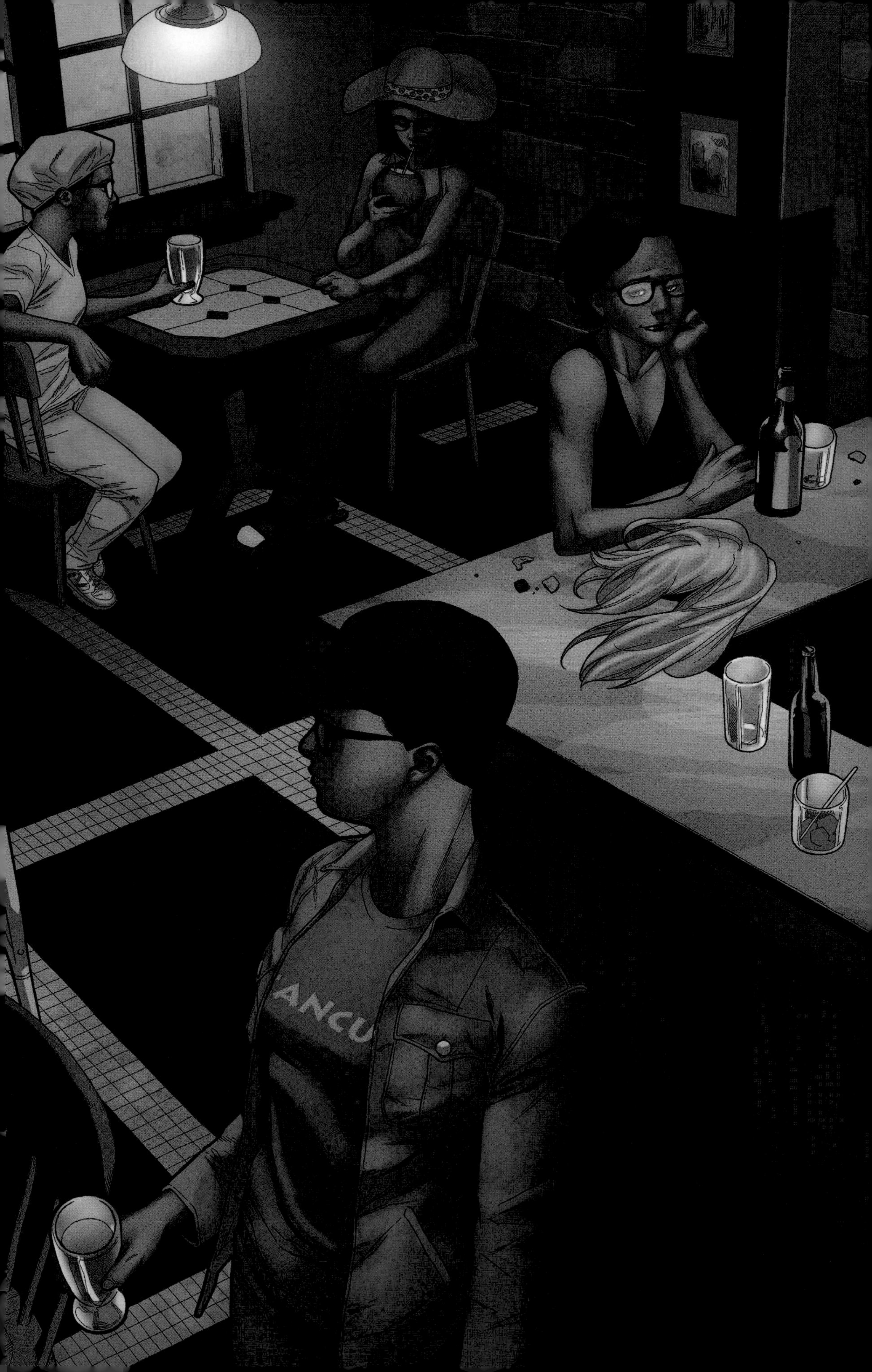
ANCU

DID IVAR SEND YOU? I DON'T CARE WHAT HE SAYS, I'M NOT LISTENING TO HIM ANYMORE--

OF COURSE SHE *ISN'T*. BECAUSE SHE ISN'T LISTENING TO *ANYONE*.

HARD TO WHEN YOUR *HEAD* IS SO FAR UP YOUR--

SHUT UP, YOU LUSH! *SOME* OF US STILL HAVE HOPE. *SOME* OF US HAVEN'T GIVEN UP, LIKE--

YOU KNOW, I REMEMBER THINKING MAYBE I WOULD *HIT* YOU WHEN I *WAS* YOU.

AND MAYBE I *SHOULD* HAVE. MAYBE I SHOULD KNOCK YOU THE EFF OUT. IT'S THE ONLY WAY TO STOP YOU FROM MAKING *STUPID* GODDAMN *DECISIONS*--

HEY! THE BEST MAN I EVER KNEW IS ABOUT TO DIE BECAUSE OF SOMETHING I CAN *STOP*.

BUT I HAVE A VERY SMALL WINDOW TO DO IT IN.

THAT'S HER. SHE'S THE FIRST! LET HER GO!

OH, OKAY. YOU'RE RIGHT. SORRY, I DIDN'T RECOGNIZE YOU AT FIRST.

GO FOR IT! SEE YOU LATER--OR-- I GUESS... *YOU'LL* SEE *US* LATER!

NOPE! IF I GET MY WAY, MY WHOLE *LIFE* WILL CHANGE-- SO I HOPE YOU ALL ENJOY FADING FROM THE PHOTOGRAPH!

"FADING FROM THE PHOTOGRAPH"?

BACK TO THE FUTURE REFERENCE.

OH, SURE. RIGHT.

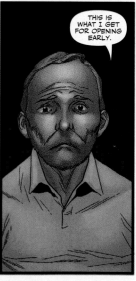

THIS IS WHAT I GET FOR OPENING EARLY.

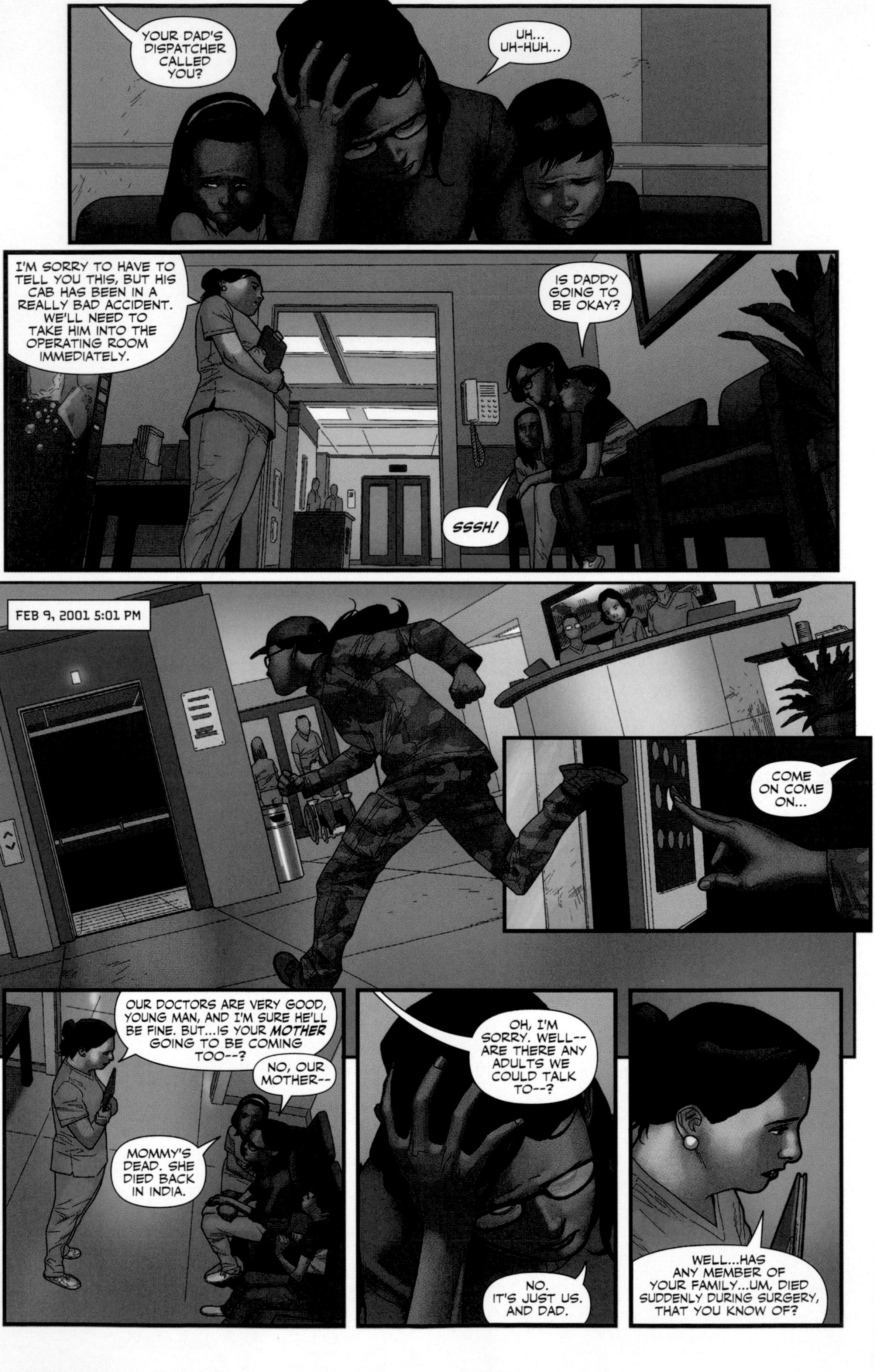
YOUR DAD'S DISPATCHER CALLED YOU?
UH... UH-HUH...
I'M SORRY TO HAVE TO TELL YOU THIS, BUT HIS CAB HAS BEEN IN A REALLY BAD ACCIDENT. WE'LL NEED TO TAKE HIM INTO THE OPERATING ROOM IMMEDIATELY.
IS DADDY GOING TO BE OKAY?
SSSH!
FEB 9, 2001 5:01 PM
COME ON COME ON...
OUR DOCTORS ARE VERY GOOD, YOUNG MAN, AND I'M SURE HE'LL BE FINE. BUT...IS YOUR *MOTHER* GOING TO BE COMING TOO--?
NO, OUR MOTHER--
MOMMY'S DEAD. SHE DIED BACK IN INDIA.
OH, I'M SORRY. WELL--ARE THERE ANY ADULTS WE COULD TALK TO--?
NO. IT'S JUST US. AND DAD.
WELL...HAS ANY MEMBER OF YOUR FAMILY...UM, DIED SUDDENLY DURING SURGERY, THAT YOU KNOW OF?

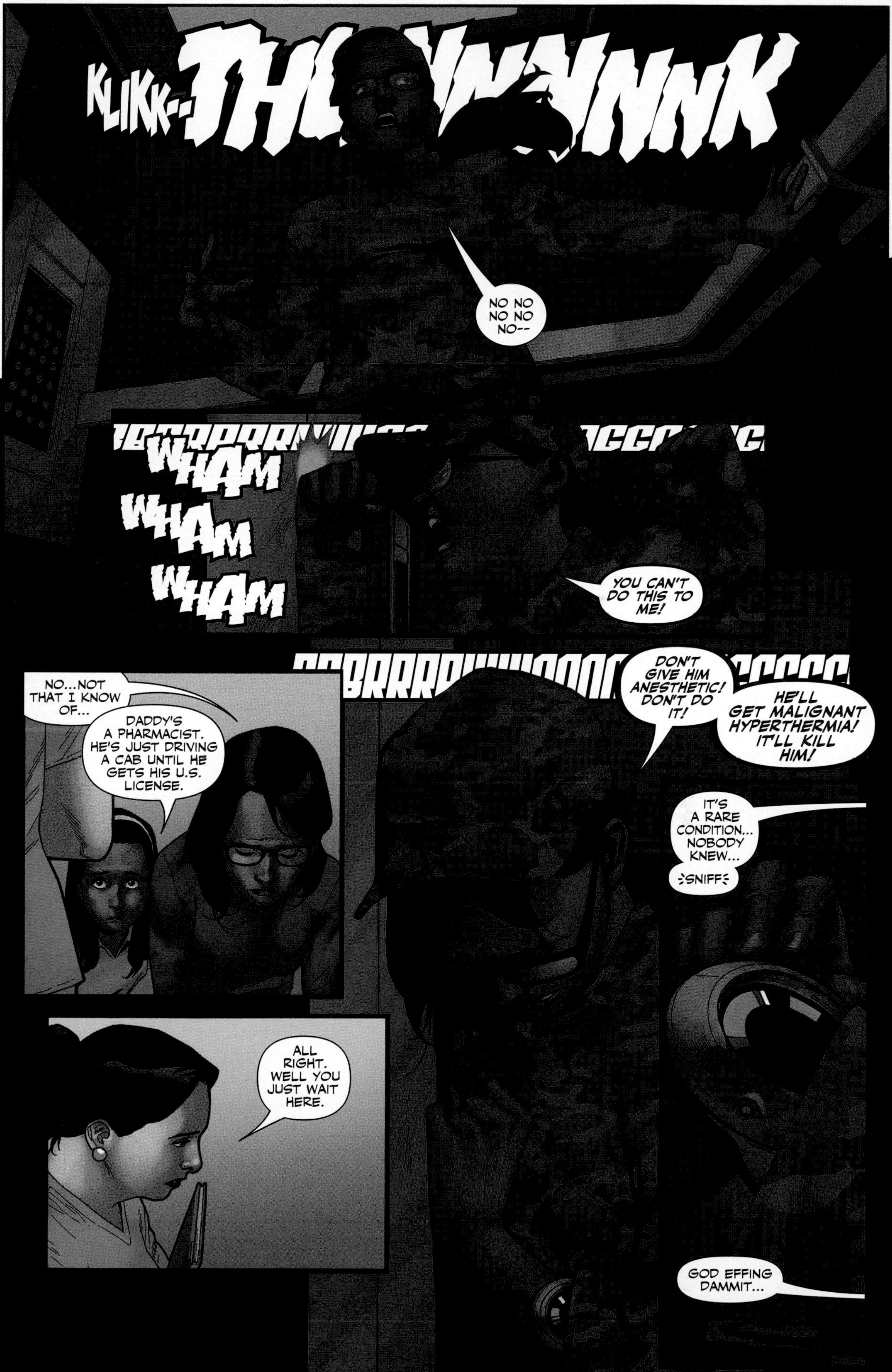
KLIKK-
NO NO NO NO NO--
WHAM
WHAM
WHAM
YOU CAN'T DO THIS TO ME!
DON'T GIVE HIM ANESTHETIC! DON'T DO IT!
HE'LL GET MALIGNANT HYPERTHERMIA! IT'LL KILL HIM!
NO...NOT THAT I KNOW OF...
DADDY'S A PHARMACIST. HE'S JUST DRIVING A CAB UNTIL HE GETS HIS U.S. LICENSE.
IT'S A RARE CONDITION... NOBODY KNEW...
SNIFF
ALL RIGHT. WELL YOU JUST WAIT HERE.
GOD EFFING DAMMIT...

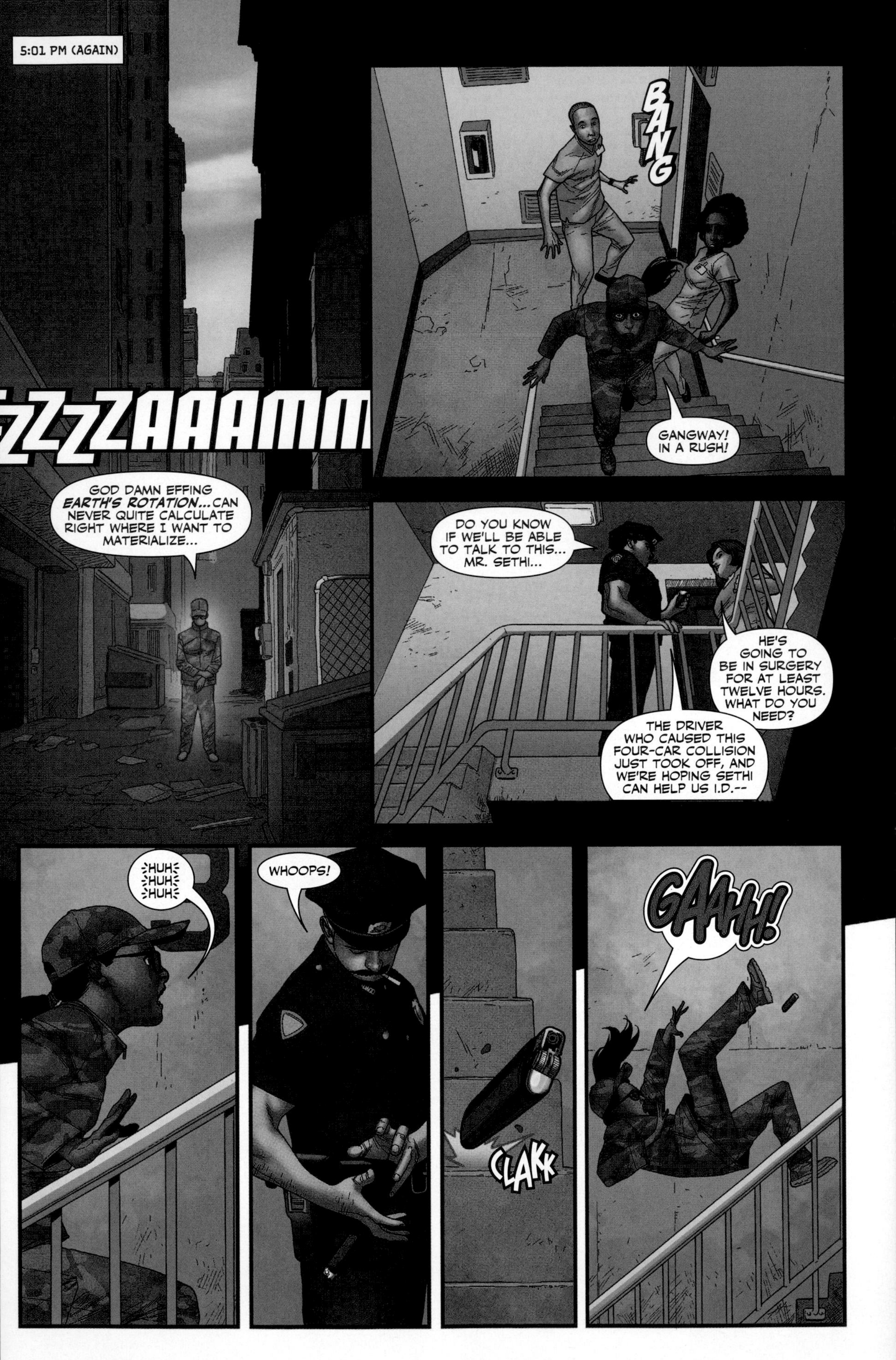
5:01 PM (AGAIN)
ZZZZAAAAMM
BANG
GANGWAY! IN A RUSH!
GOD DAMN EFFING EARTH'S ROTATION... CAN NEVER QUITE CALCULATE RIGHT WHERE I WANT TO MATERIALIZE...
DO YOU KNOW IF WE'LL BE ABLE TO TALK TO THIS... MR. SETHI...
HE'S GOING TO BE IN SURGERY FOR AT LEAST TWELVE HOURS. WHAT DO YOU NEED?
THE DRIVER WHO CAUSED THIS FOUR-CAR COLLISION JUST TOOK OFF, AND WE'RE HOPING SETHI CAN HELP US I.D.--
HUH HUH HUH
WHOOPS!
CLAKK
GAAHH!

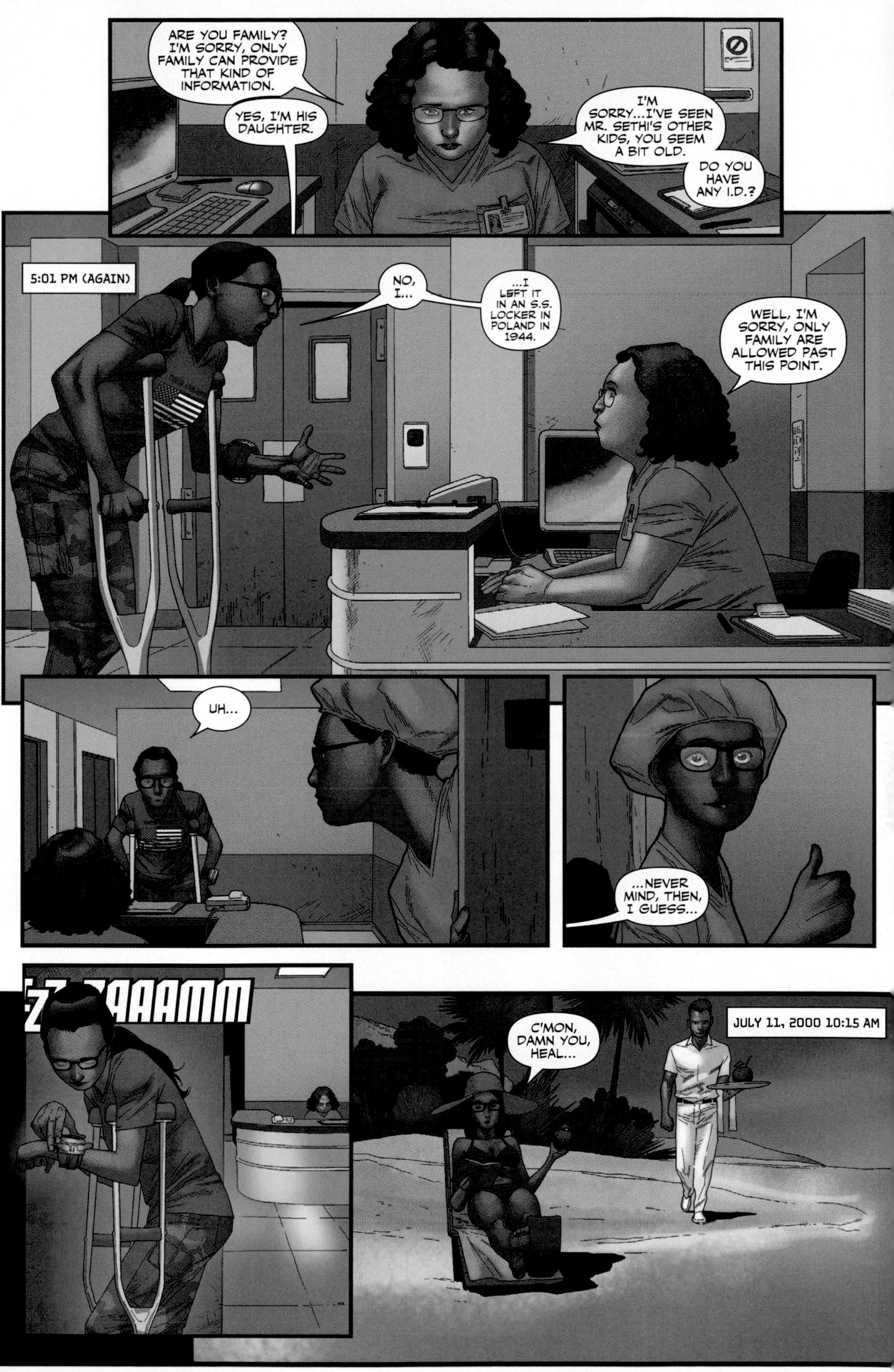
ARE YOU FAMILY? I'M SORRY, ONLY FAMILY CAN PROVIDE THAT KIND OF INFORMATION.
YES, I'M HIS DAUGHTER.
I'M SORRY...I'VE SEEN MR. SETHI'S OTHER KIDS, YOU SEEM A BIT OLD.
DO YOU HAVE ANY I.D.?
5:01 PM (AGAIN)
NO, I...
...I LEFT IT IN AN S.S. LOCKER IN POLAND IN 1944.
WELL, I'M SORRY, ONLY FAMILY ARE ALLOWED PAST THIS POINT.
UH...
...NEVER MIND, THEN, I GUESS...
ZZAAAAMM
JULY 11, 2000 10:15 AM
C'MON, DAMN YOU, HEAL...

FZZZZ...M

FEB 9, 2001 4:58 PM

NAILED IT! YES!

5:01 PM (YES, AGAIN)

UH...NEVER MIND, THEN, I GUESS...

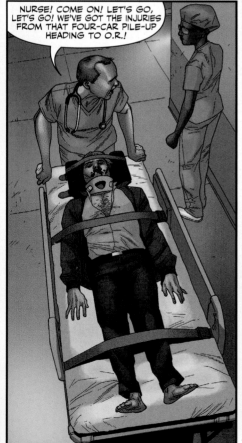

NURSE! COME ON! LET'S GO, LET'S GO! WE'VE GOT THE INJURIES FROM THAT FOUR-CAR PILE-UP HEADING TO O.R.!

ONE OF THEM, *ANISH SETHI*, IS SUSCEPTIBLE TO MALIGNANT HYPERTHERMIA!

WHAT? HOW DO YOU KNOW THAT? DID HE REGAIN CONSCIOUS- NESS?

NO, I'M A FRIEND OF MR. SETHI'S FAMILY, AND--

SETHI? THIS GUY'S NAME IS OOSTING.

SETHI IS DOWN THE HALL--

I'M SO SORRY...

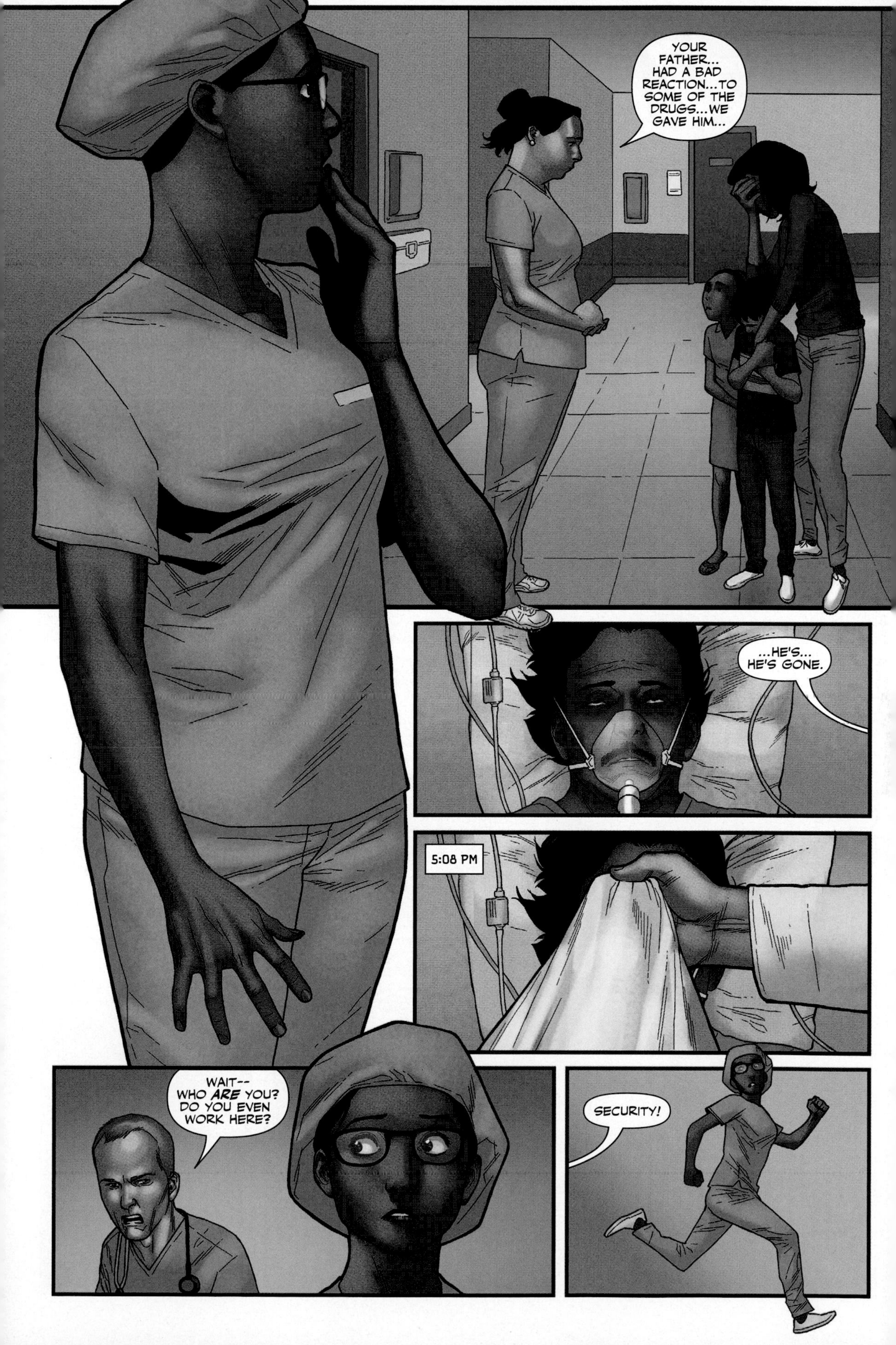
YOUR FATHER... HAD A BAD REACTION...TO SOME OF THE DRUGS...WE GAVE HIM...
...HE'S... HE'S GONE.
5:08 PM
WAIT-- WHO *ARE* YOU? DO YOU EVEN WORK HERE?
SECURITY!

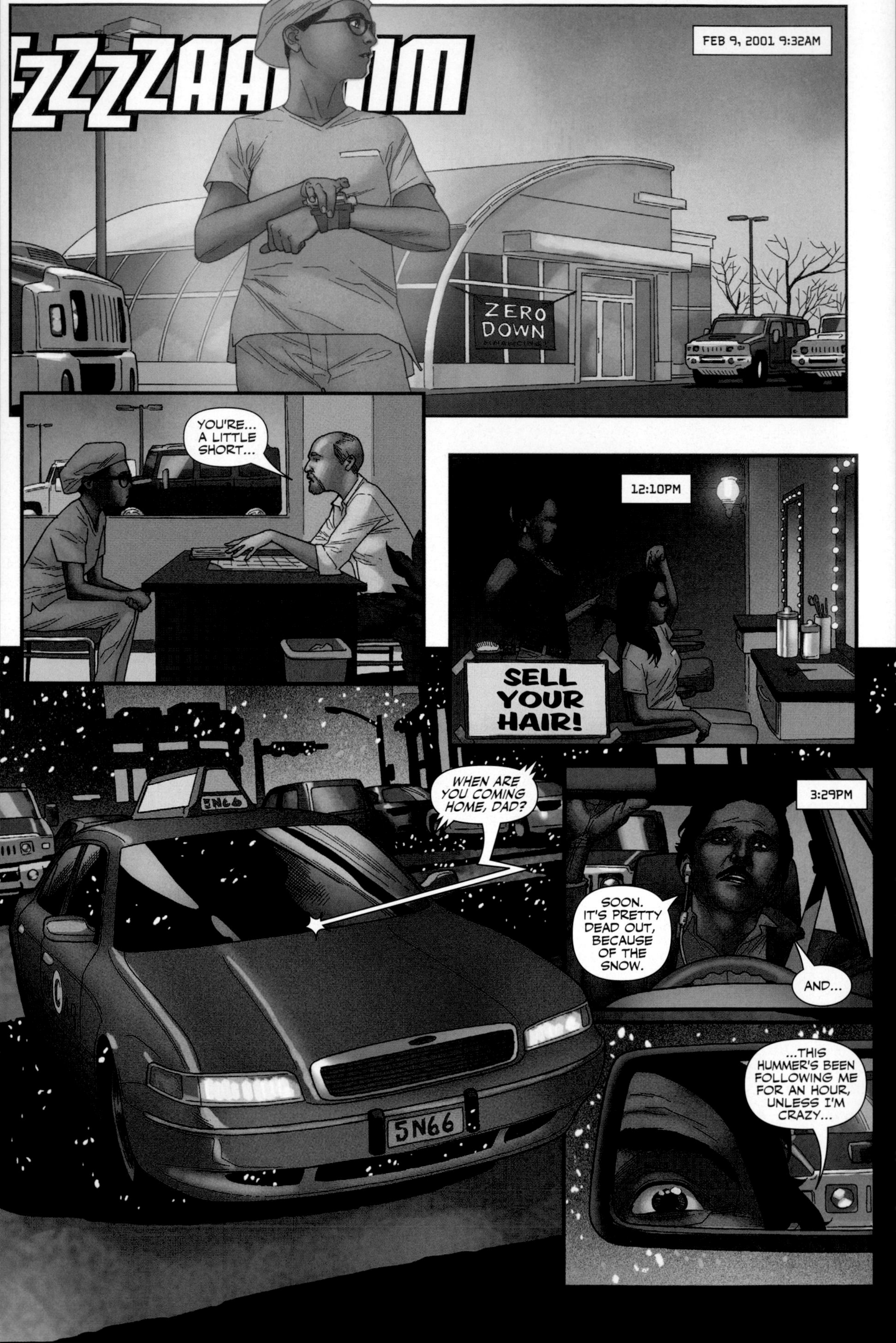
FEB 9, 2001 9:32AM
ZERO DOWN
YOU'RE... A LITTLE SHORT...
12:10PM
SELL YOUR HAIR!
WHEN ARE YOU COMING HOME, DAD?
5N66
3:29PM
SOON. IT'S PRETTY DEAD OUT, BECAUSE OF THE SNOW.
AND...
...THIS HUMMER'S BEEN FOLLOWING ME FOR AN HOUR, UNLESS I'M CRAZY...

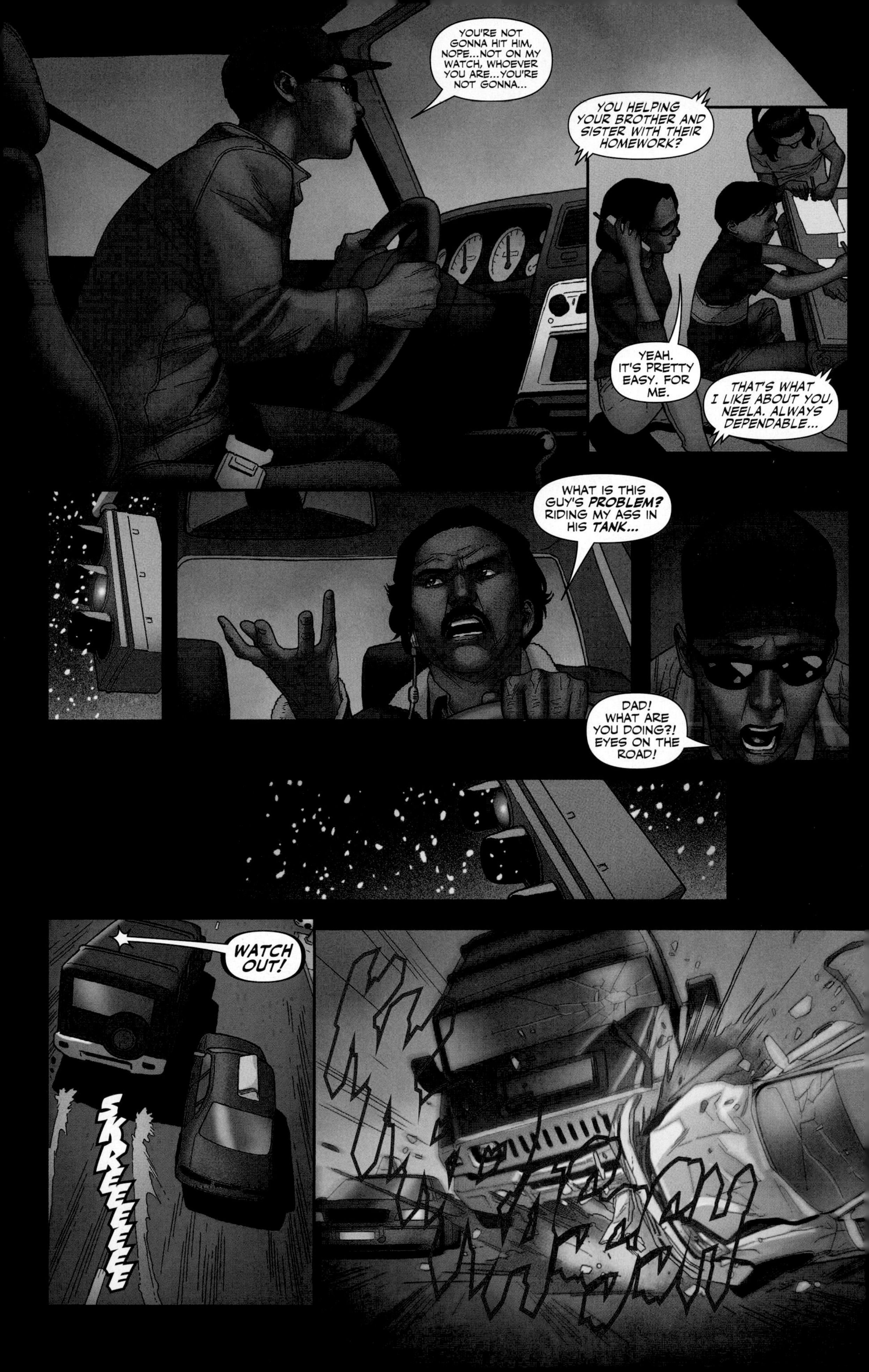
YOU'RE NOT GONNA HIT HIM, NOPE...NOT ON MY WATCH, WHOEVER YOU ARE...YOU'RE NOT GONNA...
YOU HELPING YOUR BROTHER AND SISTER WITH THEIR HOMEWORK?
YEAH. IT'S PRETTY EASY. FOR ME.
THAT'S WHAT I LIKE ABOUT YOU, NEELA. ALWAYS DEPENDABLE...
WHAT IS THIS GUY'S PROBLEM? RIDING MY ASS IN HIS TANK...
DAD! WHAT ARE YOU DOING?! EYES ON THE ROAD!
WATCH OUT!
SKREEEEEE

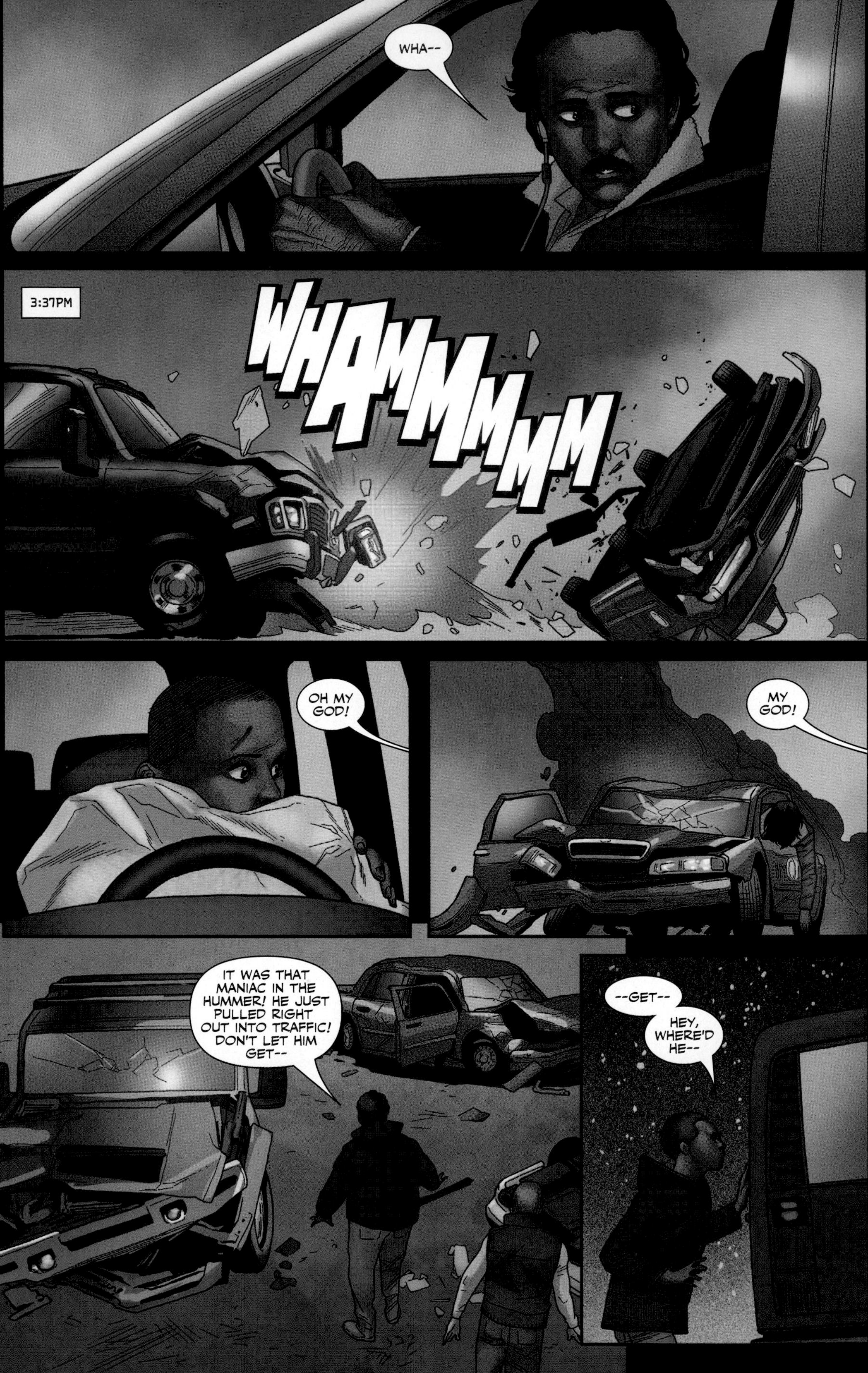
WHA--
3:37PM
WHAMMMMMM
OH MY GOD!
MY GOD!
IT WAS THAT MANIAC IN THE HUMMER! HE JUST PULLED RIGHT OUT INTO TRAFFIC! DON'T LET HIM GET--
--GET--
HEY, WHERE'D HE--

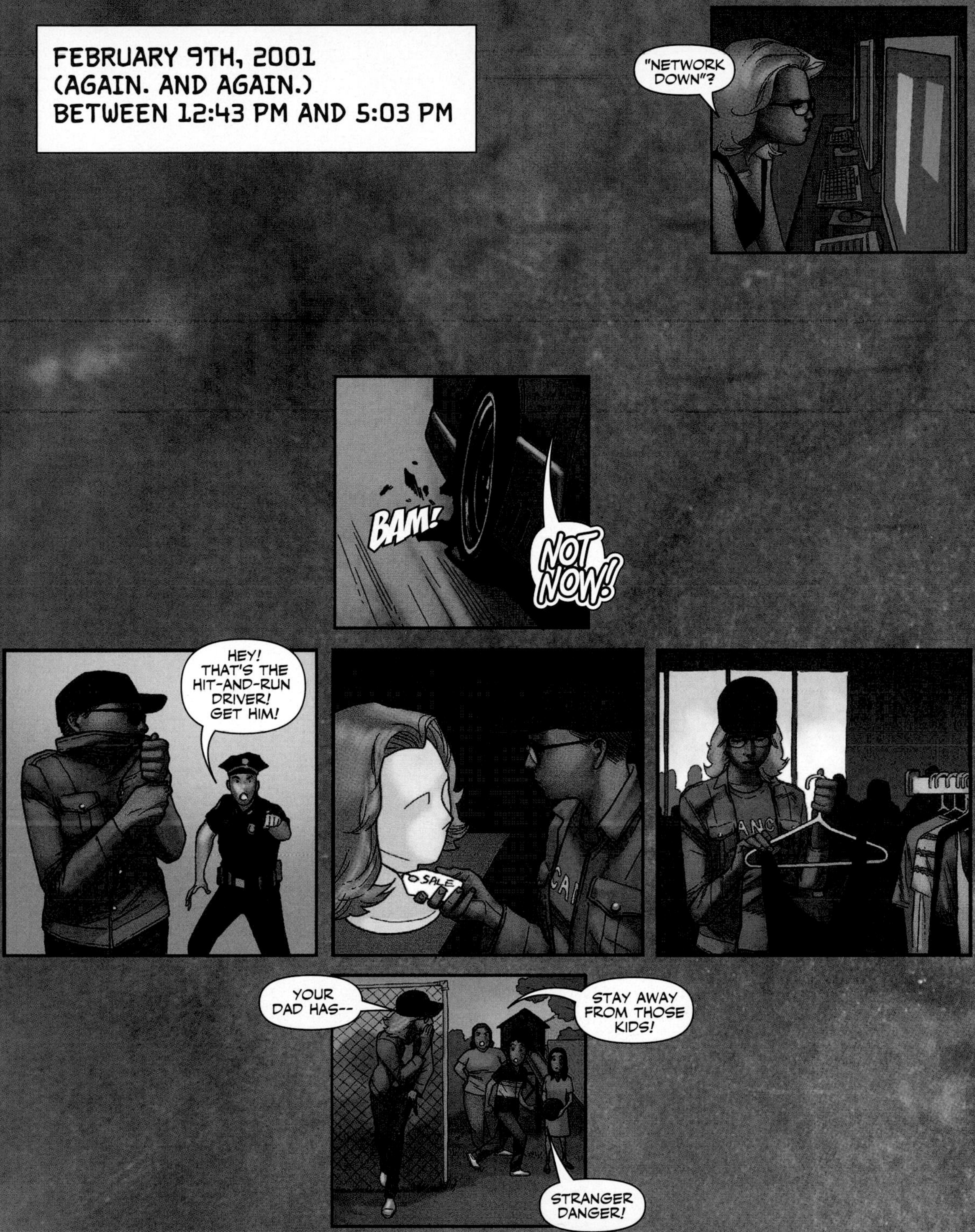
FEBRUARY 9TH, 2001
(AGAIN. AND AGAIN.)
BETWEEN 12:43 PM AND 5:03 PM
"NETWORK DOWN"?
BAM!
NOT NOW!
HEY! THAT'S THE HIT-AND-RUN DRIVER! GET HIM!
YOUR DAD HAS--
STAY AWAY FROM THOSE KIDS!
STRANGER DANGER!

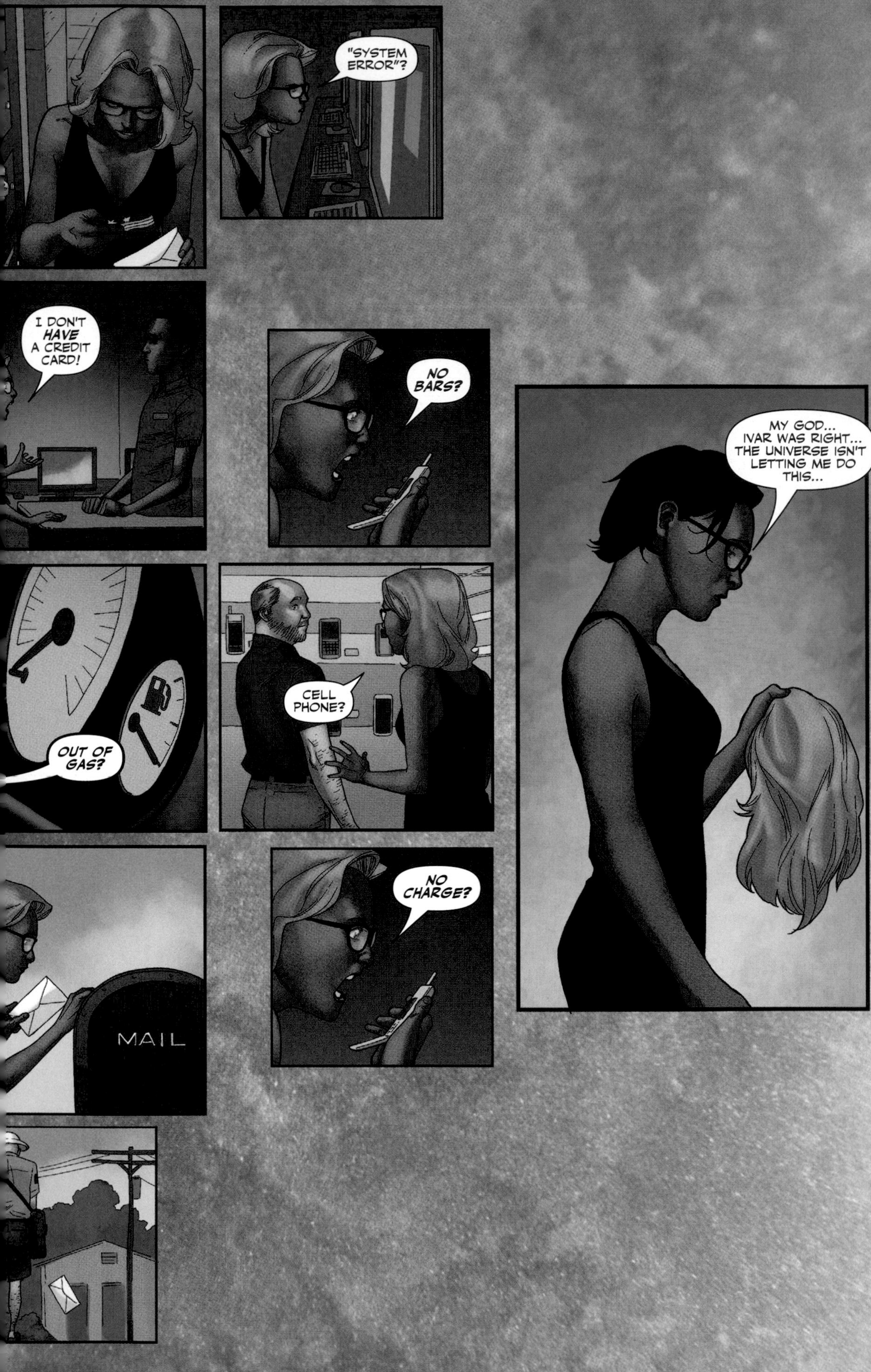
"SYSTEM ERROR"?
I DON'T *HAVE* A CREDIT CARD!
NO BARS?
OUT OF GAS?
CELL PHONE?
NO CHARGE?
MAIL
MY GOD... IVAR WAS RIGHT... THE UNIVERSE ISN'T LETTING ME DO THIS...

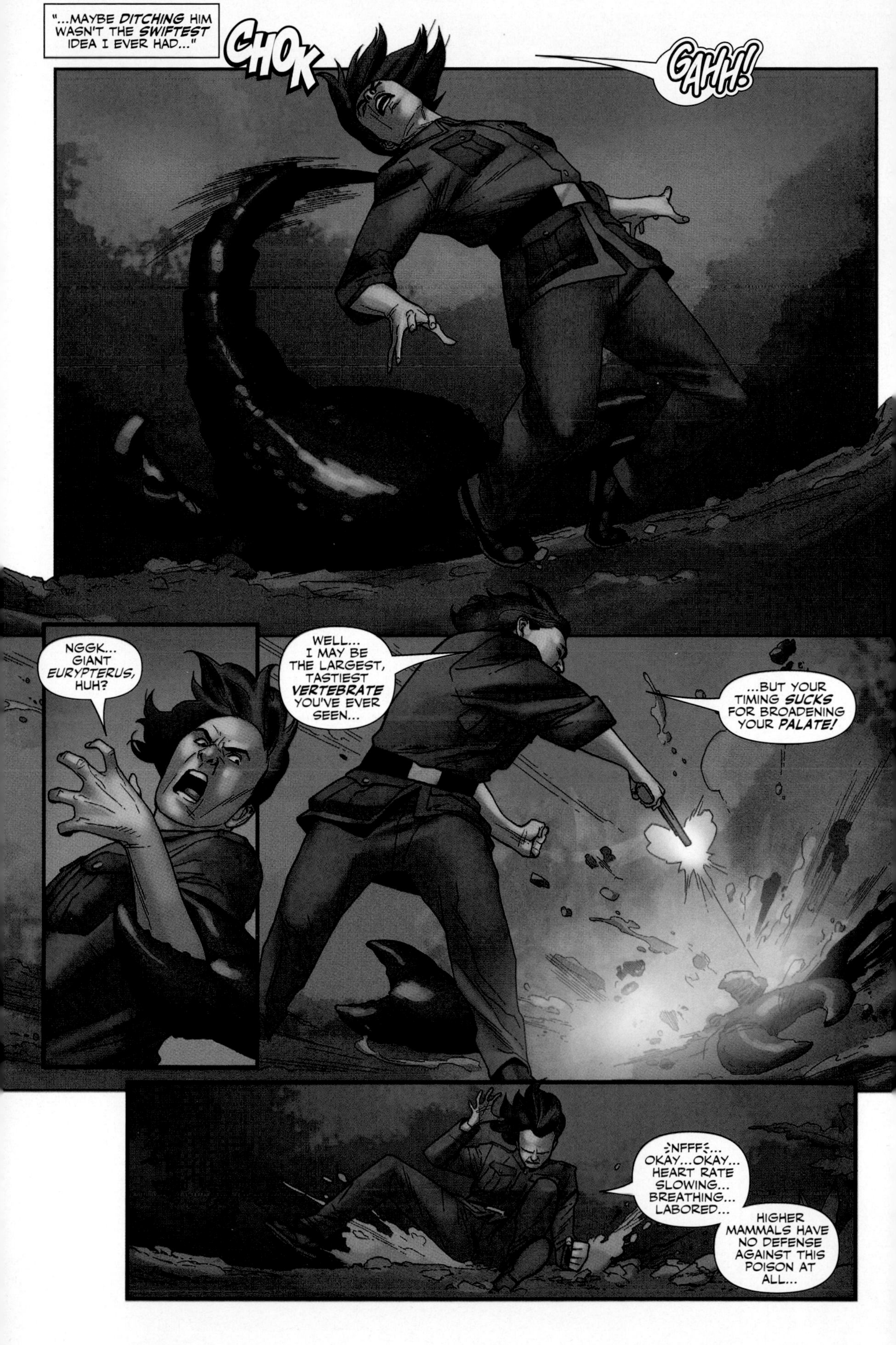
"...MAYBE DITCHING HIM WASN'T THE SWIFTEST IDEA I EVER HAD..."
CHOK
GAHH!
NGGK... GIANT EURYPTERUS, HUH?
WELL... I MAY BE THE LARGEST, TASTIEST VERTEBRATE YOU'VE EVER SEEN...
...BUT YOUR TIMING SUCKS FOR BROADENING YOUR PALATE!
NFFF... OKAY...OKAY... HEART RATE SLOWING... BREATHING... LABORED...
HIGHER MAMMALS HAVE NO DEFENSE AGAINST THIS POISON AT ALL...

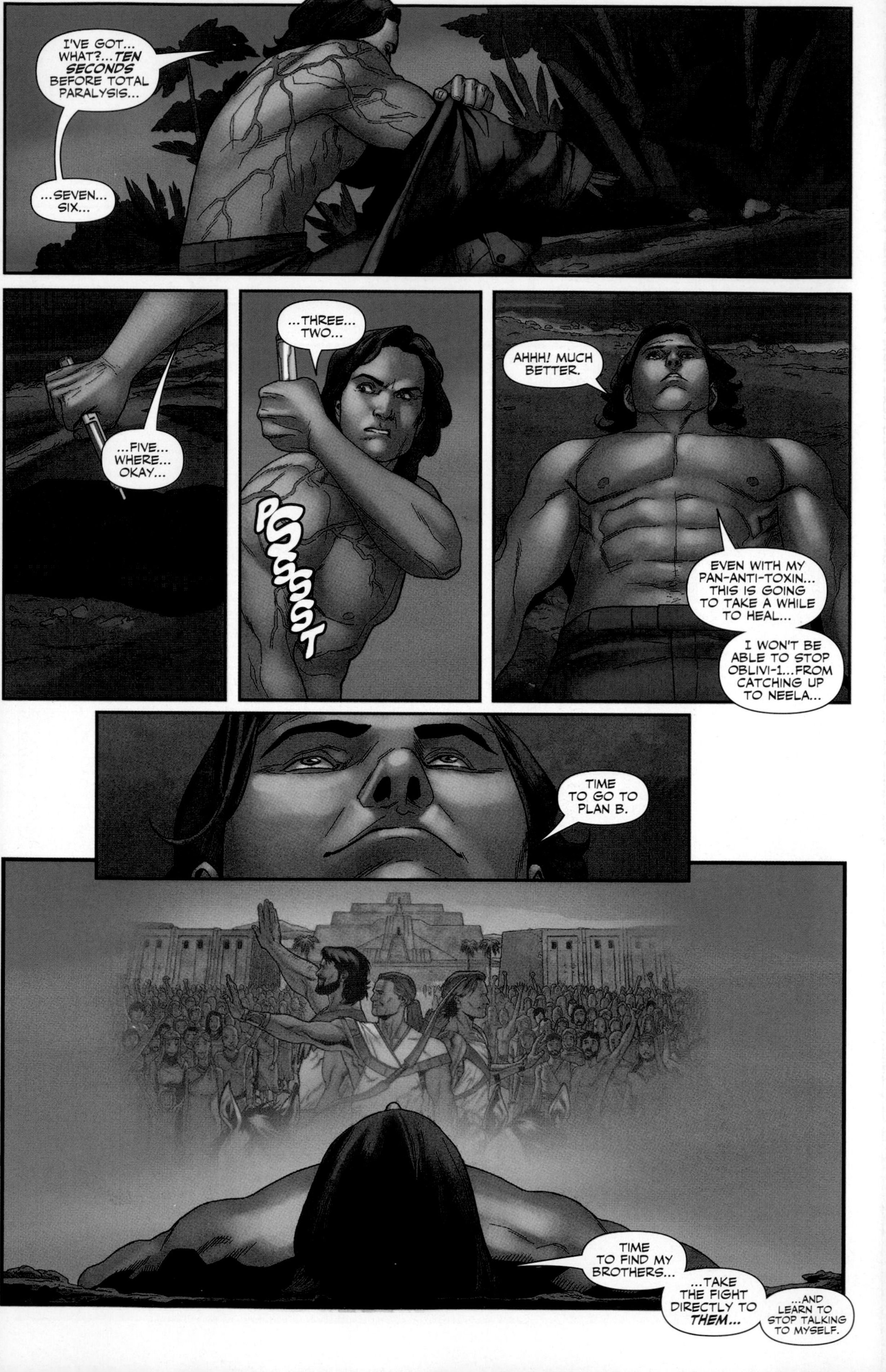
I'VE GOT... WHAT?...TEN SECONDS BEFORE TOTAL PARALYSIS...
...SEVEN... SIX...
...FIVE... WHERE... OKAY...
...THREE... TWO...
PSSSST
AHHH! MUCH BETTER.
EVEN WITH MY PAN-ANTI-TOXIN... THIS IS GOING TO TAKE A WHILE TO HEAL...
I WON'T BE ABLE TO STOP OBLIVI-1...FROM CATCHING UP TO NEELA...
TIME TO GO TO PLAN B.
TIME TO FIND MY BROTHERS...
...TAKE THE FIGHT DIRECTLY TO THEM...
...AND LEARN TO STOP TALKING TO MYSELF.

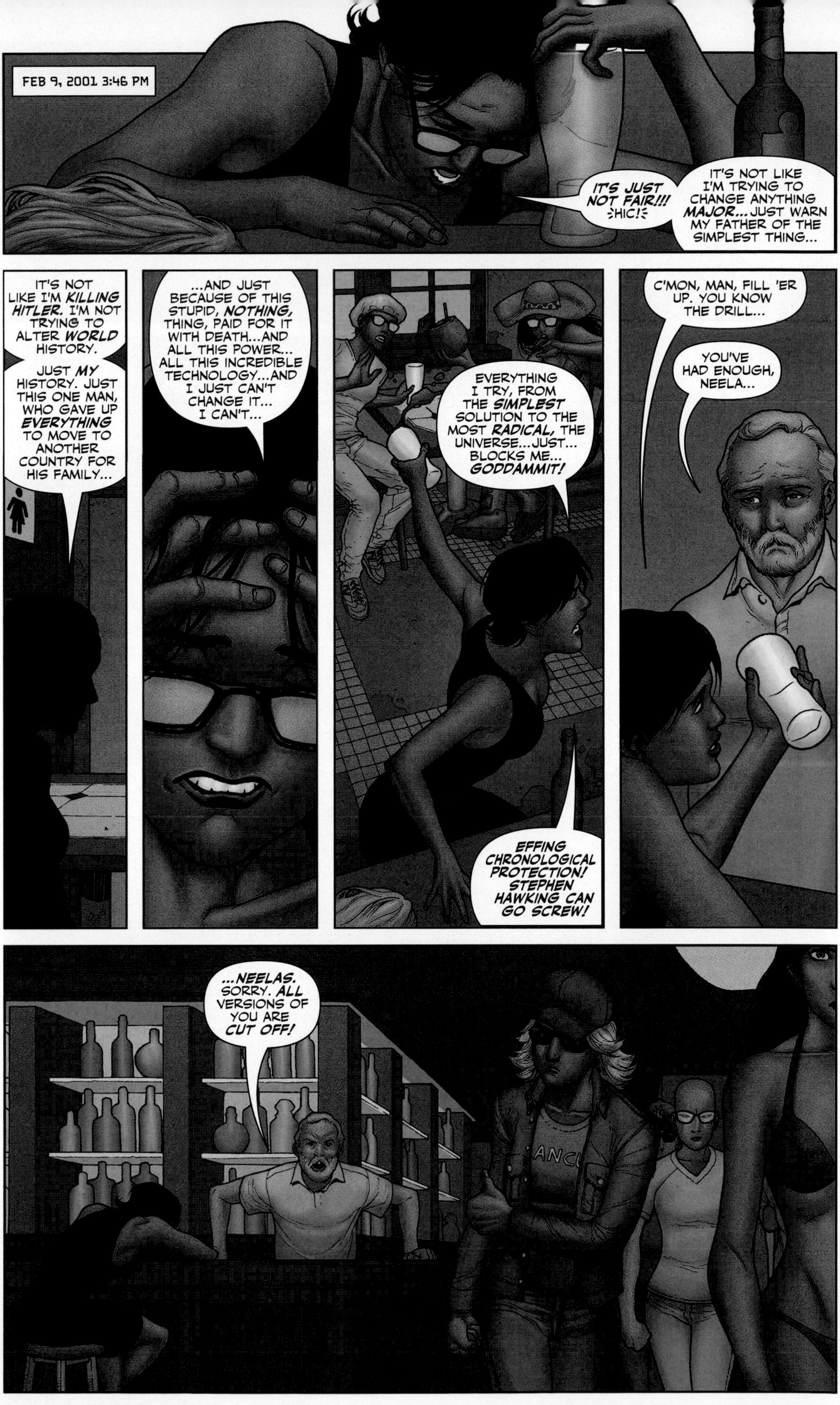
FEB 9, 2001 3:46 PM
IT'S JUST NOT FAIR!!! HIC!
IT'S NOT LIKE I'M TRYING TO CHANGE ANYTHING MAJOR... JUST WARN MY FATHER OF THE SIMPLEST THING...
IT'S NOT LIKE I'M KILLING HITLER. I'M NOT TRYING TO ALTER WORLD HISTORY.
JUST MY HISTORY. JUST THIS ONE MAN, WHO GAVE UP EVERYTHING TO MOVE TO ANOTHER COUNTRY FOR HIS FAMILY...
...AND JUST BECAUSE OF THIS STUPID, NOTHING, THING, PAID FOR IT WITH DEATH...AND ALL THIS POWER... ALL THIS INCREDIBLE TECHNOLOGY...AND I JUST CAN'T CHANGE IT... I CAN'T...
EVERYTHING I TRY, FROM THE SIMPLEST SOLUTION TO THE MOST RADICAL, THE UNIVERSE...JUST... BLOCKS ME... GODDAMMIT!
EFFING CHRONOLOGICAL PROTECTION! STEPHEN HAWKING CAN GO SCREW!
C'MON, MAN, FILL 'ER UP. YOU KNOW THE DRILL...
YOU'VE HAD ENOUGH, NEELA...
...NEELAS. SORRY. ALL VERSIONS OF YOU ARE CUT OFF!

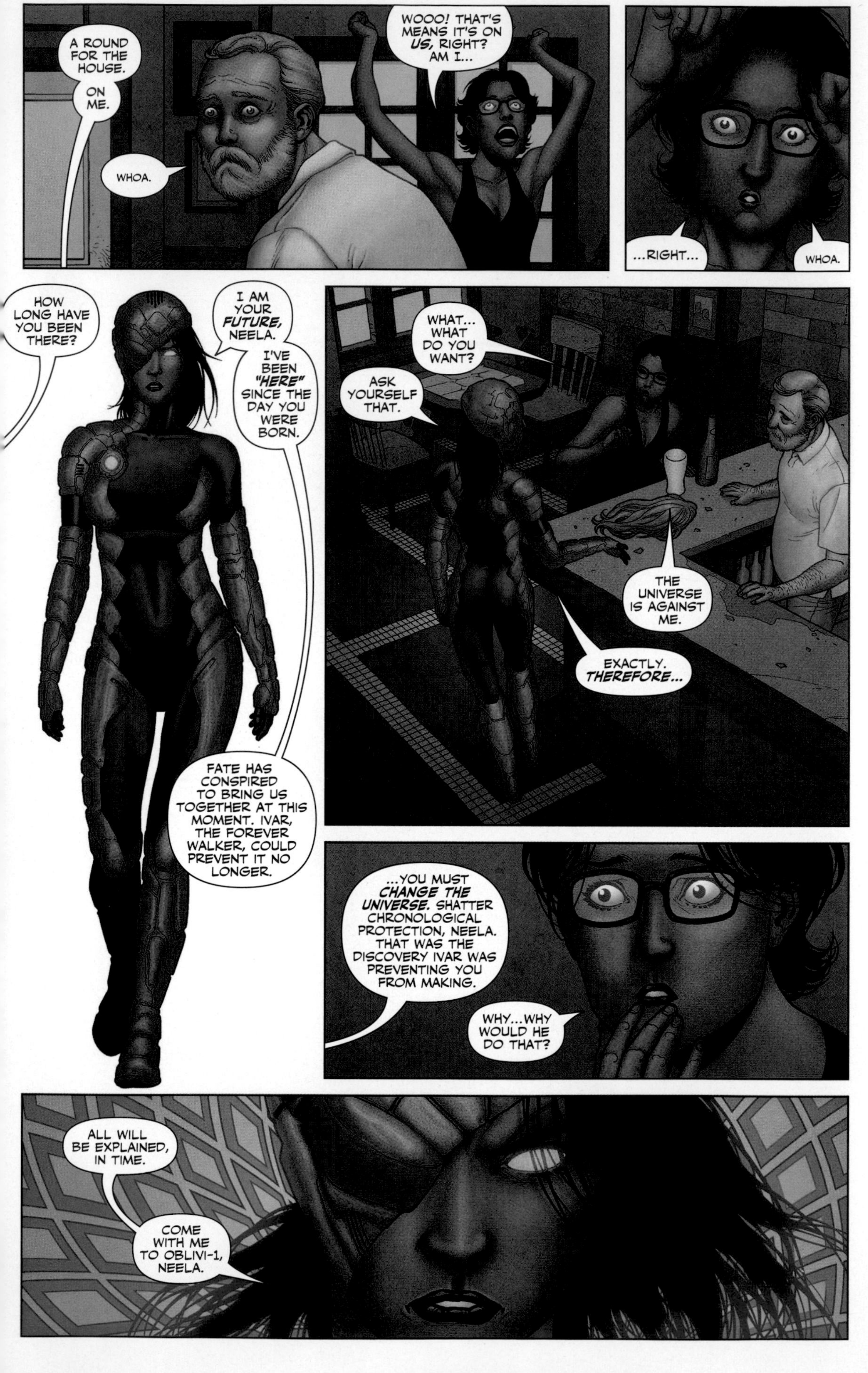
A ROUND FOR THE HOUSE.
ON ME.
WHOA.
WOOO! THAT'S MEANS IT'S ON US, RIGHT? AM I...
...RIGHT...
WHOA.
HOW LONG HAVE YOU BEEN THERE?
I AM YOUR FUTURE, NEELA.
I'VE BEEN "HERE" SINCE THE DAY YOU WERE BORN.
FATE HAS CONSPIRED TO BRING US TOGETHER AT THIS MOMENT. IVAR, THE FOREVER WALKER, COULD PREVENT IT NO LONGER.
WHAT... WHAT DO YOU WANT?
ASK YOURSELF THAT.
THE UNIVERSE IS AGAINST ME.
EXACTLY. THEREFORE...
...YOU MUST CHANGE THE UNIVERSE. SHATTER CHRONOLOGICAL PROTECTION, NEELA. THAT WAS THE DISCOVERY IVAR WAS PREVENTING YOU FROM MAKING.
WHY...WHY WOULD HE DO THAT?
ALL WILL BE EXPLAINED, IN TIME.
COME WITH ME TO OBLIVI-1, NEELA.

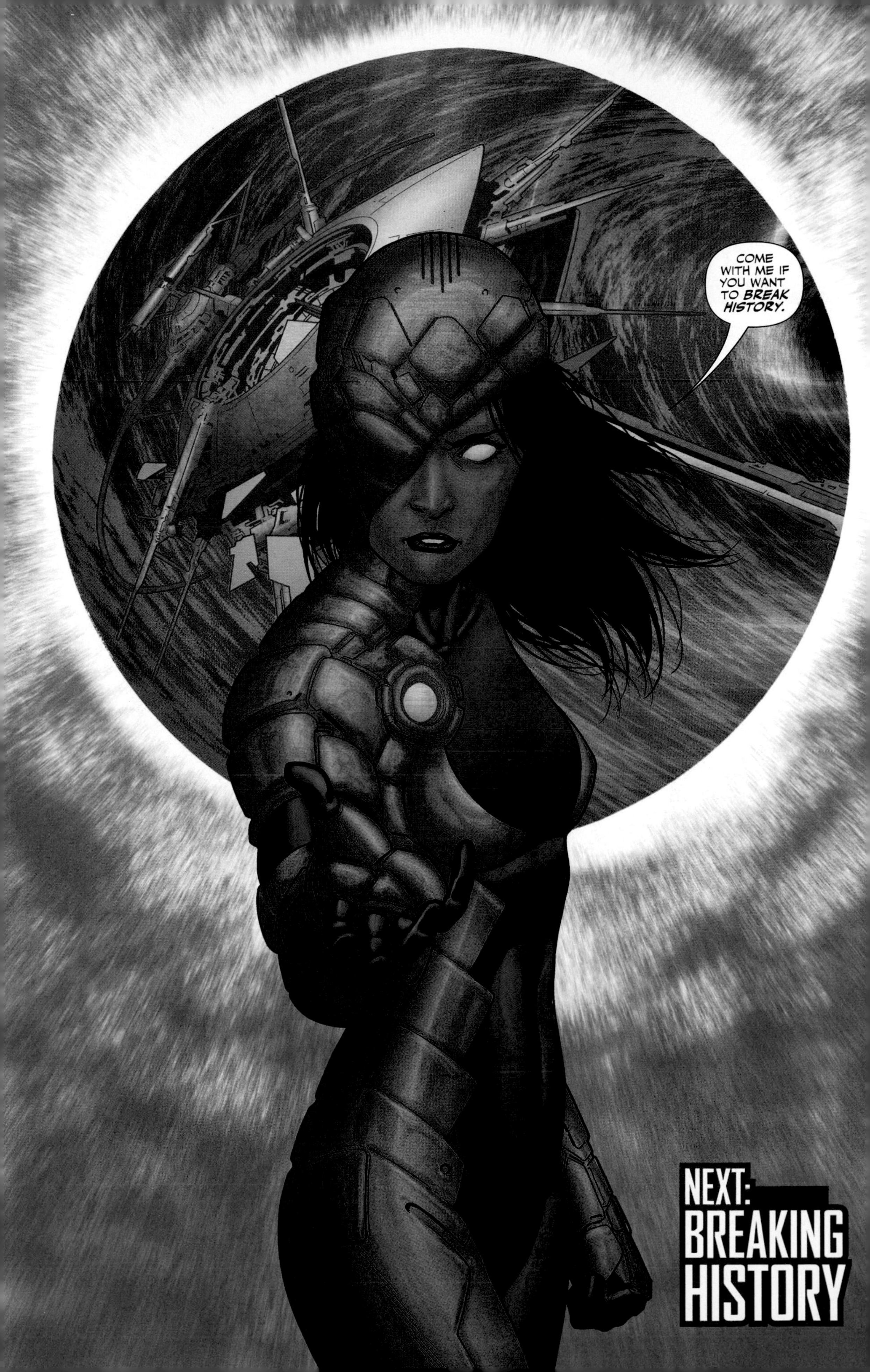
COME WITH ME IF YOU WANT TO BREAK HISTORY.
NEXT: BREAKING HISTORY

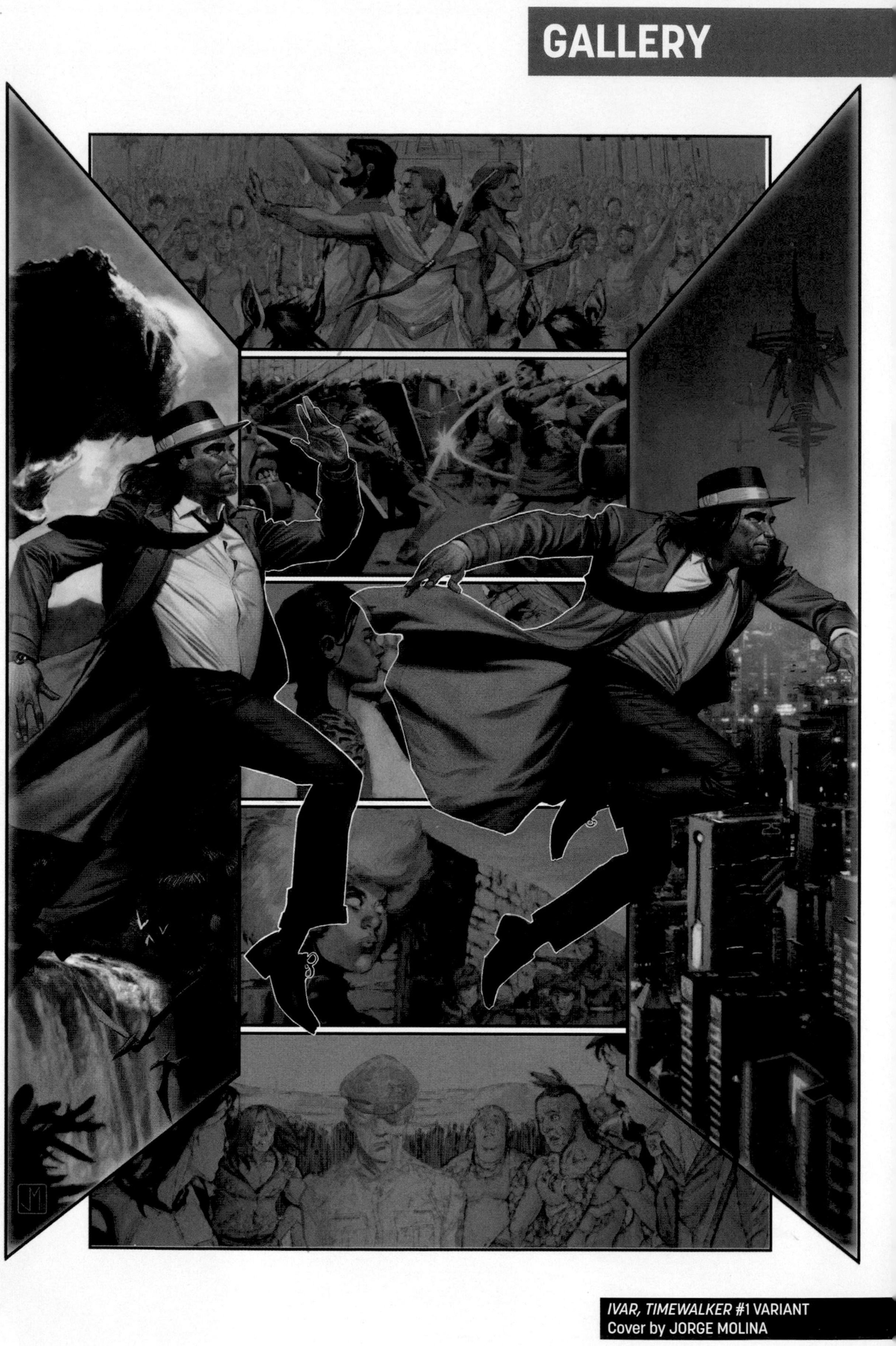

IVAR, TIMEWALKER #1 VARIANT
Cover by JORGE MOLINA

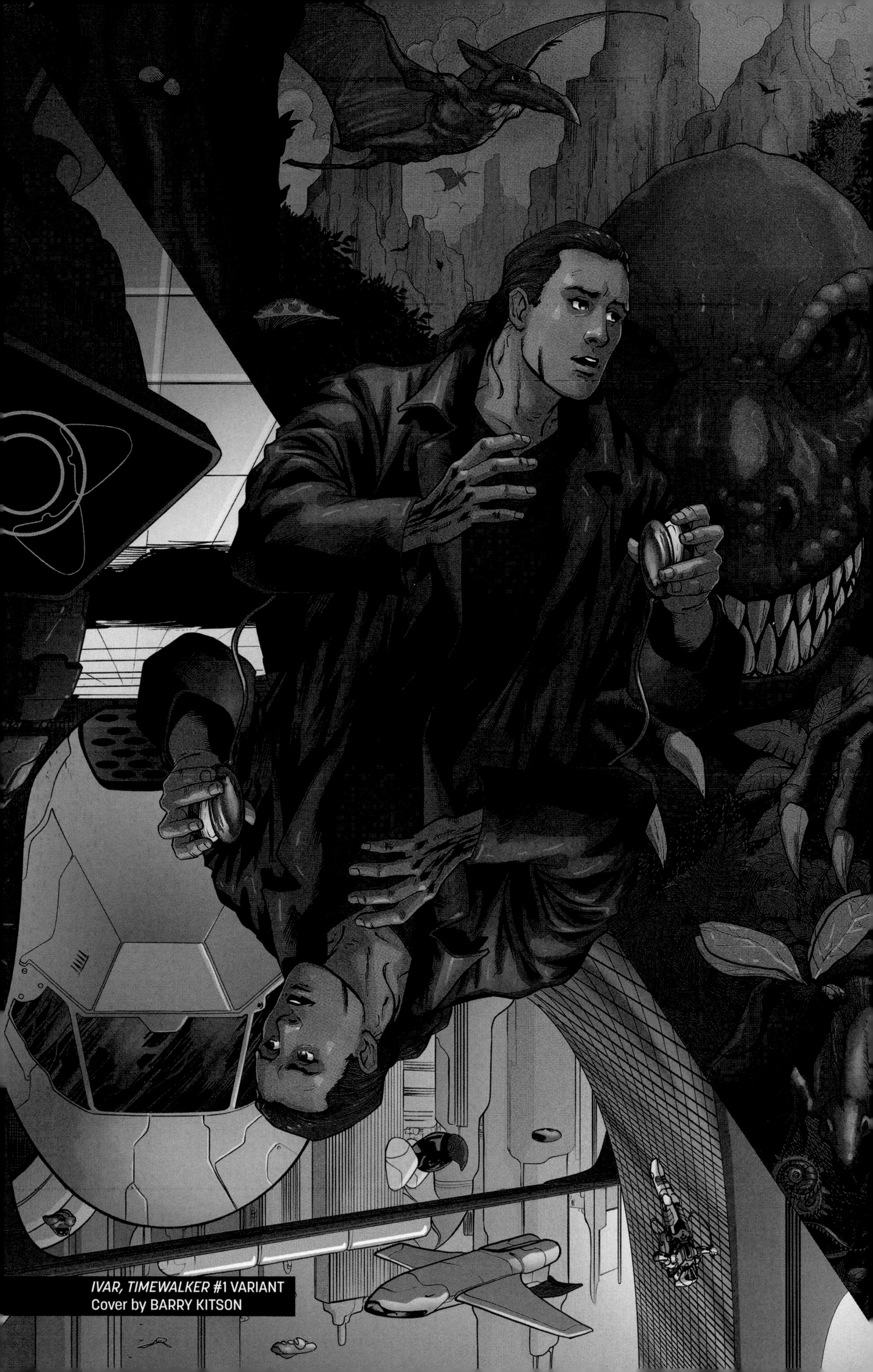

IVAR, TIMEWALKER #1 VARIANT
Cover by BARRY KITSON

IVAR, TIMEWALKER #1
CHARACTER DESIGN VARIANT
Cover by DAVID AJA

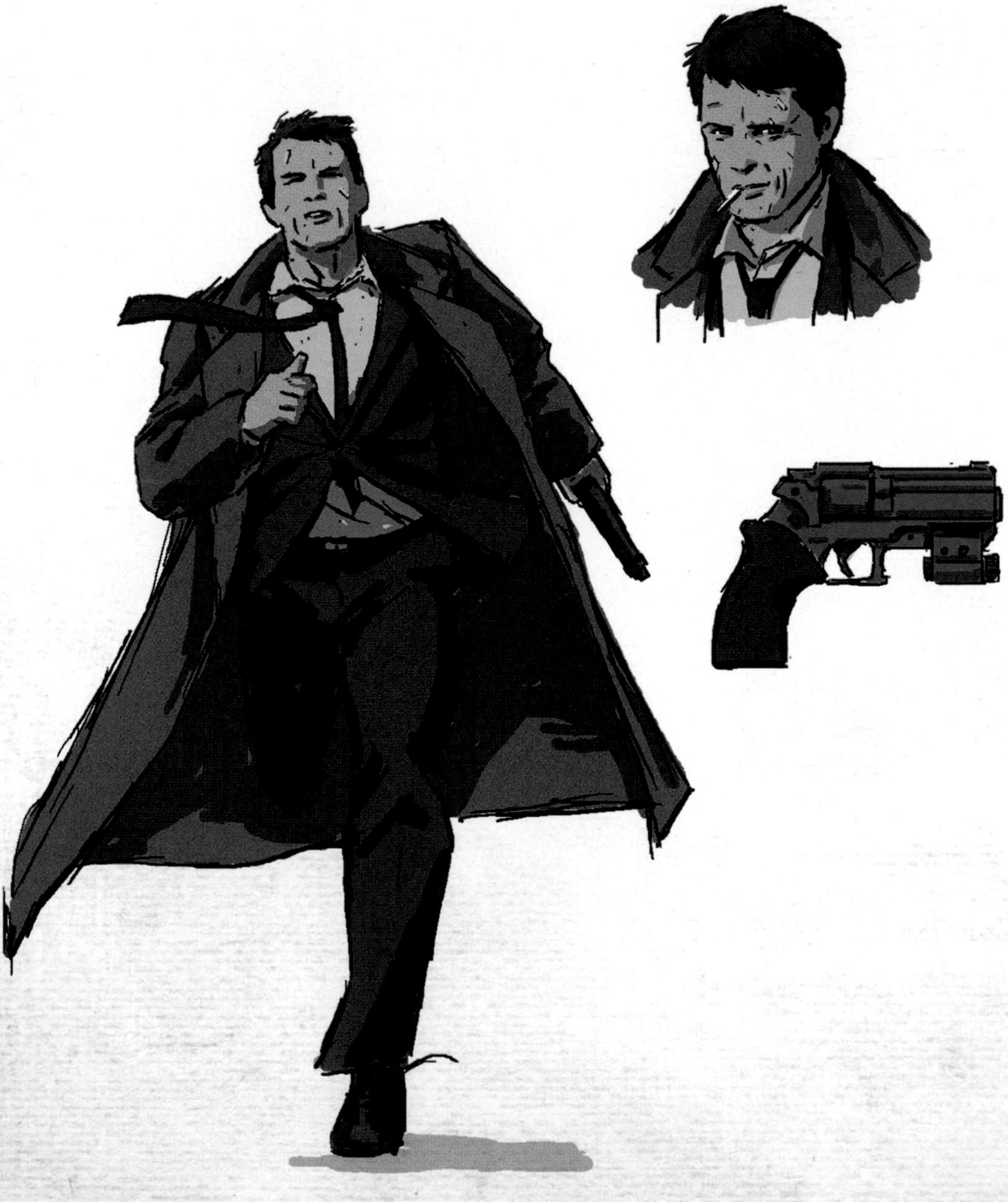

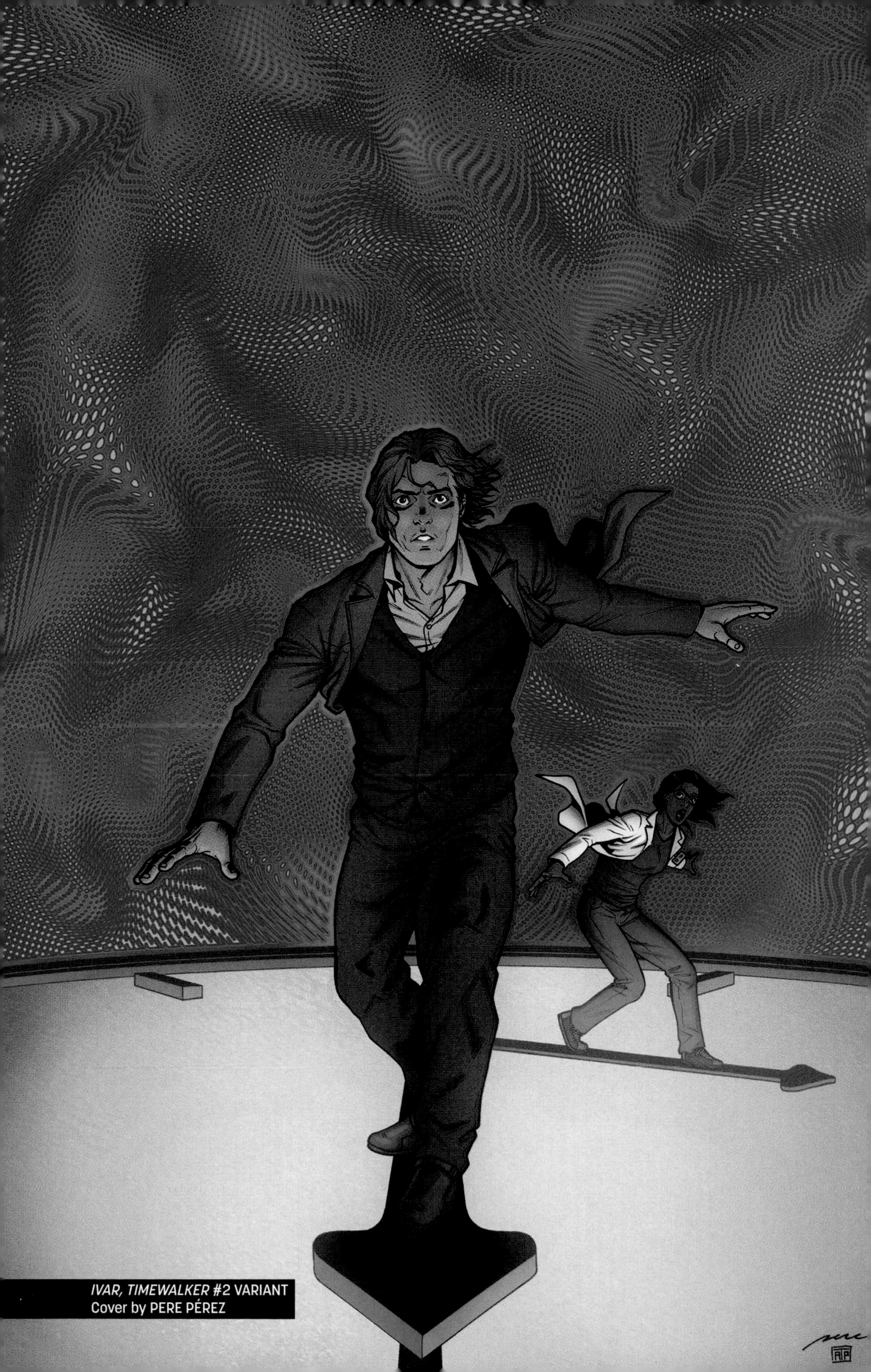

IVAR, TIMEWALKER #2 VARIANT
Cover by PERE PÉREZ

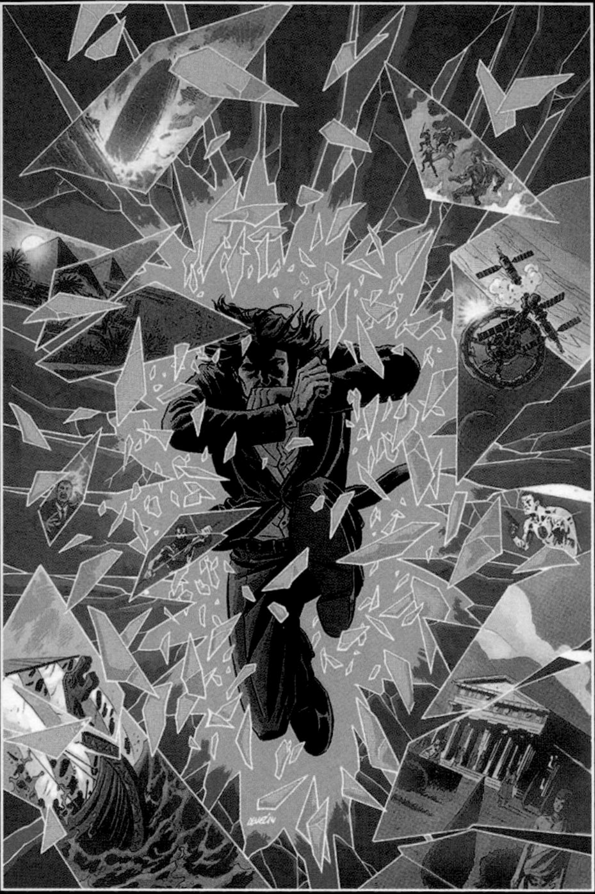

IVAR, TIMEWALKER #2 VARIAN
Cover by BRIAN LEVEL

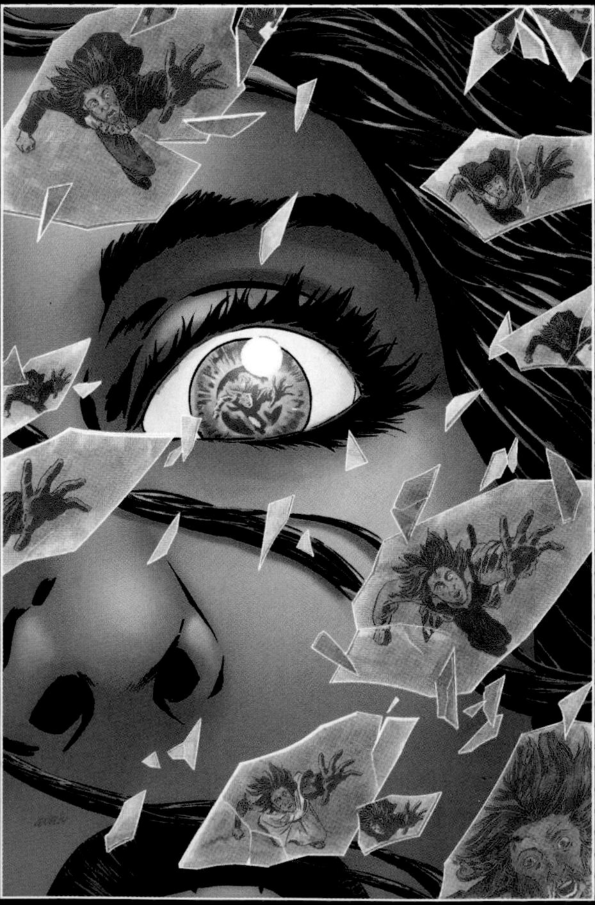

IVAR, TIMEWALKER #3 VARIAN
Cover by BRIAN LEVEL

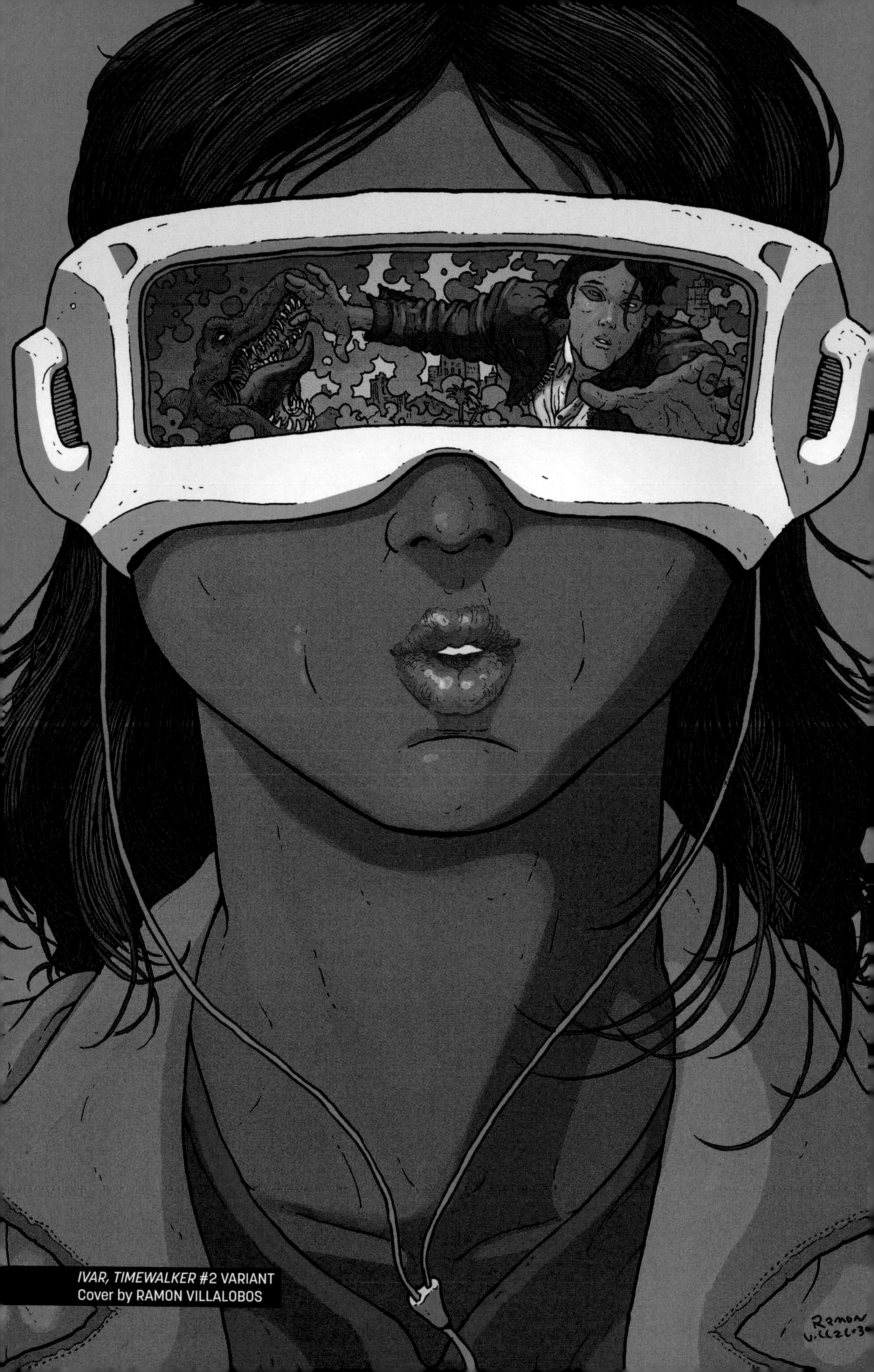

IVAR, TIMEWALKER #2 VARIANT
Cover by RAMON VILLALOBOS

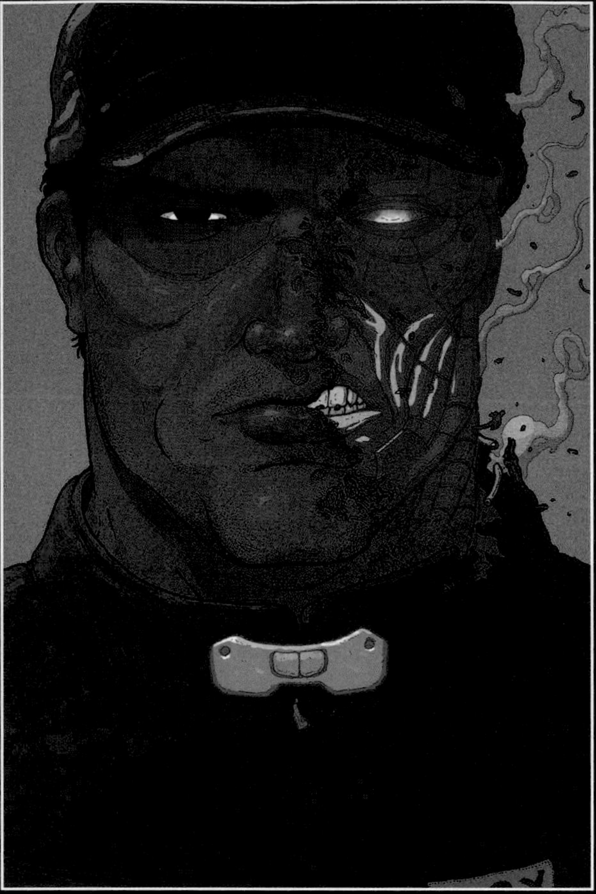

IVAR, TIMEWALKER #3 VARIANT
Cover by RAMON VILLALOBOS

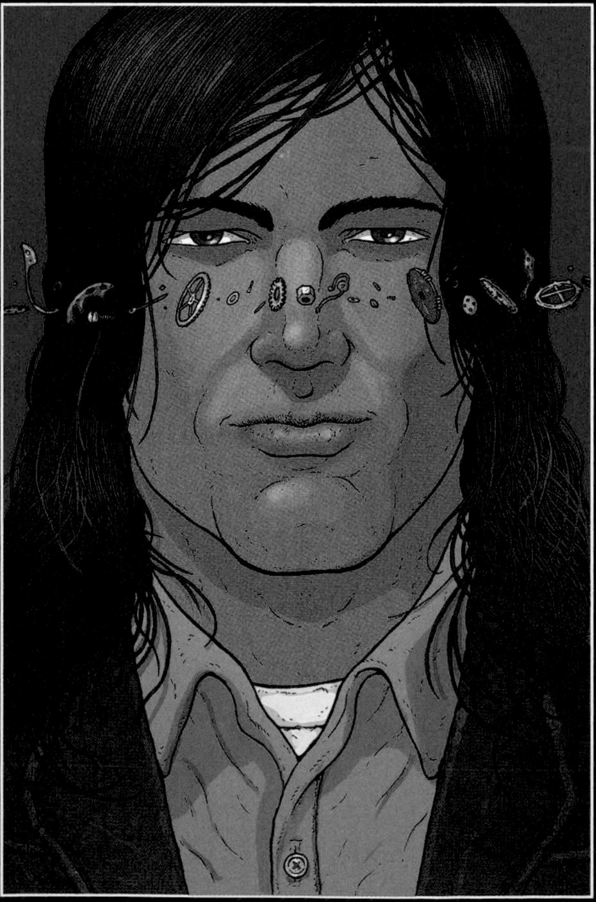

IVAR, TIMEWALKER #4 VARIANT
Cover by RAMON VILLALOBOS

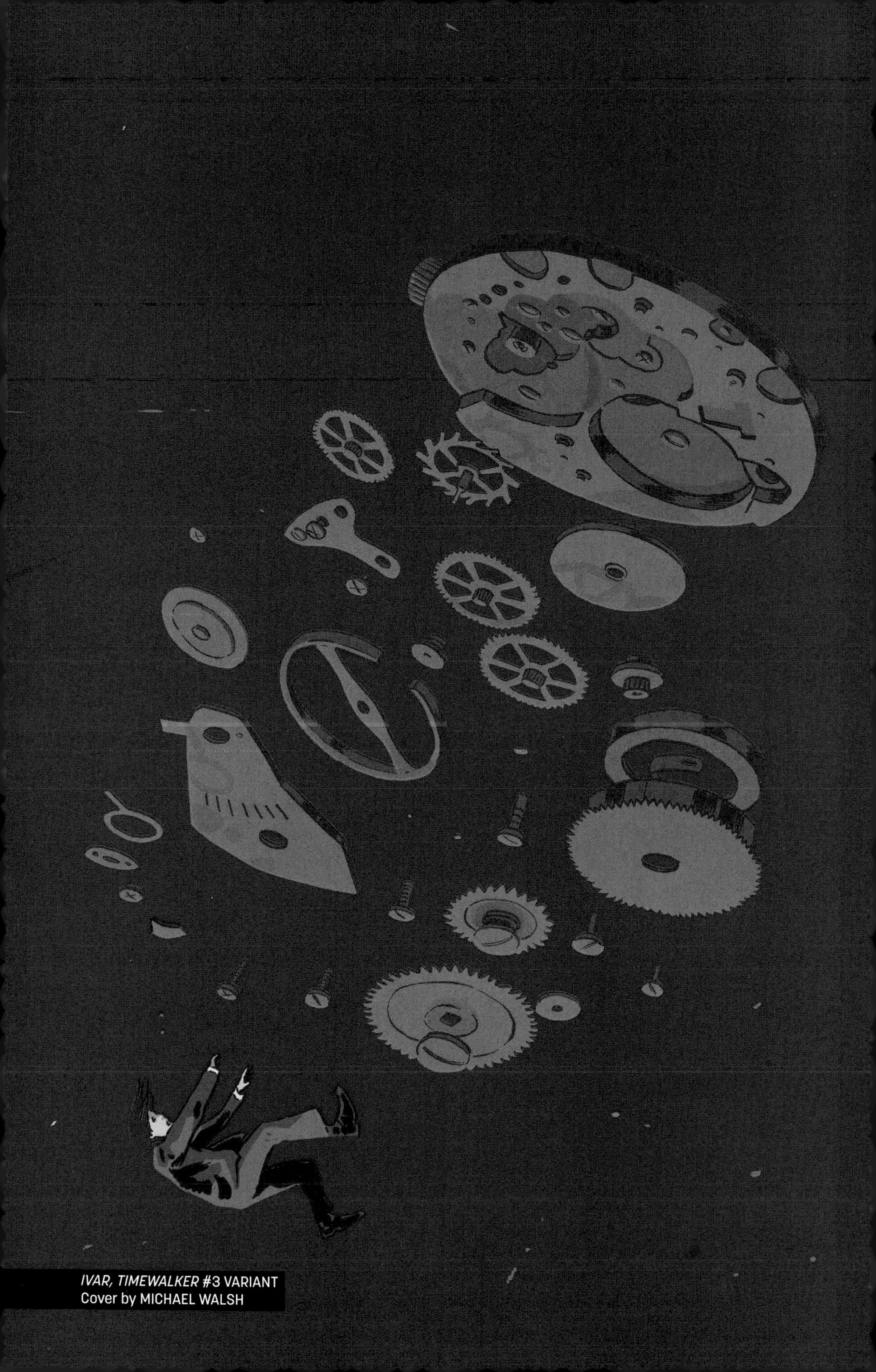

IVAR, TIMEWALKER #3 VARIANT
Cover by MICHAEL WALSH

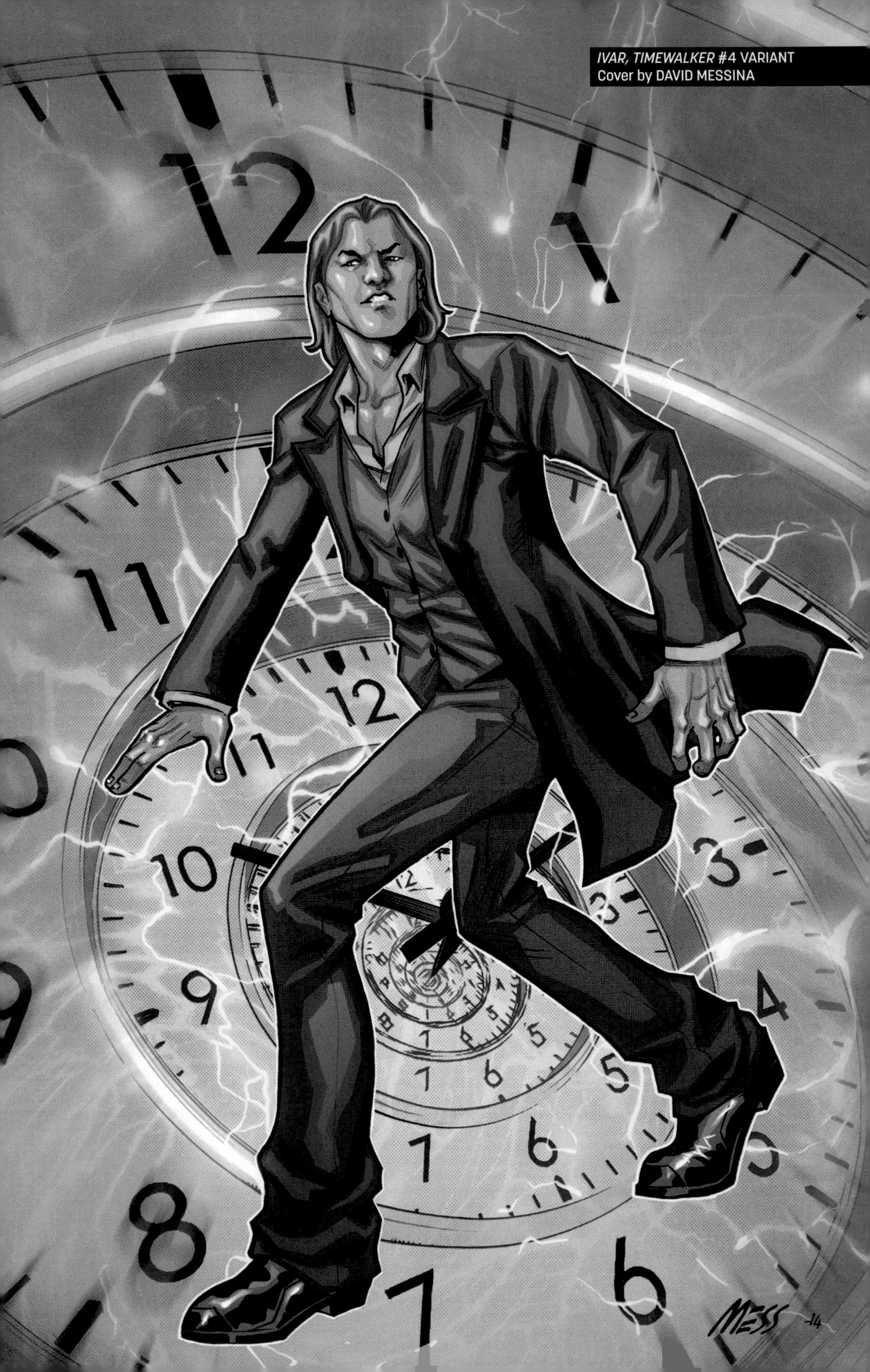
IVAR, TIMEWALKER #4 VARIANT
Cover by DAVID MESSINA
MESS -14

IVAR, TIMEWALKER #1, p. 8
Art by CLAYTON HENRY

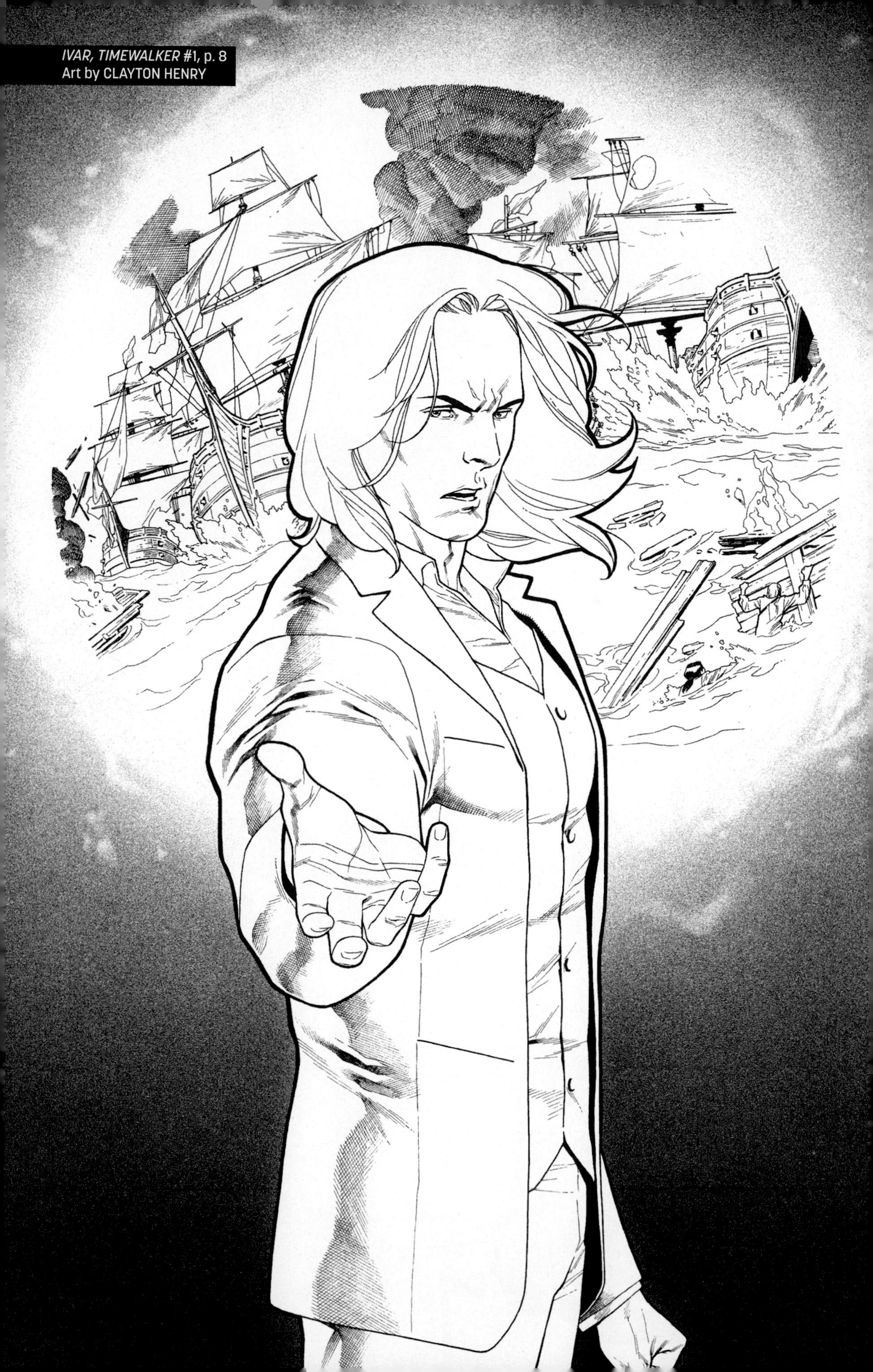

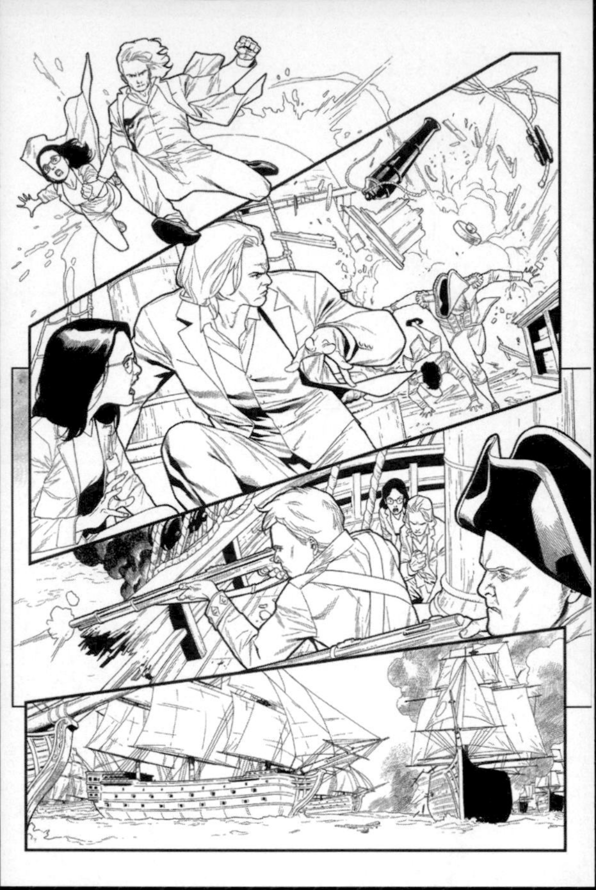

IVAR, TIMEWALKER #1, p. 9
Art by CLAYTON HENRY

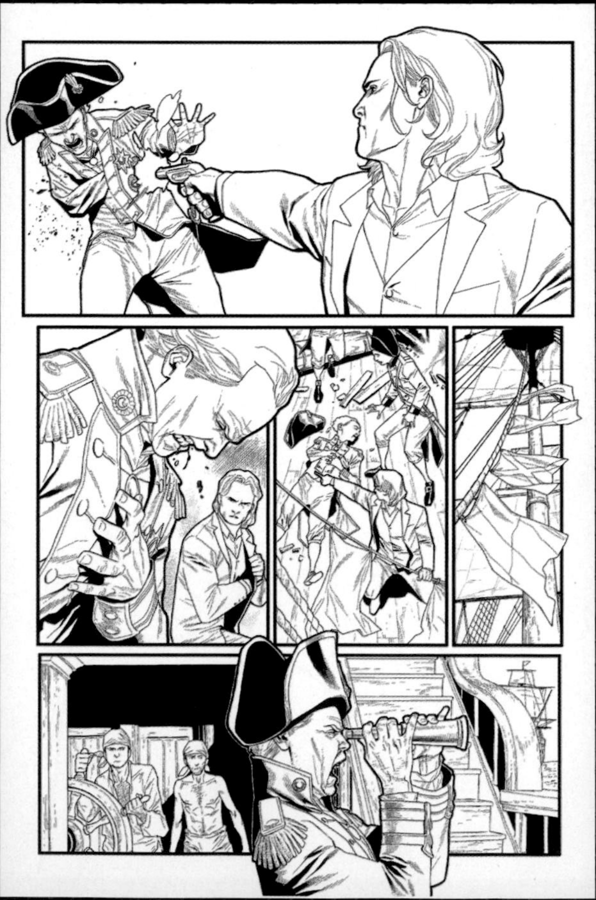

IVAR, TIMEWALKER #1, p. 12
Art by CLAYTON HENRY

TIMEWALKER #1 PAGE 14

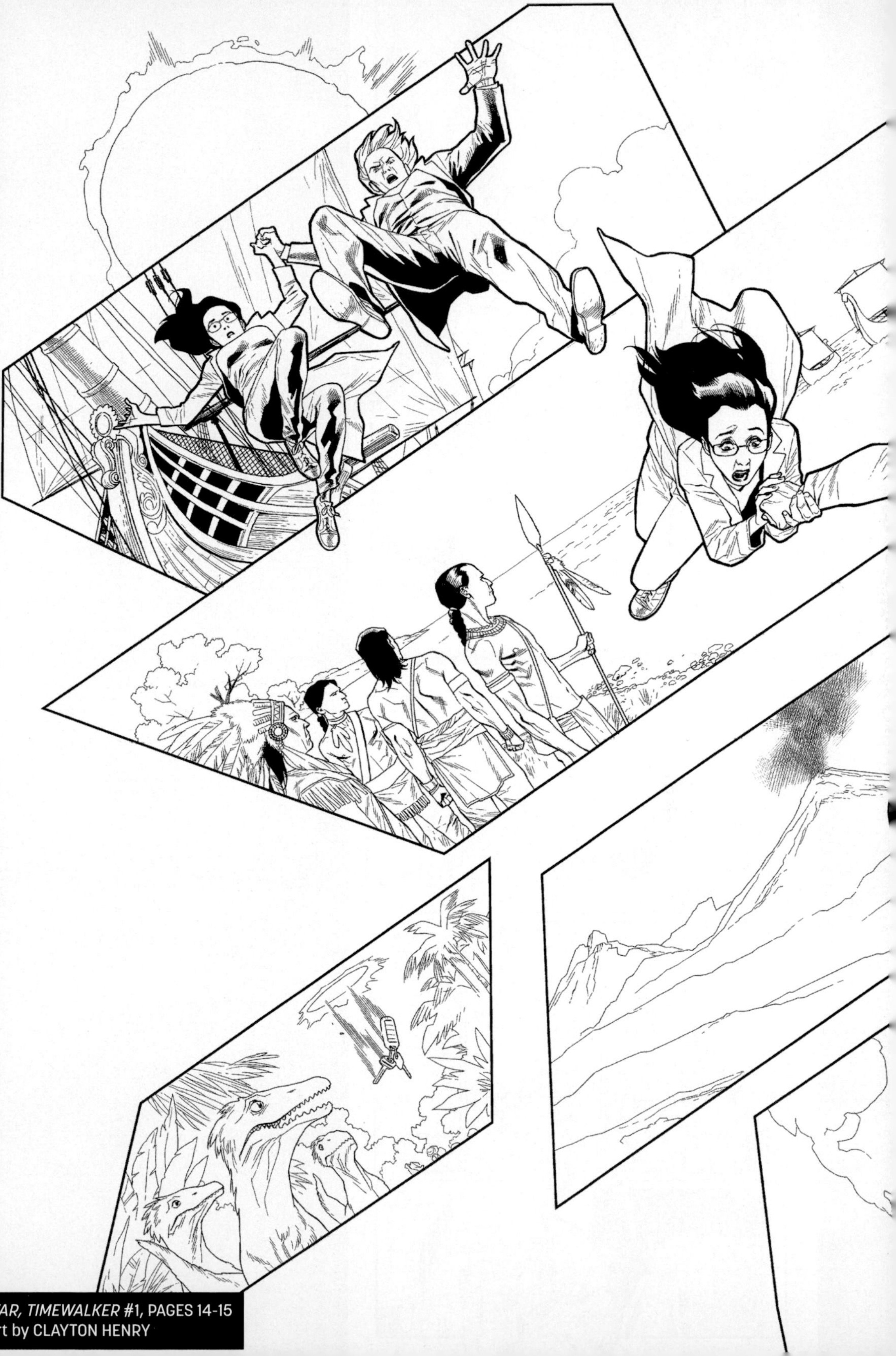

IVAR, TIMEWALKER #1, PAGES 14-15
Art by CLAYTON HENRY

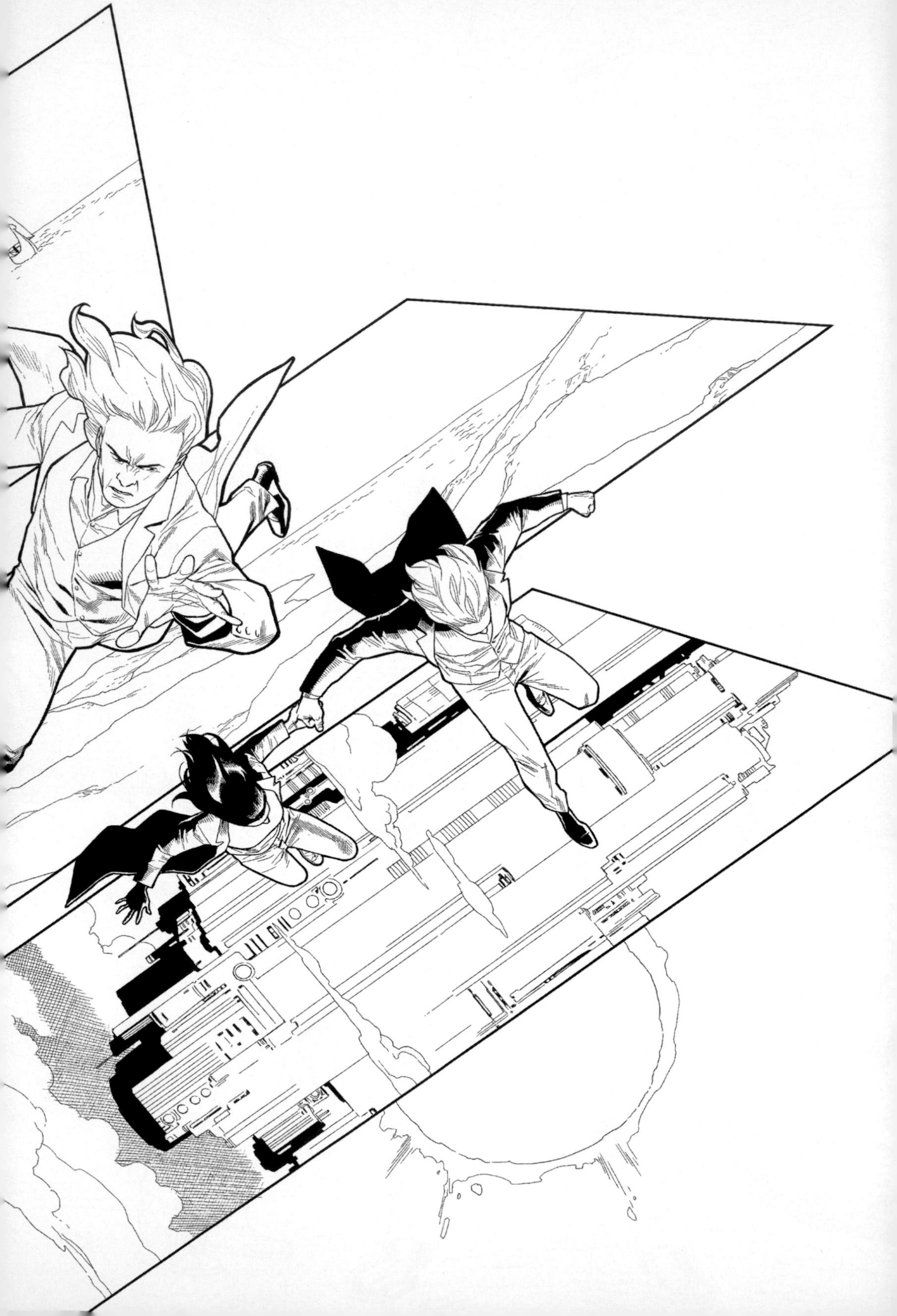

IVAR, TIMEWALKER #2, p. 5
Art by CLAYTON HENRY

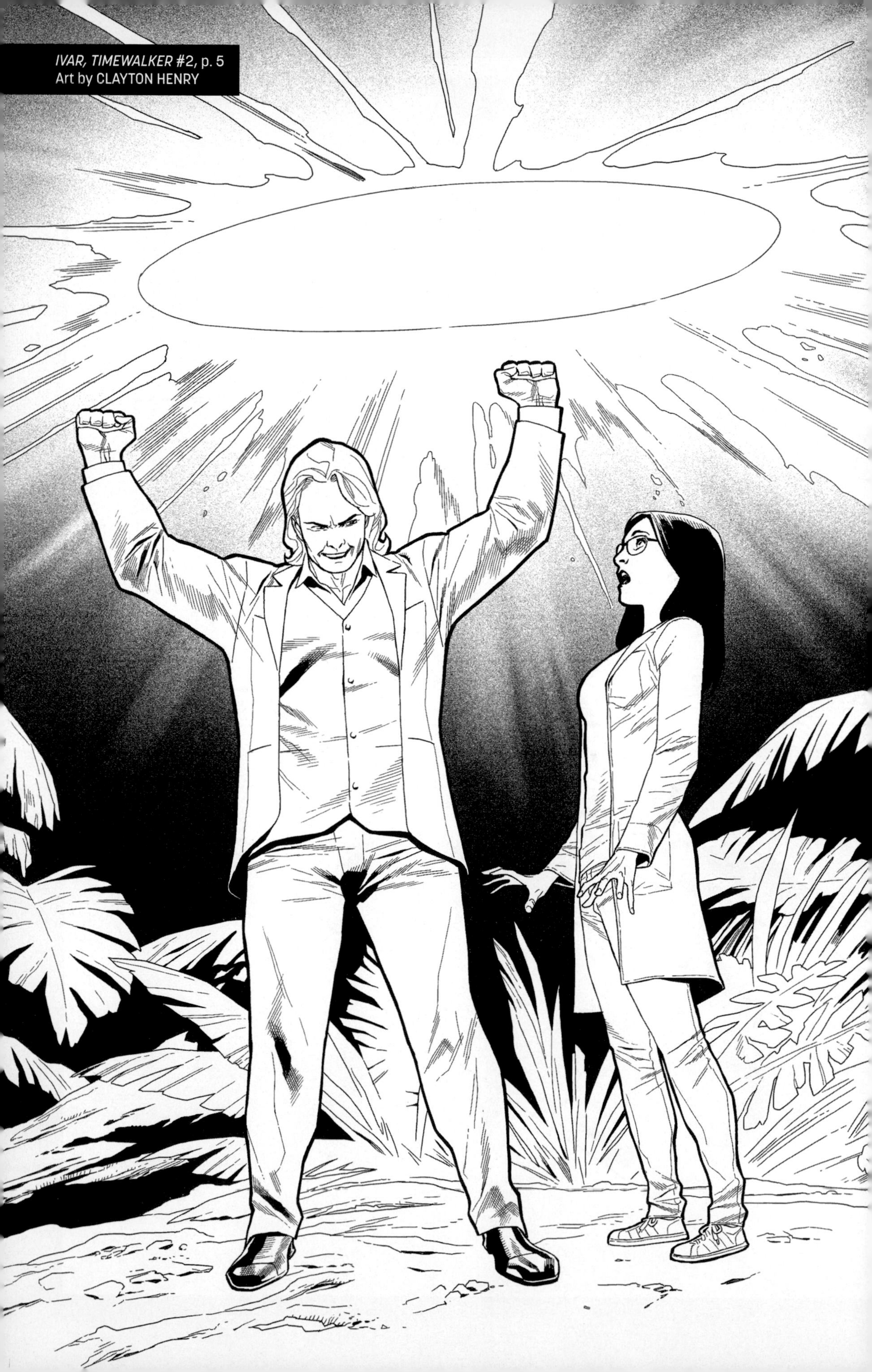

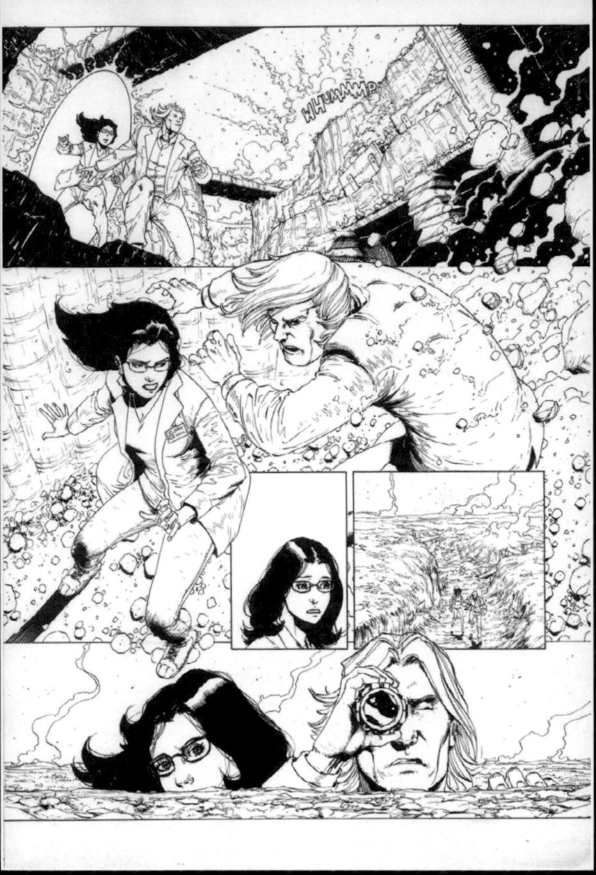

IVAR, TIMEWALKER #2, p. 10
Art by ROBERT GILL

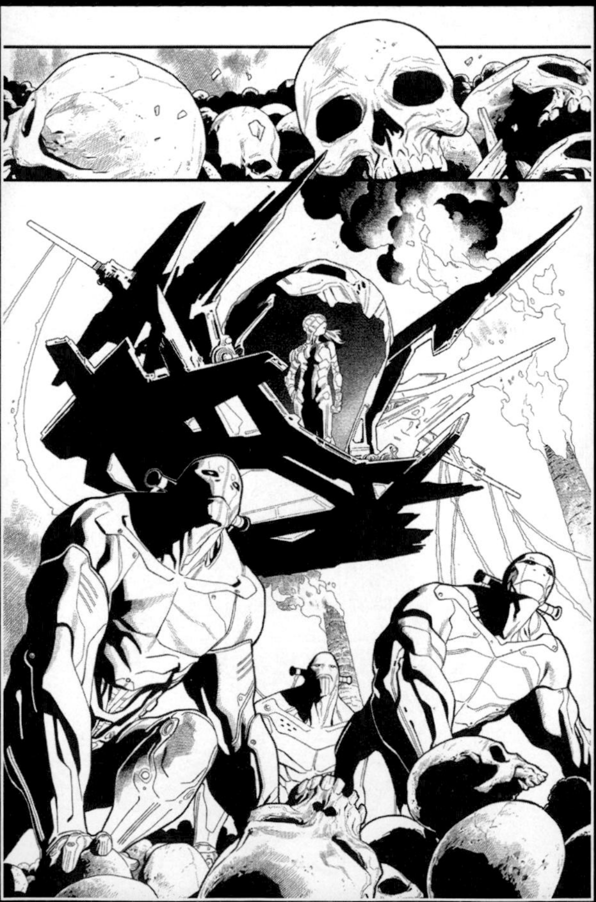

IVAR, TIMEWALKER #2, p. 13
Art by CLAYTON HENRY

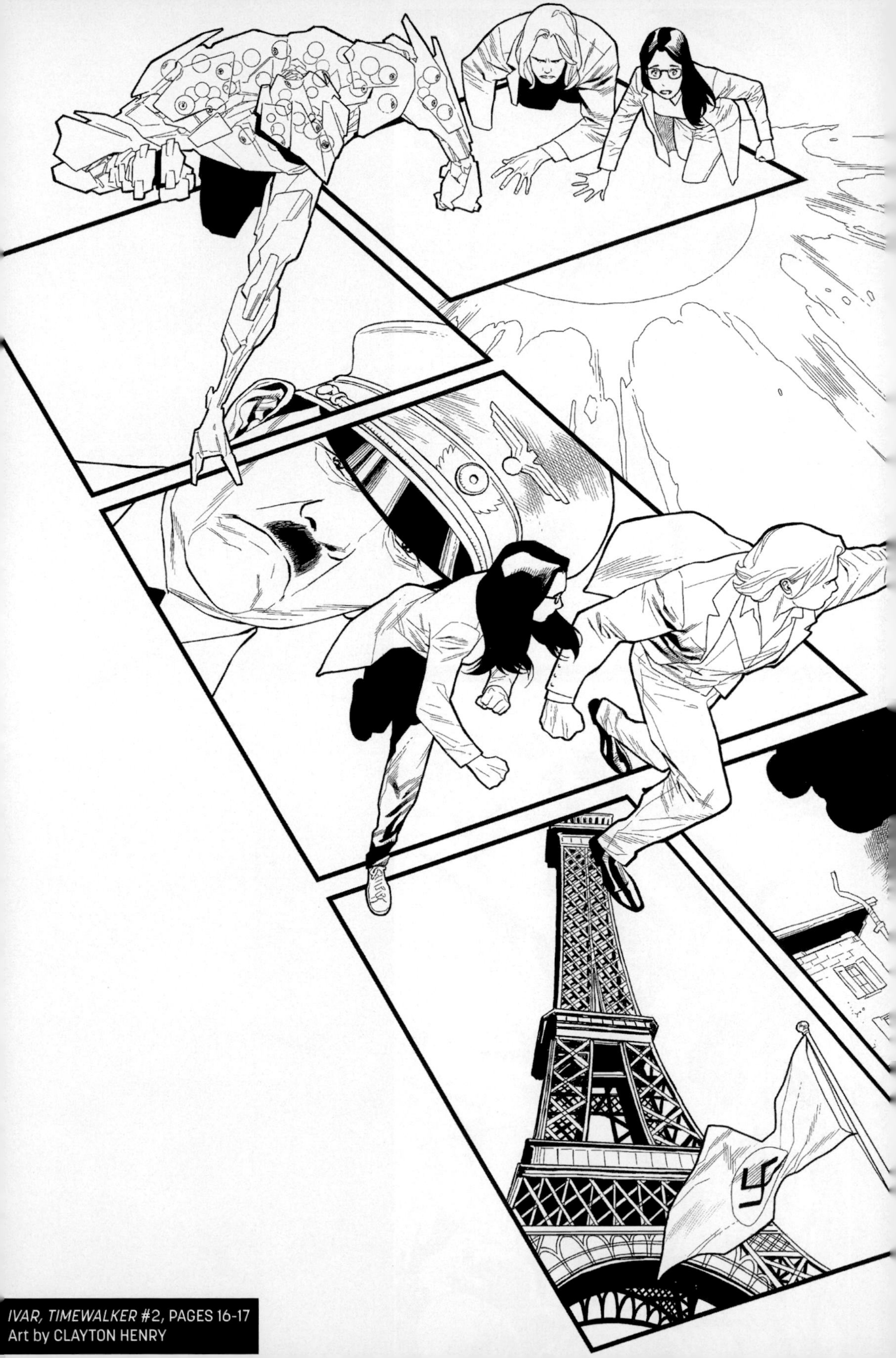

IVAR, TIMEWALKER #2, PAGES 16-17
Art by CLAYTON HENRY

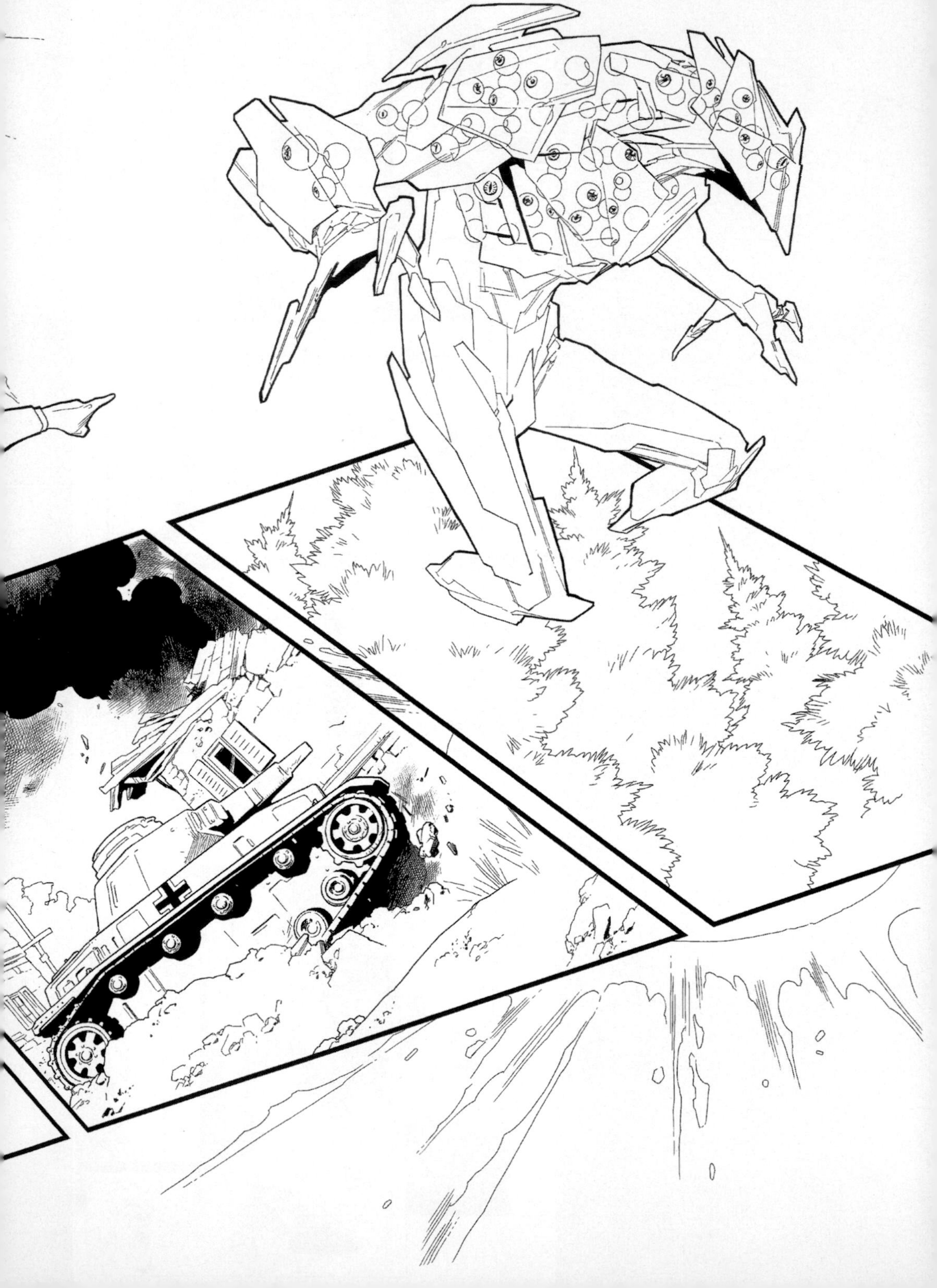

IVAR, TIMEWALKER #3, p. 2
Art by CLAYTON HENRY

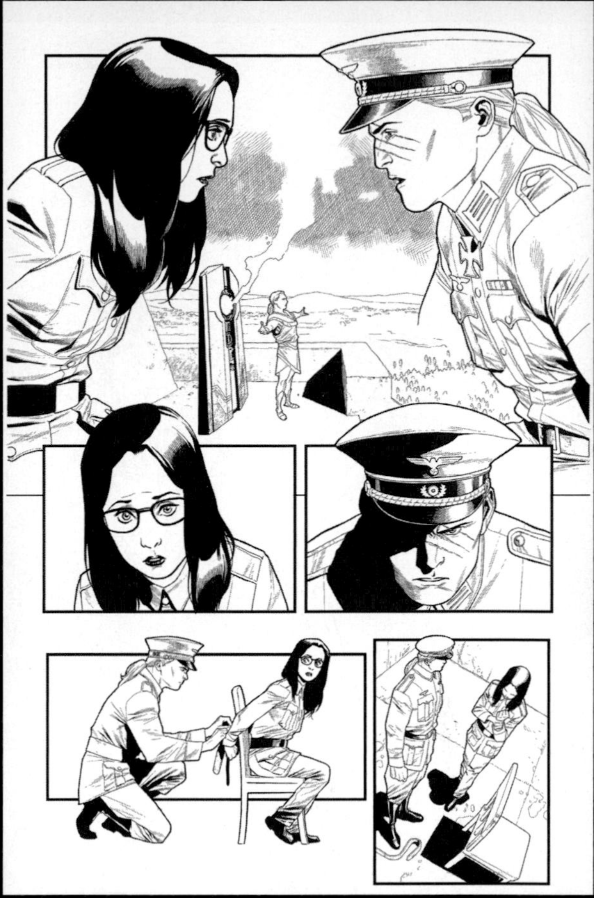

IVAR, TIMEWALKER #3, p. 3
Art by CLAYTON HENRY

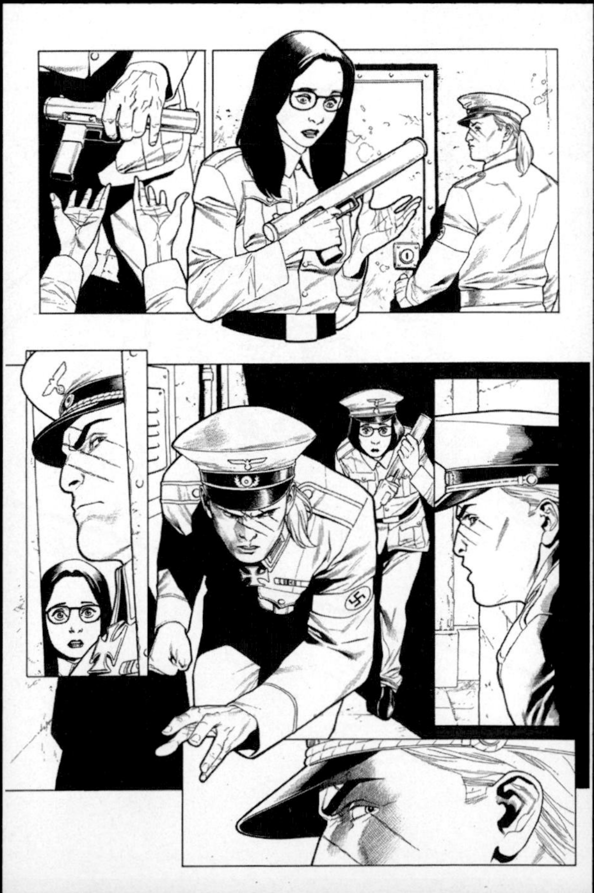

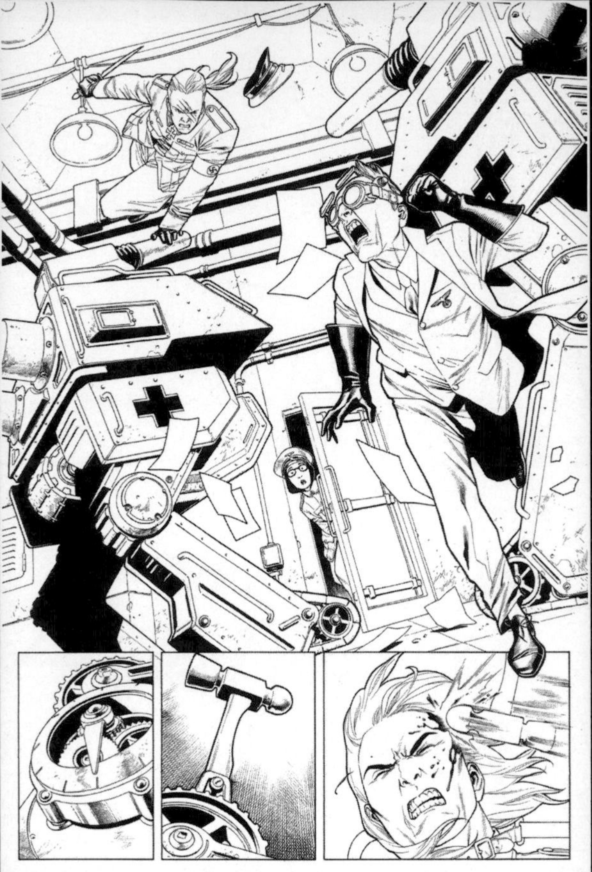

IVAR, TIMEWALKER #3, p. 5
Art by CLAYTON HENRY

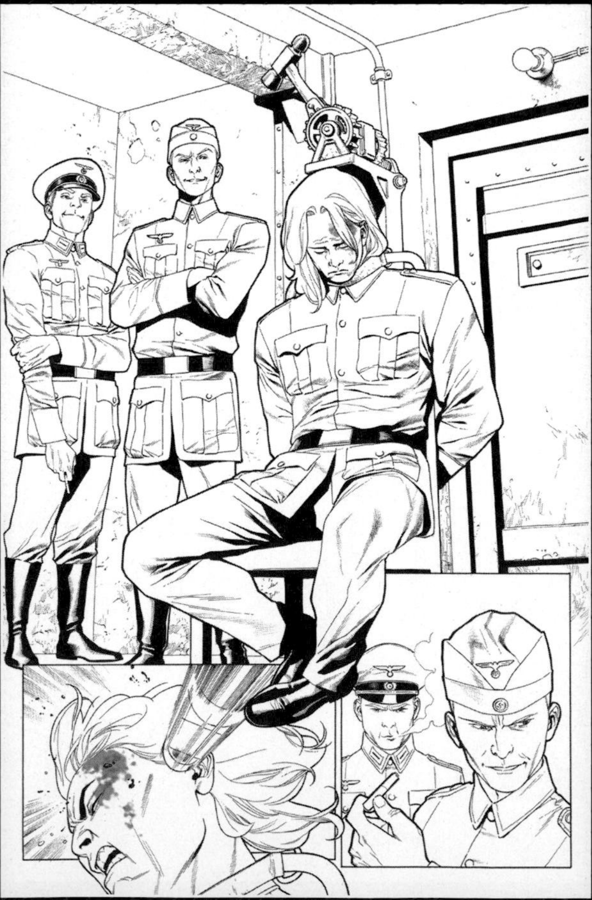

IVAR, TIMEWALKER #3, p. 6
Art by CLAYTON HENRY

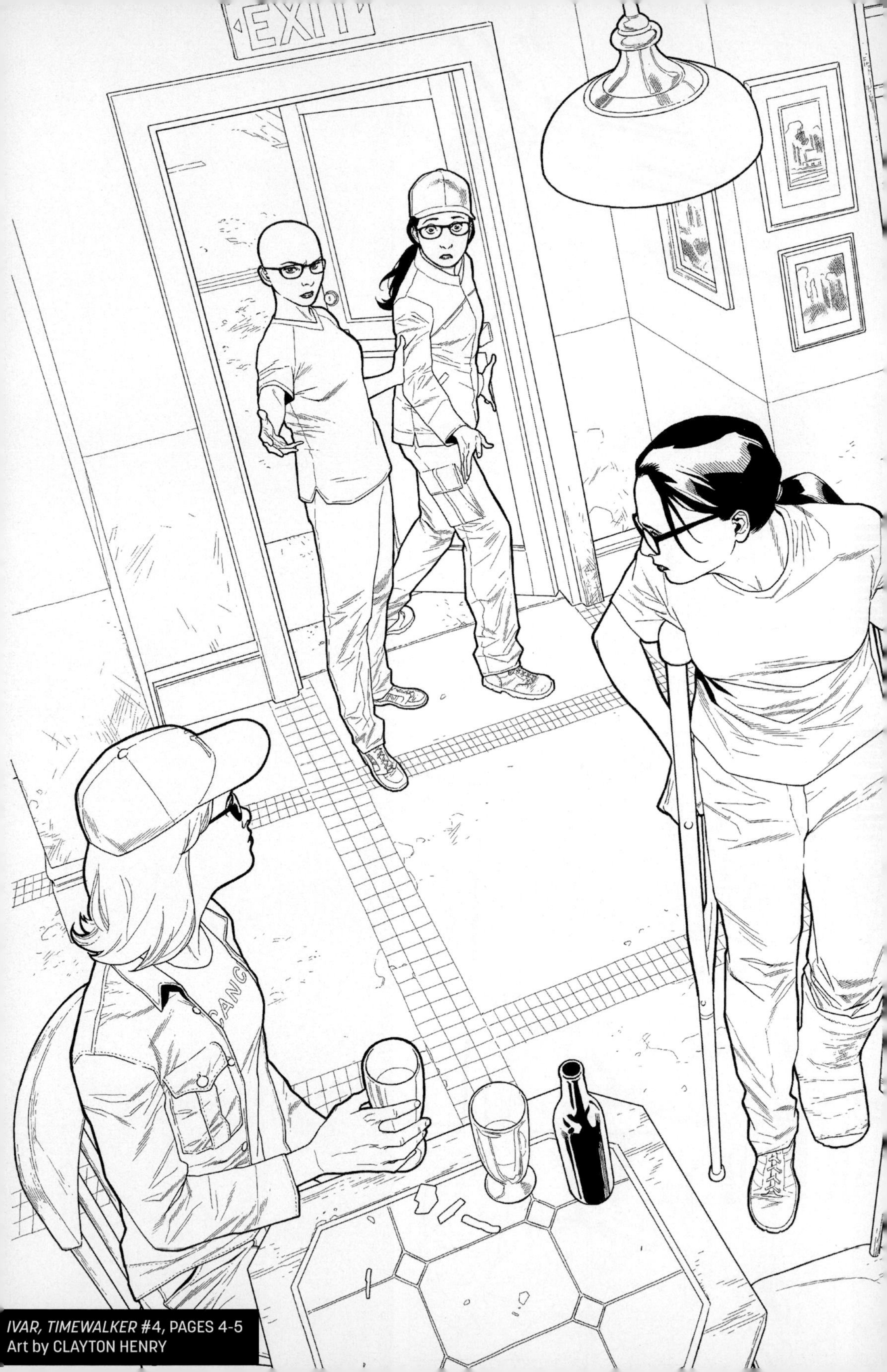
EXIT

IVAR, TIMEWALKER #4, PAGES 4-5
Art by CLAYTON HENRY

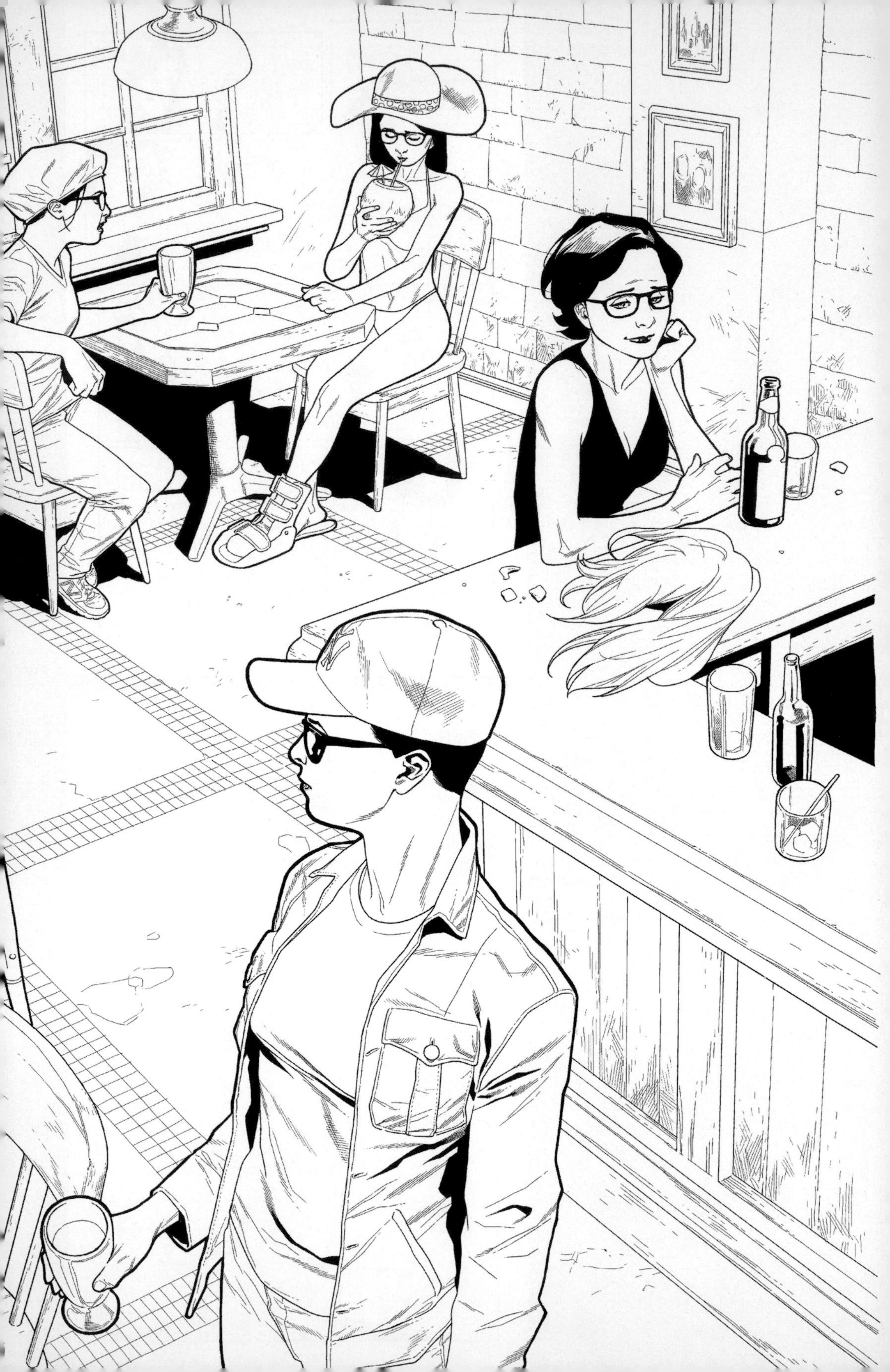

IVAR, TIMEWALKER #4, p. 6
Art by CLAYTON HENRY

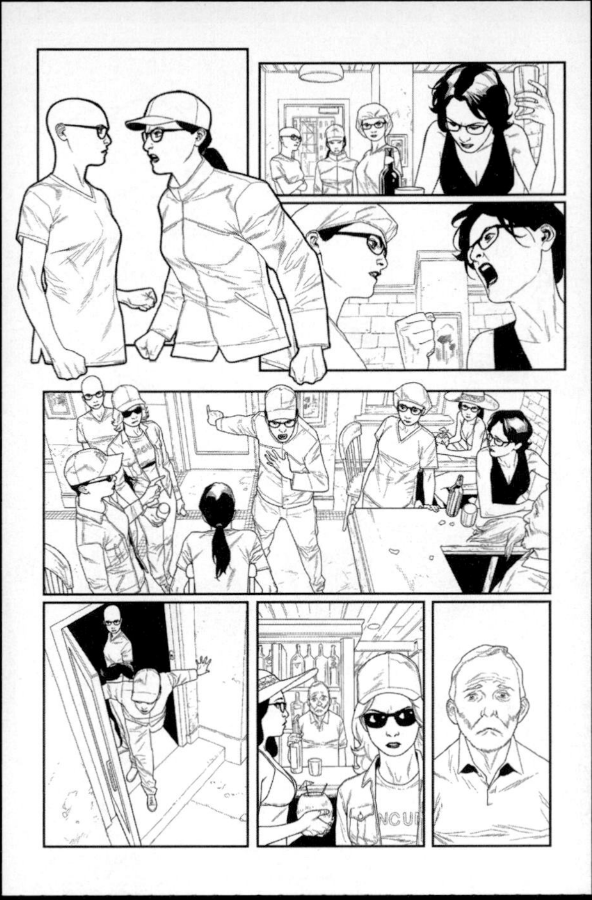

IVAR, TIMEWALKER #4, p. 11
Art by CLAYTON HENRY

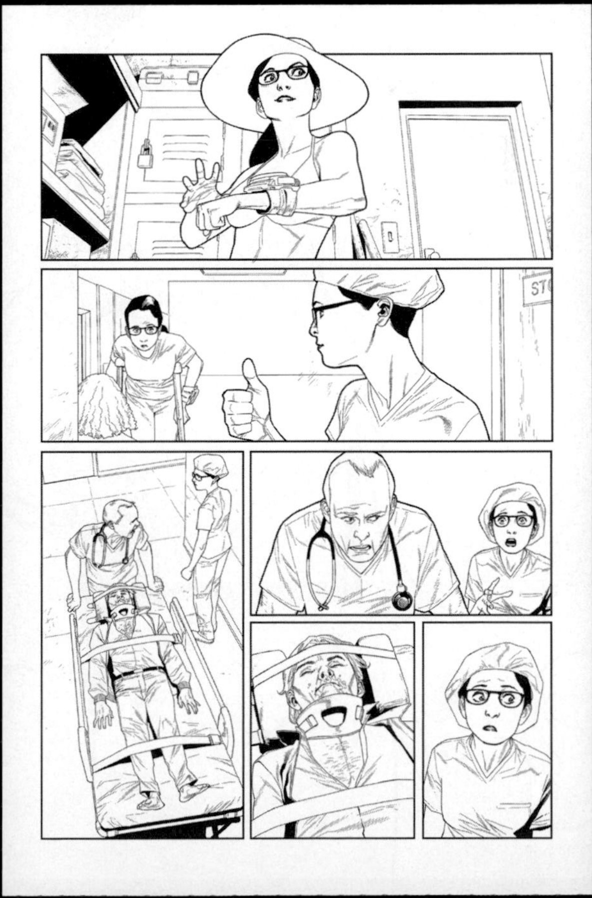

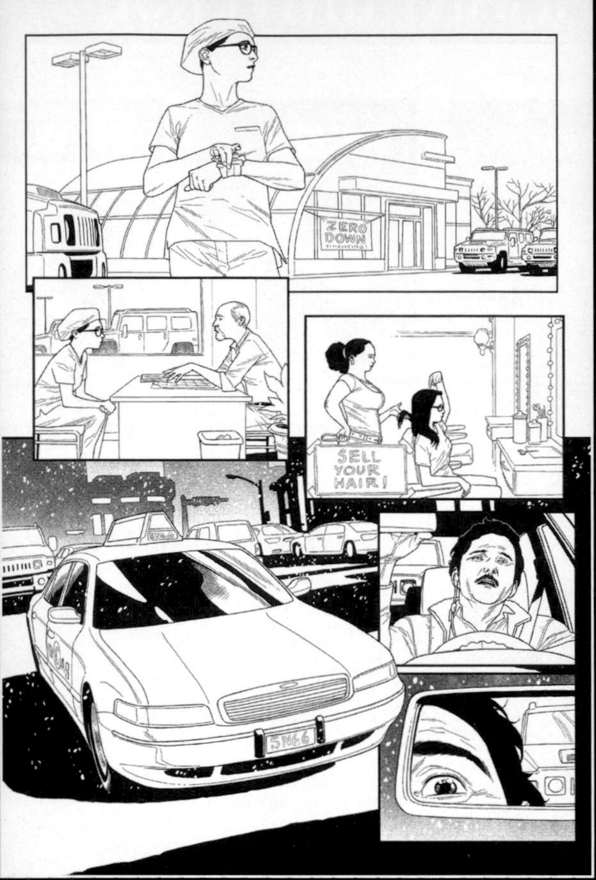
ZERO DOWN
SELL YOUR HAIR!

IVAR, TIMEWALKER #4, p. 13
Art by CLAYTON HENRY

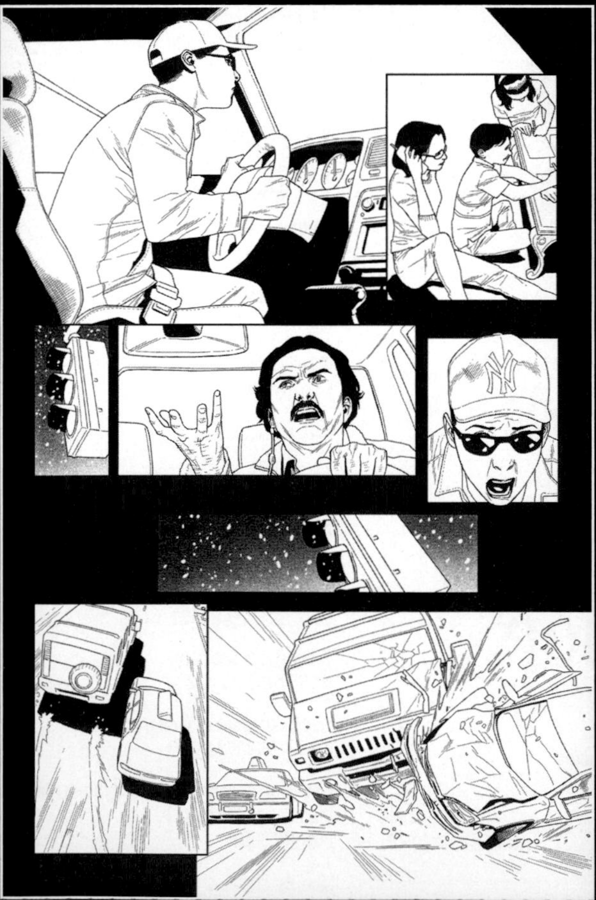

IVAR, TIMEWALKER #4, p. 14
Art by CLAYTON HENRY

EXPLORE THE VALIANT UNIVERSE

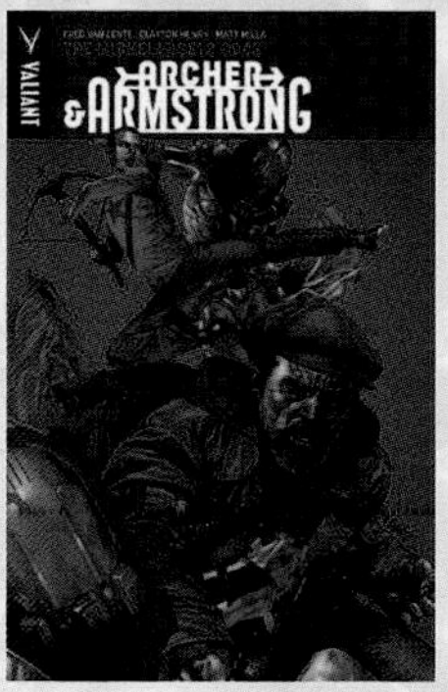
VALIANT
ARCHER & ARMSTRONG

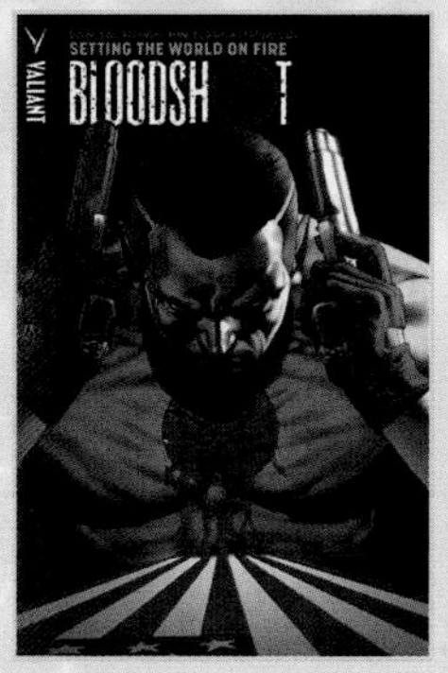
VALIANT
SETTING THE WORLD ON FIRE

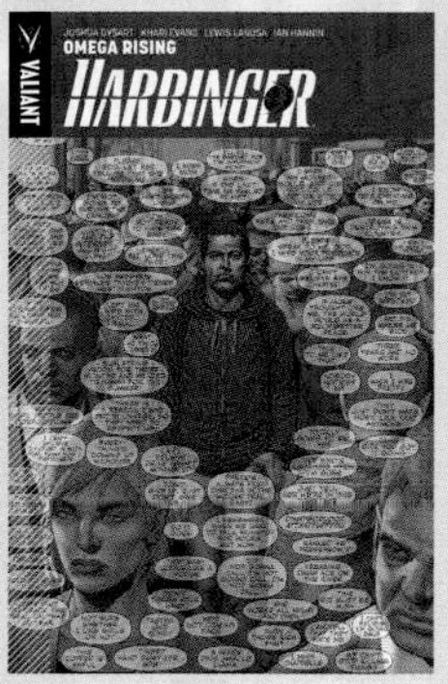
VALIANT
OMEGA RISING
HARBINGER

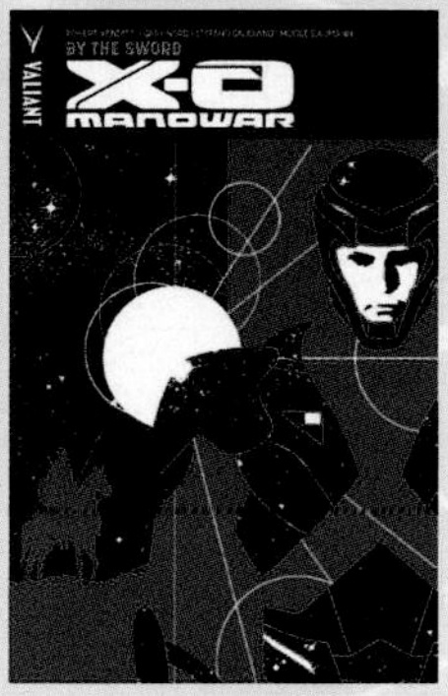
VALIANT
BY THE SWORD
X-O MANOWAR

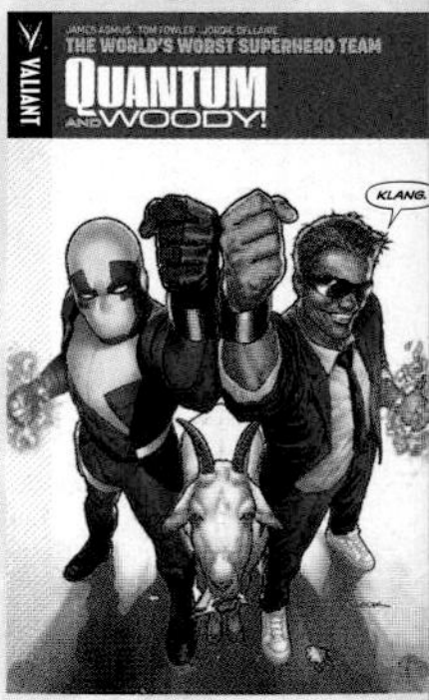
VALIANT
THE WORLD'S WORST SUPERHERO TEAM
QUANTUM AND WOODY!
KLANG

ARCHER & ARMSTRONG

Volume 1: The Michelangelo Code
ISBN: 9780979640988

Volume 2: Wrath of the Eternal Warrior
ISBN: 9781939346049

Volume 3: Far Faraway
ISBN: 9781939346148

Volume 4: Sect Civil War
ISBN: 9781939346254

Volume 5: Mission: Improbable
ISBN: 9781939346353

Volume 6: American Wasteland
ISBN: 9781939346421

ARMOR HUNTERS

Armor Hunters
ISBN: 9781939346452

Armor Hunters: Bloodshot
ISBN: 9781939346469

Armor Hunters: Harbinger
ISBN: 9781939346506

Unity Vol. 3: Armor Hunters
ISBN: 9781939346445

X-O Manowar Vol. 7: Armor Hunters
ISBN: 9781939346476

BLOODSHOT

Volume 1: Setting the World on Fire
ISBN: 9780979640964

Volume 2: The Rise and the Fall
ISBN: 9781939346032

Volume 3: Harbinger Wars
ISBN: 9781939346124

Volume 4: H.A.R.D. Corps
ISBN: 9781939346193

Volume 5: Get Some!
ISBN: 9781939346315

Volume 6: The Glitch and Other Tales
ISBN: 9781939346711

THE DEATH-DEFYING DOCTOR MIRAGE

The Death-Defying Dr. Mirage
ISBN: 9781939346490

THE DELINQUENTS

The Delinquents
ISBN: 9781939346513

ETERNAL WARRIOR

Volume 1: Sword of the Wild
ISBN: 9781939346209

Volume 2: Eternal Emperor
ISBN: 9781939346292

Eternal Warrior: Days of Steel
ISBN: 9781939346742

HARBINGER

Volume 1: Omega Rising
ISBN: 9780979640957

Volume 2: Renegades
ISBN: 9781939346025

Volume 3: Harbinger Wars
ISBN: 9781939346117

Volume 4: Perfect Day
ISBN: 9781939346155

Volume 5: Death of a Renegade
ISBN: 9781939346339

Volume 6: Omegas
ISBN: 9781939346384

HARBINGER WARS

Harbinger Wars
ISBN: 9781939346094

Bloodshot Vol. 3: Harbinger Wars
ISBN: 9781939346124

Harbinger Vol. 3: Harbinger Wars
ISBN: 9781939346117

QUANTUM AND WOODY!

Volume 1: The World's Worst Superhero Team
ISBN: 9781939346186

Volume 2: In Security
ISBN: 9781939346230

Volume 3: Crooked Pasts, Present Tense
ISBN: 9781939346391

Volume 4: Quantum and Woody Must Die!
ISBN: 9781939346629
COMING SOON

EXPLORE THE VALIANT UNIVERSE

VALIANT
KICK ME!!
QUANTUM AND WOODY
BY PRIEST & BRIGHT
VOL 1: KLANG

VALIANT
BATTLE FOR NEW JAPAN
RAI

VALIANT
THE VALIANT

VALIANT
THE DEATH-DEFYING
DOCTOR MIRAGE

VALIANT
VALIANT ZEROES ORIGINS

QUANTUM AND WOODY BY PRIEST & BRIGHT

Volume 1: Klang
ISBN: 9781939346780
COMING SOON

RAI

Volume 1: Welcome to New Japan
ISBN: 9781939346414

Volume 2: Battle for New Japan
ISBN: 9781939346612
COMING SOON

SHADOWMAN

Volume 1: Birth Rites
ISBN: 9781939346001

Volume 2: Darque Reckoning
ISBN: 9781939346056

Volume 3: Deadside Blues
ISBN: 9781939346162

Volume 4: Fear, Blood, And Shadows
ISBN: 9781939346278

Volume 5: End Times
ISBN: 9781939346377

Ivar, Timewalker

Volume 1: Making History
ISBN: 9781939346636
COMING SOON

UNITY

Volume 1: To Kill a King
ISBN: 9781939346261

Volume 2: Trapped by Webnet
ISBN: 9781939346346

Volume 3: Armor Hunters
ISBN: 9781939346445

Volume 4: The United
ISBN: 9781939346544

Volume 5: Homefront
ISBN: 9781939346797

THE VALIANT

The Valiant
ISBN: 9781939346605
COMING SOON

VALIANT ZEROES AND ORIGINS

Valiant: Zeroes and Origins
ISBN: 9781939346582
COMING SOON

X-O MANOWAR

Volume 1: By the Sword
ISBN: 9780979640940

Volume 2: Enter Ninjak
ISBN: 9780979640995

Volume 3: Planet Death
ISBN: 9781939346087

Volume 4: Homecoming
ISBN: 9781939346179

Volume 5: At War With Unity
ISBN: 9781939346247

Volume 6: Prelude to Armor Hunters
ISBN: 9781939346407

Volume 7: Armor Hunters
ISBN: 9781939346476

Volume 8: Enter: Armorines
ISBN: 9781939346551

Volume 9: Dead Hand
ISBN: 9781939346650

EXPLORE THE VALIANT UNIVERSE

VALIANT
HARBINGER
DELUXE EDITION 2

OMNIBUSES

Quantum and Woody: The Complete Classic Omnibus
ISBN: 9781939346360
Collecting QUANTUM AND WOODY (1997) #0, 1-21 and #32, THE GOAT: H.A.E.D.U.S. #1, and X-O MANOWAR (1996) #16

X-O Manowar Classic Omnibus Vol. 1
ISBN: 9781939346308
Collecting X-O MANOWAR (1992) #0-30, ARMORINES #0, X-O DATABASE #1, as well as material from SECRETS OF THE VALIANT UNIVERSE #1

DELUXE EDITIONS

Archer & Armstrong Deluxe Edition Book 1
ISBN: 9781939346223
Collecting ARCHER & ARMSTRONG #0-13

VALIANT
ARMOR HUNTERS
DELUXE EDITION

Armor Hunters Deluxe Edition
ISBN: 9781939346728
Collecting ARMOR HUNTERS #1-4, ARMOR HUNTERS: AFTERMATH #1, ARMOR HUNTERS: BLOODSHOT #1-3, ARMOR HUNTERS: HARBINGER #1-3, UNITY #8-11 and X-O MANOWAR #23-29

Bloodshot Deluxe Edition Book 1
ISBN: 9781939346216
Collecting BLOODSHOT #1-13

Harbinger Deluxe Edition Book 1
ISBN: 9781939346131
Collecting HARBINGER #0-14

Harbinger Deluxe Edition Book 2
ISBN: 9781939346773
Collecting HARBINGER #15-25, HARBINGER: OMEGAS #1-3, and HARBINGER: BLEEDING MONK #0

Harbinger Wars Deluxe Edition
ISBN: 9781939346322
Collecting HARBINGER WARS #1-4, HARBINGER #11-14, and BLOODSHOT #10-13

Quantum and Woody Deluxe Edition Book 1
ISBN: 9781939346681
Collecting QUANTUM AND WOODY #1-12 and QUANTUM AND WOODY: THE GOAT #0

Q2: The Return of Quantum and Woody Deluxe Edition
ISBN: 9781939346568
Collecting Q2: THE RETURN OF QUANTUM AND WOODY #1-5

JAMES ASMUS · TOM FOWLER · MING DOYLE
KANO · JORDIE BELLAIRE · DAVE LANPHEAR
VALIANT
QUANTUM AND WOODY!
DELUXE EDITION 1
MEH!

Shadowman Deluxe Edition Book 1
ISBN: 9781939346438
Collecting SHADOWMAN #0-10

X-O Manowar Deluxe Edition Book 1
ISBN: 9781939346100
Collecting X-O MANOWAR #1-14

X-O Manowar Deluxe Edition Book 2
ISBN: 9781939346520
Collecting X-O MANOWAR #15-22, and UNITY #1-4

JIM SHOOTER DAVID LAPHAM
CHILDREN OF THE EIGHTH DAY
HARBINGER
VALIANT
VALIANT MASTERS

VALIANT MASTERS

Bloodshot Vol. 1 - Blood of the Machine
ISBN: 9780979640933

H.A.R.D. Corps Vol. 1 - Search and Destroy
ISBN: 9781939346285

Harbinger Vol. 1 - Children of the Eighth Day
ISBN: 9781939346483

Ninjak Vol. 1 - Black Water
ISBN: 9780979640971

Rai Vol. 1 - From Honor to Strength
ISBN: 9781939346070

Shadowman Vol. 1 - Spirits Within
ISBN: 9781939346018

KEVIN VANHOOK | DON PERLIN
BLOOD OF THE MACHINE
VALIANT
BLOODSHOT
VALIANT MASTERS

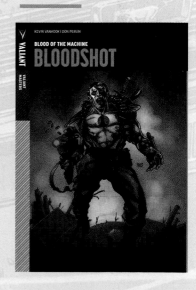

VALIANT®

Ivar, Timewalker®

VOLUME TWO: **BREAKING HISTORY**

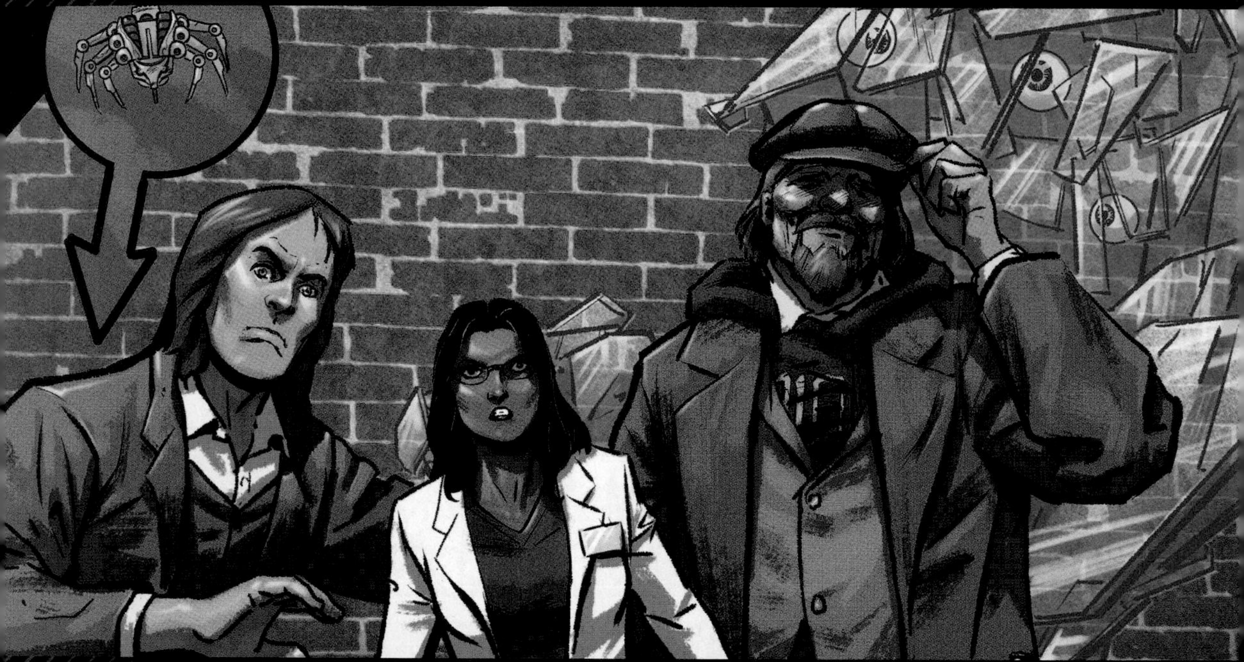

A LITTLE CONFUSED BY TIME TRAVEL? DON'T WORRY, THESE GUYS DON'T REALLY UNDERSTAND IT EITHER. SO THEY'RE *BREAKING HISTORY*!

With the universe on the brink of destruction, Ivar must turn to his closest relatives - Armstrong and Gilad Anni-Padda - to save Neela Sethi from the machinations of the Prometheans! The problem? These three guys couldn't be further apart. Time doesn't heal all wounds as the assault on Oblivi-1 begins!

Join New York Times best-selling writer Fred Van Lente (ARCHER & ARMSTRONG) and rising star Francis Portela (*Green Lantern Corps*) as they kick off the next volume of the series that io9 calls "impressively shocking!" Collecting IVAR, TIMEWALKER #5-8.

TRADE PAPERBACK
ISBN: 978-1-939346-83-4

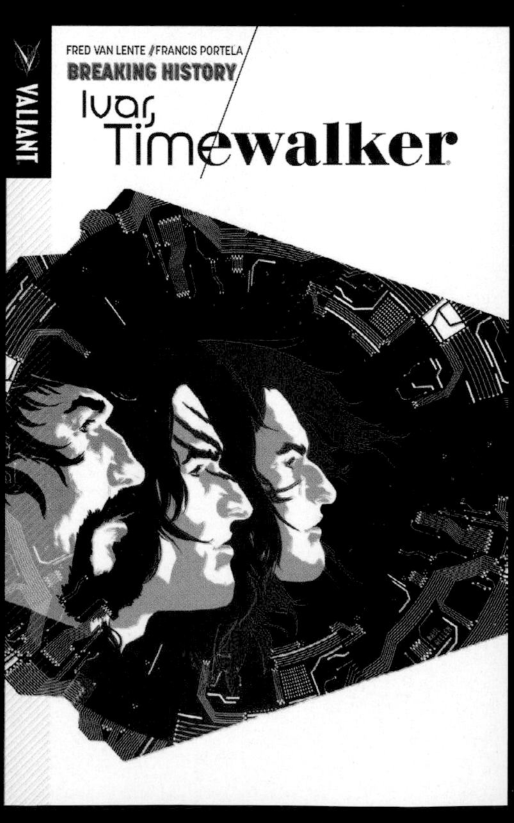
FRED VAN LENTE / FRANCIS PORTELA
BREAKING HISTORY
VALIANT
Ivar, Timewalker

Ivar, Timewalker READING ORDER

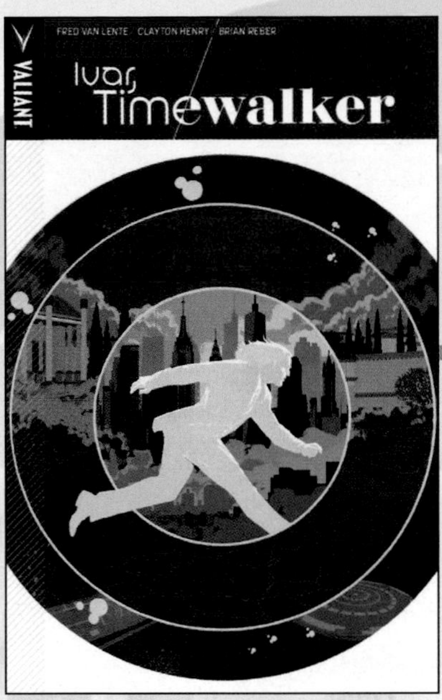
FRED VAN LENTE / CLAYTON HENRY / BRIAN REBER
VALIANT
Ivar, Timewalker

Ivar, Timewalker Vol. 1: Making History

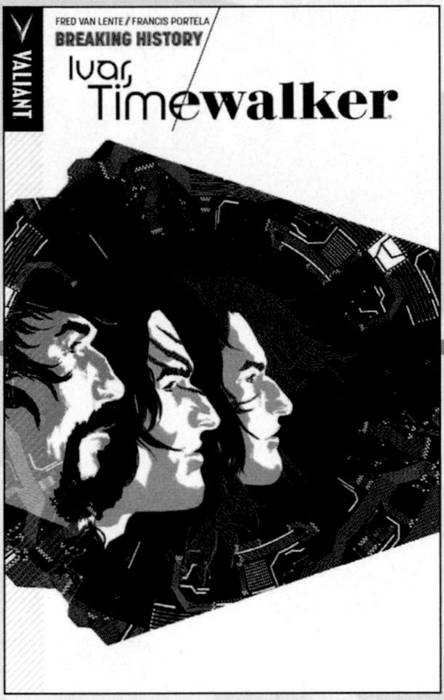
FRED VAN LENTE / FRANCIS PORTELA
BREAKING HISTORY
VALIANT
Ivar, Timewalker

Ivar, Timewalker Vol. 2: Breaking History

READ IVAR, TIMEWALKER'S EARLIEST APPEARANCES

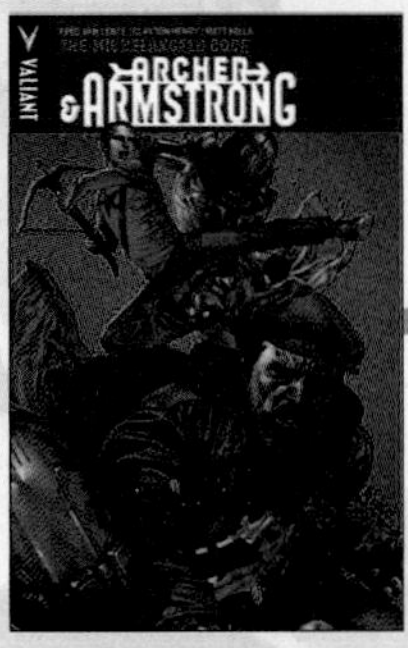
VALIANT
ARCHER & ARMSTRONG

Archer & Armstrong Vol. 1: The Michelangelo Code

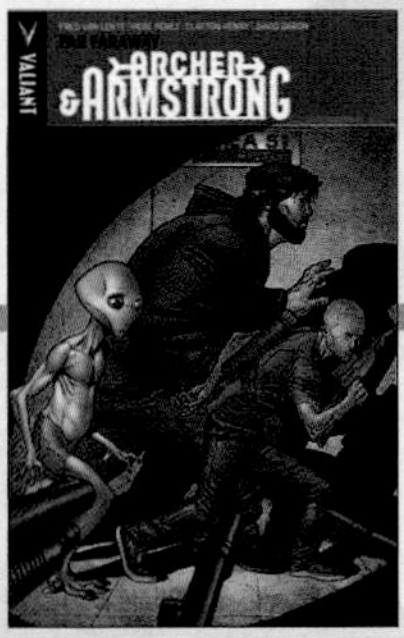
VALIANT
ARCHER & ARMSTRONG

Archer & Armstrong Vol. 3: Far Faraway

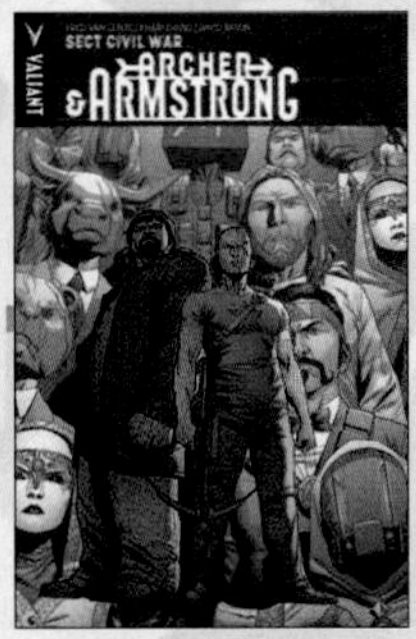
SECT CIVIL WAR
VALIANT
ARCHER & ARMSTRONG

Archer & Armstrong Vol. 4: Sect Civil War

"Big and crazy and hilarious... Ivar, Timewalker is one of a kind."
- Newsarama

"Quiet character moments, tense drama, and spectacular action..."
- The Onion/A.V. Club

Get ready for a clock-stopping adventure into the distant past and far future!
From New York Times best-selling writer

FRED VAN LENTE

And an all-star cast of artists including

CLAYTON HENRY and FRANCIS PORTELA

VALIANT.

Peter Cuneo
Chairman

Dinesh Shamdasani
CEO and Chief Creative Officer

Gavin Cuneo
Chief Operating Officer and CFO

Fred Pierce
Publisher

Warren Simons
VP Editor-in-Chief

Walter Black
VP Operations

Hunter Gorinson
Director of Marketing, Communications
& Digital Media

Atom! Freeman
Matthew Klein
Andy Liegl
Sales Managers

Josh Johns
Digital Sales & Special Projects Manager

Travis Escarfullery
Jeff Walker
Production and Design Managers

Alejandro Arbona
Editor

Tom Brennan
Associate Editor

Kyle Andrukiewicz
Associate Editor

Peter Stern
Publishing and Operations Manager

Chris Daniels
Marketing Coordinator

Ivan Cohen
Collection Editor

Steve Blackwell
Collection Designer

Rian Hughes/Device
Trade Dress and Book Design

Russell Brown
President, Consumer Products,
Promotions and Ad Sales

Jason Kothari
Vice Chairman

Editors: Tom Brennan (#1-4) and Josh Johns (#1)
Editor-in-Chief: Warren Simons

CONTENTS

Collection Cover Art: Raúl Allén

IVAR, TIMEWALKER

MAKING HISTORY

FRED VAN LENTE | CLAYTON HENRY | BRIAN REBER